WE ARE ALL CRIMINALS

Emily Baxter

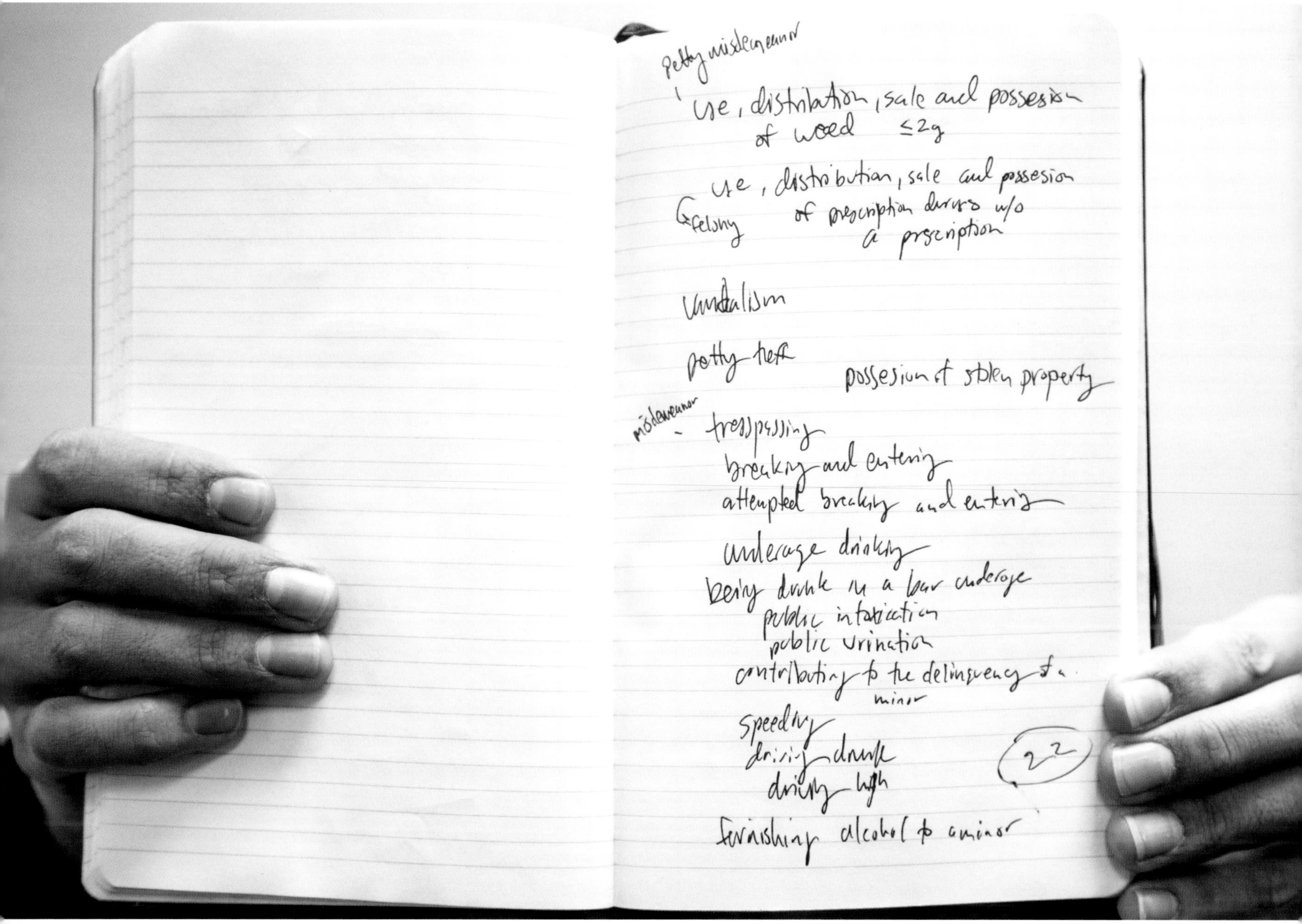

Petty misdemeanor

use, distribution, sale and possesion
of weed ≤2g

use, distribution, sale and possesion
Felony   of prescription drugs w/o
a prescription

vandalism

petty teft
                    possesion of stolen property

misdemeanor
- tresspassing
   breaking and entering
   attempted breaking and entering

   underage drinking
   being drunk in a bar underage
      public intoxication
      public urination
   contributing to the delinquency of a
                    minor

   speeding
   driving drunk   22
      driving high

   furnishing alcohol to minor

||| FOR ANTHONY |||

WE ARE ALL CRIMINALS

Copyright © 2017 We Are All Criminals, Saint Paul, Minnesota.
FIRST EDITION.

No part of this publication may be reproduced or transmitted
in any form or by any means without prior written permission of
We Are All Criminals or as permitted by law.

All photos by Emily Baxter

Book design by Emily Christensen

Typefaces are Lato and Open Sans

Printed by Sexton Printing, Saint Paul, Minnesota

weareallcriminals.org

ISBN 978-0-9992090-0-4
LCCN 2017948807

CONTENTS

Equal Justice for All. It is the hallmark of our democracy, repeated in so many legal documents and treatises. The question before us today is, *Does justice apply equally to everyone?* I can answer that question with a resounding "no."

I am inspired by Emily Baxter and her work in this book because she dares to shine a light on what many of us know: justice applies differently if you are poor, black, brown, or labeled. Many people in our society commit criminal acts and are never held accountable because of who they are. Laws can be written in a racially neutral fashion and yet applied in a discriminatory way; by over-policing of poor communities of color, we cause an imbalance between who is and who is not held accountable. We know that affluent, predominately white communities have just as many drug users and sellers as any other communities, but who we see in jails and prisons reflects where we choose to patrol, arrest, and incarcerate.

Policies and procedures have even been put into place to make *sure* that the law does not equally apply to everyone. In the early 1990s, I was asked to rule on a case involving the possession of crack cocaine. The defense lawyers argued that those who possessed "crack" were mostly black and sentenced to prison, while those who possessed "powder" were mostly white and typically sentenced to probation. Dramatically different consequences for essentially the same substance. I heard testimony about how crack was made (basically, cooking powder cocaine with baking soda to create a rock form) and how it had the same effect on the body as powder cocaine, snorted or liquefied and injected with a needle. I saw that there was absolutely no reason for the penalties to be different, so I held the law unconstitutional on equal protection grounds. Unfortunately, it took 20 years before the criminal justice system nationwide acknowledged this disparity that had so unfairly targeted African-American and Latino individuals. Thousands of individuals were incarcerated with this unjust law, labeled "criminal/felon." Communities and families were torn apart and will feel the effects of this for years to come.

Equal justice? I think not.

The unfortunate part is that we start this process early: many schools have a large police presence and suspension rates that are disproportionally high among children of color. We have chosen the children we believe are worth saving and those we do not believe are worth saving.

Equal justice? Are we fulfilling our declarations that all men (and women) are created equal and entitled to all rights and privileges, or does this only apply to the people already armed to the teeth with privilege in the form of whiteness and wealth, accidental armor against aggressive policing, strident sentencing, and accountability?

This book vividly shows us the contrast and what we must do as human beings living in a democracy to ensure that we are living up to our pledge of "equal justice for all." For all of us to be free, freedom must be available to all. Rather than "Just Us," we must work to achieve *justice for all.*

—*Judge Pamela G. Alexander*
Minnesota District Court
4th Judicial District
Minnesota, 2017

We Are All Criminals is a compassionate and fresh look at the modern day prison industrial complex. WAAC explores the American ideology that creates, profits from, and perpetuates a divisive narrative that for the "good" people to be free, "bad" people must be in bondage. This false narrative permeates our society, even though all of us have traversed that line between "bad" action and "good" lives. It is the luxury to forget that divides us: only some—typically not people of color—get to move on.

We Are All Criminals does an amazing job shining a light on this through the stories of real people. This text is more than an indictment of the criminal justice system, it is an indictment of the moral conscience of our society.

I read this powerful book as a currently incarcerated black male. I am from the generation of children who inhaled the radiation from the bombs dropped on our communities during the War on Drugs, which landed great swaths of poor black and brown youth in prisons and jails throughout this country. Most of us don't know a world that does not include prison fences, a school that does not have a law enforcement presence. America has told generations that bondage is their station in life. Merely to dream of anything outside captivity is, itself, almost criminal.

History will not be kind to mass incarceration, nor to the profiteers, politicians, corrections personnel, and citizens who turned a blind eye to this human rights crisis.

We Are All Criminals is a necessary read for all who believe that in order for any of us to be free we must all be free, and for any of us to dream we must all be able to dream.

—*Kevin Reese*
prison justice organizer
and founder of BRIDGE
Minnesota, 2017

FOUR IN FOUR

Several years ago, I was living in Minneapolis, Minnesota, working at an overstretched and underfunded legal advocacy organization. I had recently left my job as an assistant public defender, and I was hungry to change the system that had been so relentlessly stacked against my clients. My daily work concerned legislative and policy change, while at night and on the weekends my colleagues and I met with people who couldn't wait for the trickle down of a statutory shift. These men, women, and youth—all economically disadvantaged, overwhelmingly black, brown, and Indigenous—had lost their jobs, homes, opportunities for education, and licensure because of a past mistake. With so much else taken away, I wanted them to be able to hold onto hope.

Twice a month, we held criminal records clinics: the first in an open community room on the Northside, the second in the drab, windowless basement of a downtown government center. In these spaces, Minnesotans would wait for hours to speak with an attorney who could help decipher their criminal record and determine their eligibility for expungement (the court-ordered sealing of a criminal record). It was a lengthy process. Criminal records are notoriously difficult to read and frequently rife with error, and a mix of statutory limitations and subjective measures determine the likelihood of expungements. When it comes to a court's decision to seal your records, it matters why you committed the crime (of course many of the participants were haunted by records of wrongful arrests, dismissals, and acquittals); it matters what you've done since the offense (as evidenced by rehabilitation, education, employment, and civic engagement); and it matters how the record has affected you (essentially, how it has prevented you from doing all those things that might provide your redemption).

I'm sure the sun had long since set when our last participant arrived one night. Anthony was tall, thin, black, and clearly distraught. He walked hesitantly toward the front of the room. As he sat across the table from me, he pulled from his back pocket the copy of his criminal record he'd printed from a computer terminal two flights up.

The dread and defeat on his face were heavy. I opened it, expecting to see a recent aggravated robbery, multiple felony assaults, or substantial fraud. Maybe he was still eyeball-deep in probation or restitution. Whatever it was, it must have been egregious to warrant his worry. It wasn't: instead, it was a minor theft. I let out a small laugh of relief. *Even if the judge didn't expunge the matter*, I said—*it's not like your life is over.*

And with that, Anthony started to cry. Earlier that day, he had considered taking his own life. You see, while it was "just a theft" to me, to Anthony it was a lost job, missed housing payments, and skipped meals. It was the loss of respect from his friends and family, the loss of hope, and the loss of a sense of self.

Around this same time, I had been driving around the state, reaching out to employers and landlords, legislators and licensing boards, asking them to make second chances possible for individuals with criminal records. I knew that the overwhelming majority of decision-makers used background checks as shortcuts for assessing character and worth, and I knew just how difficult it was to move on and up from a criminal record. Time and again I would hear *You can't trust a con* or *Once a criminal, always a criminal.*

Those words came back to me as I sat across from Anthony, who was folding and opening and staring at the paper, refolding, reopening, and staring again at the paper—as if expecting what was written inside to suddenly change or disappear.

I wondered *How many times had I taken something that wasn't mine?* Sure, I'd considered my own criminality before—but not like this. I hadn't really thought about what life would be like in the shadow of that record, the suffocating stigma of being caught.

What would life be like if I didn't have the luxury to forget?

I thought about my friends, my family, my colleagues. I thought about my college classmates, my high school coworkers, my neighbors. Time and again, I had either witnessed them violate the law or had joined in the offense myself. From petty to serious, recent to ancient, each among us had broken the law. I thought about where we were now: lawyers, doctors, architects, accountants, academics, engineers, and entrepreneurs; mothers, fathers, leaders, and creators. Men and women defined by our professional and personal status, not by our criminal history.

So, for the past few years, I've been asking people like me—the 75 percent of people in the U.S. with criminal histories but no record, *What have you had the luxury to forget?* Many of the people whose stories I've collected are—like I am—white and middle-class. So I ask a follow-up question: *What roles did race and class play in your ability to get away with it?*

Since 2012, I've been traveling across the country, sharing and collecting more stories—deconstructing the "us versus them" dichotomy that plagues both our private thoughts and public discourse about crime and criminality. I ask students and scholars, police and prosecutors, employers and policymakers to challenge and change the divisive and destructive narrative that dominates our concept of the criminal justice system. Those stories became the We Are All Criminals (WAAC) project, and in 2014, that project became an organization.

Since that time, WAAC has been used as a catalyst for conversations about race and class, privilege, punishment, and second chances around the world. The project has assisted in "ban the box" efforts, education equity demands, and calls for a compassionate criminal justice system.

I've heard from cops who have told me their approach to policing has changed since realizing not just a shared criminality but a common humanity.

I've heard from policymakers who are taking it upon themselves to say that if voters are calling for tired "tough on crime" approaches, it's their turn to stand up and educate the electorate.

I've heard from professors who say that WAAC is a tool that finally illustrates privilege for their students and communicates their duty to do something about it.

And I've heard from employers that second chances have given them first-rate employees, people they would have rejected had they not considered their own histories.

WATCHING ANTHONY, I COULDN'T HELP BUT THINK: HOW MANY TIMES HAD I TAKEN SOMETHING THAT WASN'T MINE?

And here's more good news: WAAC is just one part of a much larger movement. Many political and faith leaders of all stripes are joining business and advocacy leaders in saying that mass criminalization and mass incarceration do not work, that they make us less safe as they eviscerate our nation's economy and communities.

In addition to these remarkable efforts, I've continued to ask those of us lucky enough to live without the shadow of a criminal record to answer the same, simple question:

What have you had the luxury to forget?

After all, this isn't about supporting a single petition or policy. It's about shifting the way we see others by altering the way we view ourselves. This is a call for reason, equity, and mercy across the board. Together, we own the problem and the solution.

Someday soon, when Anthony opens the folded page that is used to define his character, I hope that he finds not THIEF, but *father, caregiver, nurse, cook, speaker of multiple languages, survivor of genocide, volunteer coach, and avid reader*: the mark of a man no longer tethered to his past, but wholly able to live in the present and dream of his future. Anthony and millions of others deserve to be defined not through their worst moments, but by their true worths. They deserve, as much as any of us, the opportunity to be forgiven, and the luxury to forget.

I just keep telling myself: one in four, one in four, one in four. I'm not alone. I'm not broken.

Four in four, four in four, four in four. We may all be criminals, but that's not all we are.

Anthony in his kitchen

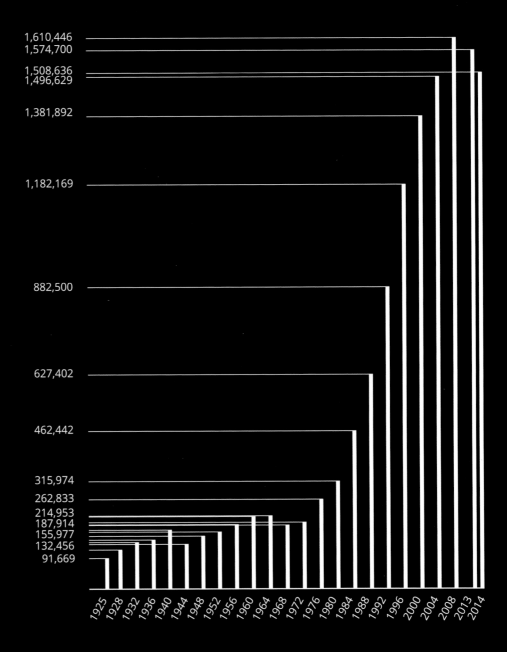

U.S. State and Federal Prison Population, 1925–2014

(Source: U.S. Bureau of Justice Statistics)

1,610,446
1,574,700
1,508,636
1,496,629
1,381,892
1,182,169
882,500
627,402
462,442
315,974
262,833
214,953
187,914
155,977
132,456
91,669

1925 1928 1932 1936 1940 1944 1948 1952 1956 1960 1964 1968 1972 1976 1980 1984 1988 1992 1996 2000 2004 2008 2013 2014

THE LANDSCAPE

We haven't always been an incarceration nation. Decades of bipartisan tough-on-crime approaches at the state and federal levels have directed the deliberate and regrettable march toward caging millions of people. Nearly half a century of "wars" on drugs, mental illness, and poverty; three-strike rules, mandatory minimum sentences, private prisons, and concentrated policing in minority communities; and the proliferation of both criminal code and collateral sanctions attached to criminal records have contributed to this catastrophe.

Mass criminalization cuts deep and wide for some, while scraping the surface for others. Black men are more likely to be arrested, charged, convicted, and incarcerated than their white counterparts. Black women and children, Native Americans, Latinos, and people in poor communities are also profoundly and disproportionately devastated. Whether in fiscal or human terms, the system is unjust and too costly to sustain. Meanwhile, many non-directly affected people have settled into a disturbing apathy, as if to suggest that mass incarceration and its accompanying disparities are both inexorable and acceptable to the great many who have never been caught.

Note that the human toll of mass incarceration reaches far beyond the squad car, courtroom, or prison walls: it swallows individuals, families, and communities whole. One in four people in this country has been arrested, arraigned, ticketed, charged, or fingerprinted for something other than a minor traffic violation—and that's a *conservative* estimate.

Not everyone arrested is convicted, not everyone convicted is incarcerated, and the vast majority of those in custody will eventually return to communities. Nevertheless, records stick. Even after "doing your time," punishment continues in the form of discrimination and exclusion. Months, years, and decades can go by, but the electronic testament to your interaction with the criminal justice system remains as indelible as a forehead tattoo. The record is permanently and easily accessed in our information age, regardless of how long it has been or how far you've come.

These criminal records are used by employers, legislators, landlords, and licensing boards to craft policy and determine the presumed character of an individual. Qualified people lose jobs, sheltered people lose housing, children lose parents, people lose hope.

Woven throughout the web of mass criminalization are policies and practices that require the assumption of an inherent difference between *us* and *them*. Between people with a criminal record and people without a criminal record.

Let's start with the low-hanging fruit. How many ostensibly *clean* people have smoked pot or used someone else's prescription medication? How about those who have taken office supplies home from work, walked out of the store without paying for something, cheated on their taxes, tagged school property, piggybacked on their neighbor's Wi-Fi or cable, written a check that bounced, or illegally downloaded music and movies? How many have driven home drunk, bought booze for someone underage, thrown a punch, or given leftover pain medication to a friend?

The criminal justice system ensnares thousands of people for precisely this kind of conduct. Those caught will pay for it for decades to come, through exacerbated marginalization, broken families and communities, and countless precluded opportunities to move on and move up. And for what? Mass criminalization has made our nation no safer. Meanwhile, facing few options and laboring under the crippling beasts of hunger, debt, and despair, some are left with few legal options for putting food in their bellies or a roof over their families' heads while people without criminal records walk through doors otherwise closed to those with records, often without ever realizing they're crossing a threshold.

If we're honest, one in four people may have a criminal record, but four in four have a criminal history.

Treatises, documentaries, studies, biographies, memoirs, and poetry, as well as legal, sociological, and medical reviews have explored and mapped out complex themes of crime and punishment.

Here, we will hopscotch across the mass criminalization landscape while glossing over rivers and rocks, and at times, entire oceans and mountain ranges; every now and then, we'll zoom in for a closer look. While covering the general terrain, we'll hear stories of crimes caught and uncaught from our neighbors, doctors, lawyers, family, and friends. We'll hear from that guy you haven't seen since high school and the person you just passed in the street. Maybe we'll even hear from you. By the end, my hope is that you see this world as it exists for you and for others.

In these opening days of the Trump administration, the short-term trajectory of American punishment is uncertain. President Trump and his Attorney General, Jeff Sessions, have signaled a much lower tolerance for marijuana, for instance, and a desire to prosecute drug crimes by pursuing the most damning possible charges. Still, the progress made by reform and rehabilitative activists cannot wholly be undone. Moreover, meaningful and profound changes need not be Fed-led; this can start in your state, your city, in your own backyard.

Acknowledging the landscape is the first step in navigating it. Then, together, we can alter the terrain.

OUR CRIMINAL HISTORIES AFFECT NEARLY EVERY
ASPECT OF LIFE. FROM PSYCHOLOGICAL TO SOCIAL,
PERSONAL TO PROFESSIONAL: *WHO WE ARE AND
HOW WE ARE* ARE DEFINED AND CONFINED BY OUR
CRIMINAL PASTS.

BUT NOT FOR EVERYONE.

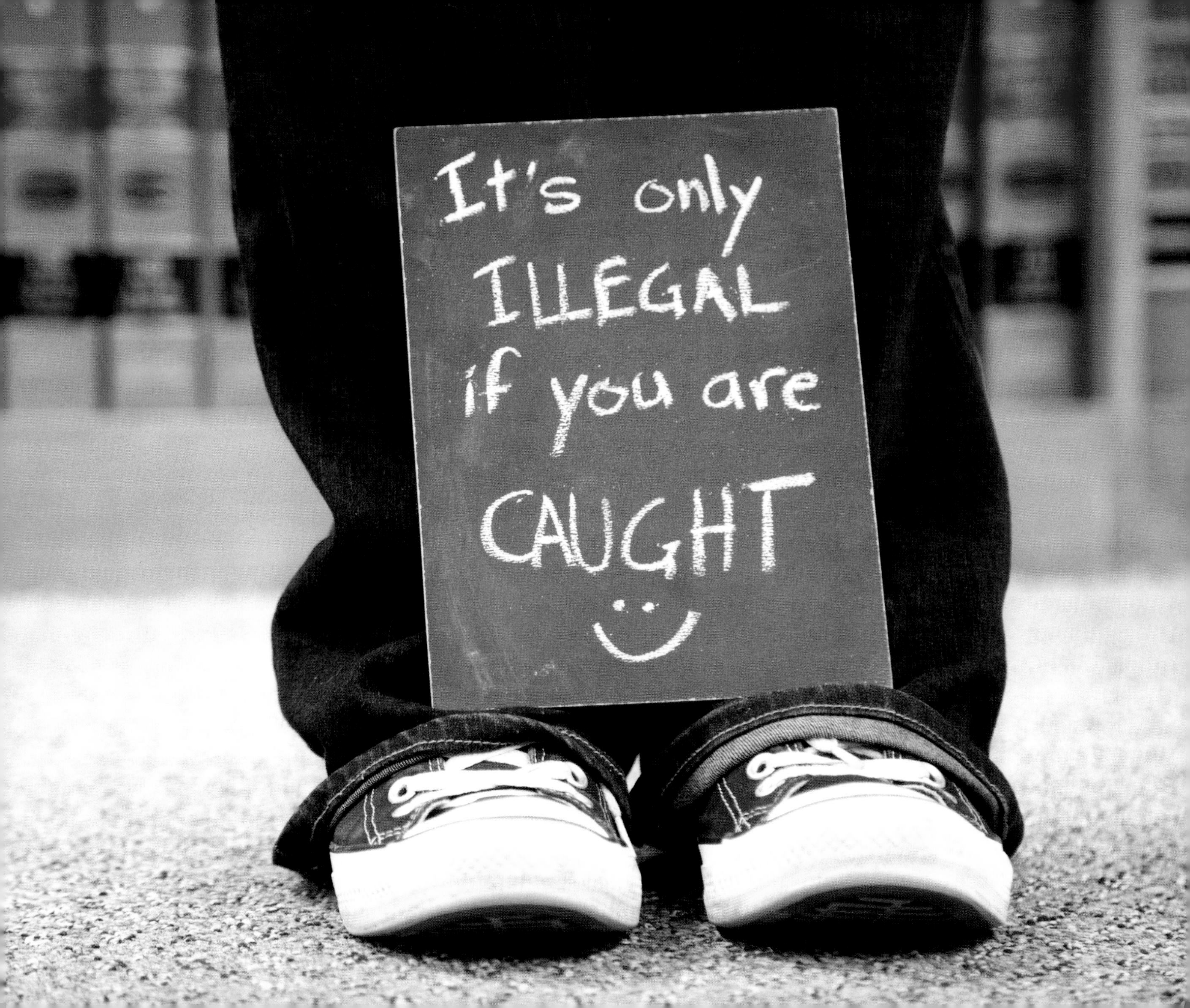
It's only
ILLEGAL
if you are
CAUGHT

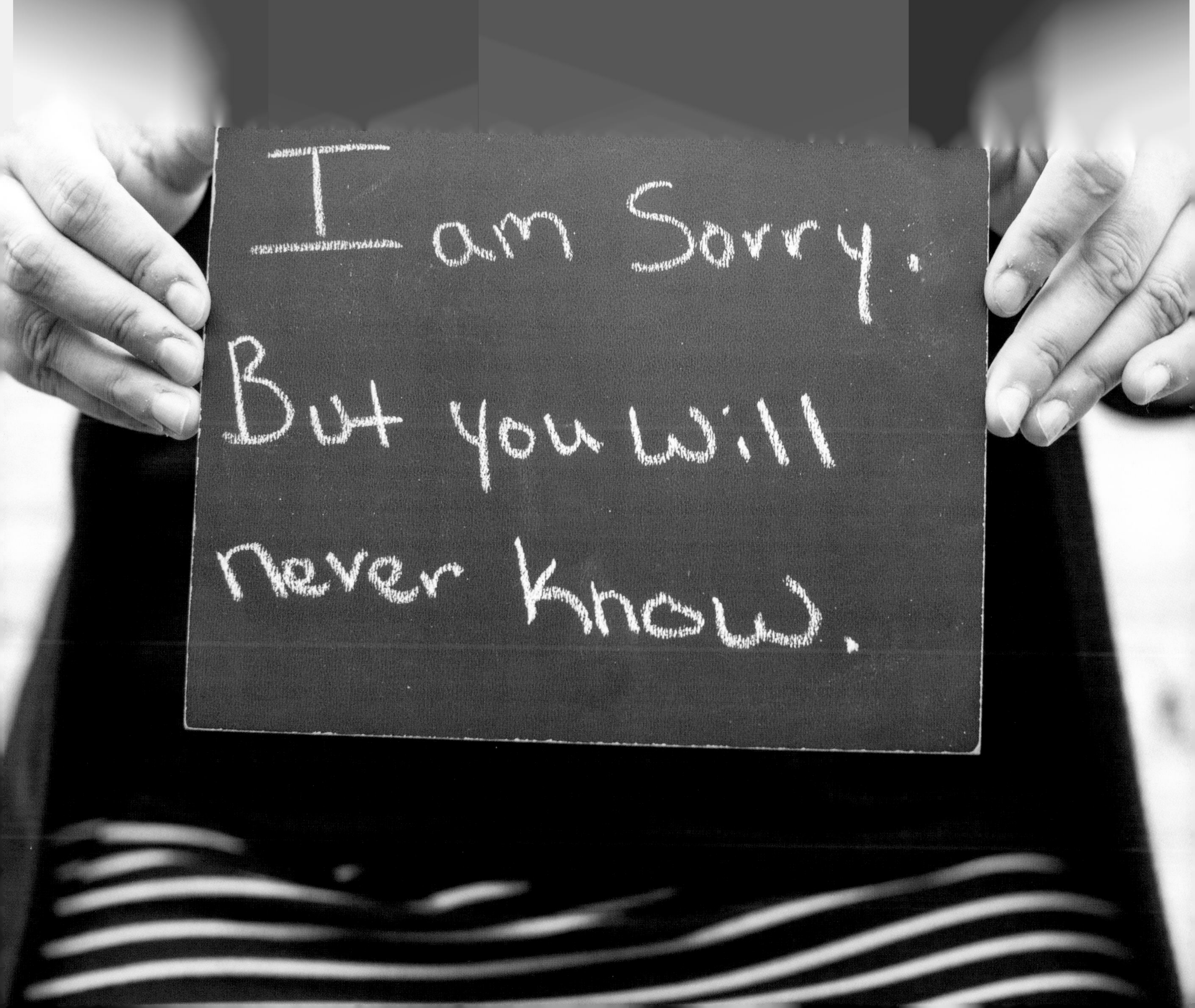
I am Sorry.
But you will
never know.

WE ARE ALL CRIMINALS

For all of us, but in particular the generations and communities that have only ever known mass arrests, mass incarceration, and mass supervision, this legalized discrimination on the basis of criminal records is a mass disaster. This is death by a thousand cuts—where a pound of flesh is no longer enough. We demand the whole person, and quite often, his or her family too.

Nearly every conceivable aspect of one's life—from personal to professional, from social to psychological—is defined and confined by past acts and accusations. Without substantial social and policy change, millions of people nationwide are not only robbed of a future, they are denied a present. Their criminal histories tether them to their pasts.

But not for everyone.

In fact, for just a few of us. Just one in four of us. What about the other 75 percent? Those of us who have committed crimes, but not been caught; those of us with criminal histories but no criminal record.

In 2012, I started asking others the questions I had begun to ask myself: *What have I had the luxury to forget? How would life be different had I been caught? What role did race and class (and to a lesser degree, other factors) play in my ability to get away with it?*

The stories that follow were shared by legislators and lawyers, cops and doctors, students and retirees from across the nation. Some of their crimes are relatively egregious, others petty; some happened recently, others decades ago. Likewise, the emotions these people experience as they recall their past transgressions vary from bemusement to relief, apologetic to proud.

There are four main types of stories in this book. The most numerous can be called *Luxury to Forget* (the participant "got away with it"). The others include *More Than My Mugshot* (in which the participant has a criminal record); *Parallel Stories* (scattered throughout the text, these are brief mentions of former clients, community members, family, and friends who were caught or accused of engaging in acts similar to what the *Luxury to Forget* participants got away with); and *Ripple Effect* (stories from people whose loved ones have been incarcerated).

Each interview is complex—like the system, like the mind, like the human experience. Many are excerpted from longer conversations; some details have been changed to help protect the participants' identities, some to abbreviate their stories for clarity and flow; and some have been transcribed from recordings, while others are written in collaboration with the participant. The majority of the *Luxury to Forget* participants relayed numerous offenses, but in most cases, only one event is cataloged.

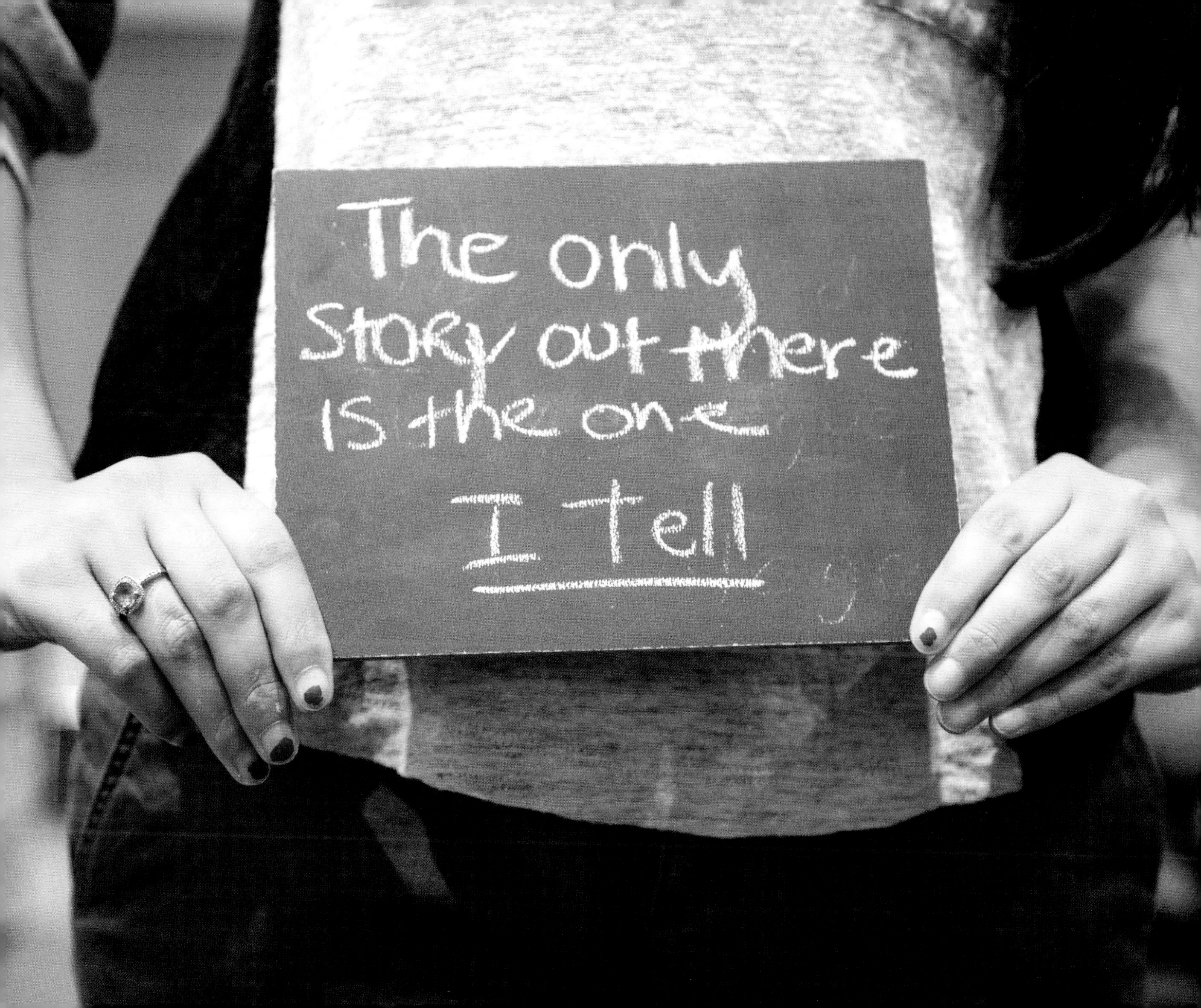
The only
Story out there
is the one
I tell

Many of the parallel stories are recollections of conversations I had with people while in public defense and later in individual rights restoration work.

The photographs, while protecting participants' identities, convey personality and location, sometimes in the participant's home, office, crime scene, or neighborhood. A few participants requested that neither they nor their surroundings be photographed; at times, photography was not feasible during the interview. In such cases, I have selected photographs that merely support the story.

Out of curiosity or compassion or catharsis, hundreds of people have shared their stories. In these pages you'll read their recollections, which touch upon race and class, pain and pride, drugs and alcohol, boredom and loneliness, love and hormones, and perhaps most frequently, the need to belong. Together they show the commonality and divergence of life across the country.

We'll start where the discussion usually ends: with the collateral consequences of a criminal record. After we've spent some time contemplating the legal and social morass created by perpetual punishments, we'll move to the launch of the War on Drugs. From there, we'll discuss how swelling criminal codes across the country swept up millions in their growing tides before we return for an updated look at the ever-evolving drug war. We'll examine what mass incarceration actually looks like before moving to the consideration of juvenile crimes committed before these perpetrators' brains are fully developed. We'll pause to discuss how policing and presumptions of innocence change with the color of one's skin. Next we'll consider what mass criminalization is costing us, in cash and in humanity, and then take a look at the ripple effect of incarceration upon loved ones. Finally, we'll imagine what this nation could look like if we invested in rather than incarcerated millions of people in America.

To the people who shared their experiences with me, *thank you*. You cannot know how profoundly grateful I am to have the privilege to gather and share stories that have the power to change the conversation.

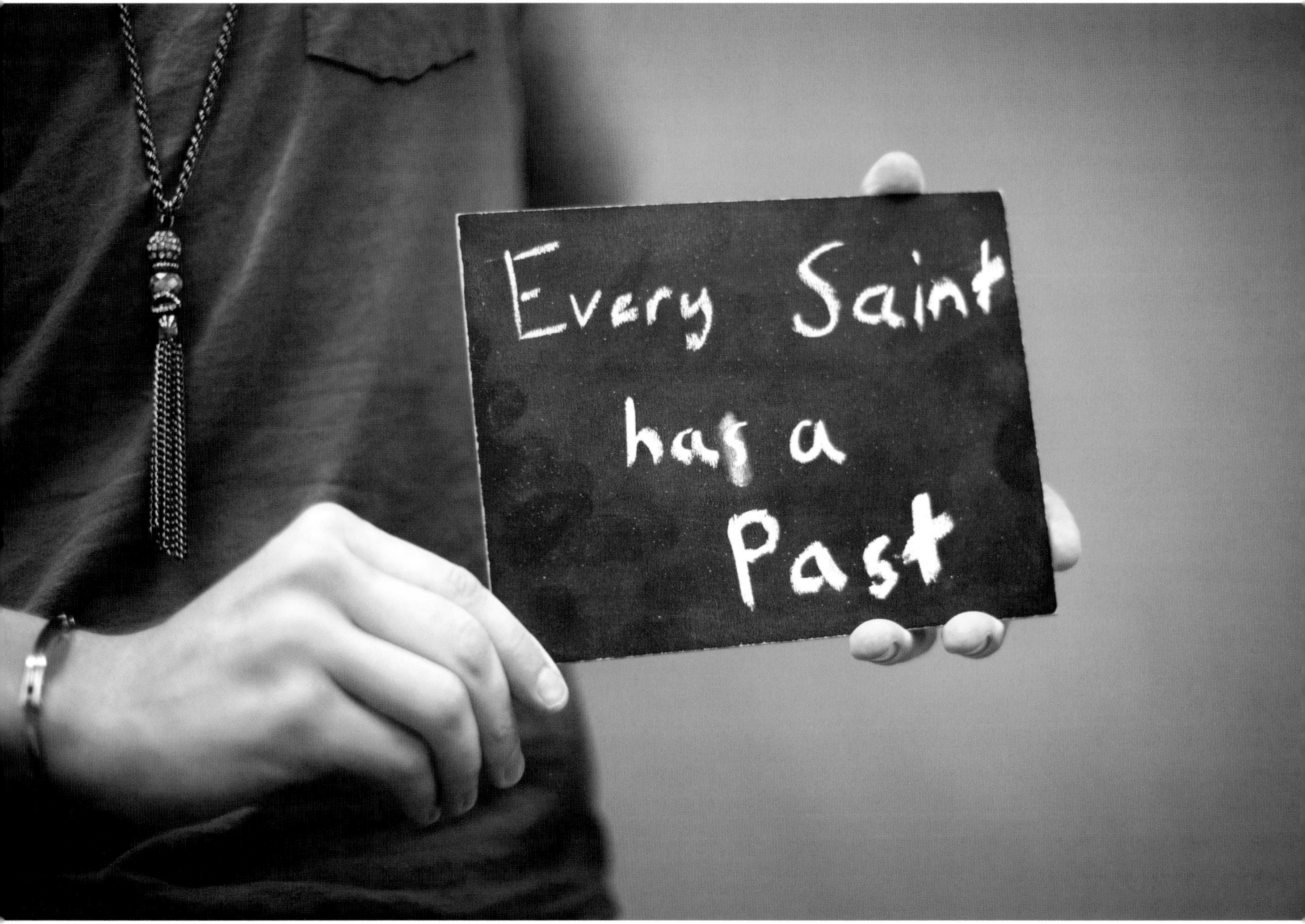
Every Saint
has a
Past

MECHANICAL ENGINEER

FRAUD; DISTRIBUTION AND POSSESSION OF CONTROLLED SUBSTANCES; ASSAULT; BURGLARY

This could go in any direction. Where do you want to start?

Let's see. Paperwork crimes? I was charged in-state tuition at an out-of-state school. That saved me tens of thousands. Drug crimes? Selling out of an apartment complex is what got me through college. Fights? Burglary? Showing up at work drunk, high? Sure. I was the smart kid always getting into trouble.

I grew up poor and am still clawing my way out of debt. At my first real internship, I made more money than my parents combined.

You know what makes the difference? My white, Christian boss sees me as his son. I may mess up, but he's not going to kick me out.

Thankfully, I don't have a record. I wouldn't be able to get this job if I did. But even if I did have a record and didn't have this job, I'd still be the same person.

I don't judge people for the bad things they've done. It's like that saying, *every saint has a past, and every sinner a future.*

I DON'T JUDGE PEOPLE FOR THE BAD THINGS THEY'VE DONE. IT'S LIKE THAT SAYING, *EVERY SAINT HAS A PAST, AND EVERY SINNER A FUTURE.*

PERPETUAL PUNISHMENT

They say a picture is worth a thousand words,
yet a single word can paint a thousand pictures.

Criminal.

A thousand pictures and none of them me.

—Delaine Snow

| BRANDED |

Beyond the bars and broader correctional control, what happens to people once they're no longer in the system is devastating. That's when a new punishment begins. People find that they may no longer be locked up, but they are effectively locked out of jobs, housing, school, and countless opportunities to move up and move on.

Criminal records activate barriers and foster a social stigma that stifles the individual; the barriers and stigma spread to his or her family and community as well.

Sociologist Devah Pager draws a contrast between the positive credentialing that enables access and upward mobility—from high school diplomas and college degrees to medical licenses—and the negative credentialing that criminal records create:

> With a criminal record comes official state certification of an individual's criminal transgressions; a wide range of social, economic, and political privileges become off-limits. Further, just as positive credentials offer the informal rewards of social status and generalized assumptions of competence, negative credentials confer the inverse: social stigma and generalized assumptions of untrustworthiness or undesirability.

Criminal records are essentially inescapable. They are in the paper, in the news, online, and on our phones; what once required a trip to the courthouse and help pulling files is now available with a few keystrokes to anyone, anytime. This accessibility and ubiquity has extended the punishments meted out to millions.

| DATA MINERS |

From employment checks to tear-off-tab flyers in bars' bathroom stalls (*Do you know who you're dating? Call now for a background report!*) our insatiable thirst for information is being met, in the data age, with unprecedented access to criminal records.

Be it a formal background report or a voyeuristic mugshot online, criminal records have fueled a multibillion dollar industry that feeds on fear and fascination. Norman Reimer, Executive Director of the National Association of Criminal Defense Lawyers, notes that this "growing obsession with background checking and commercial exploitation of arrest and conviction records makes it all but impossible for someone with a criminal record to leave the past behind."

And while there is certainly valid use for criminal history information that is recent, relevant, and perhaps above all else, *accurate*, too often that's not what is accessible. The National Employment Law Project (NELP) asserts that the records collected, cached, and disseminated by the Federal Bureau of Investigation (FBI)—widely considered to be the gold standard of criminal background checks—are wrong as frequently as they're right: fifty percent of the FBI's criminal records fail to include information on the final disposition of the case. Moreover, NELP notes, the information that is missing would often be beneficial to job seekers: for example, one-third of felony arrests in the U.S. do not result in conviction. Many others are reduced to misdemeanors. That means, if the record only reports the initial charge, millions of job applicants are routinely, profoundly, and negatively affected by clerical errors. Even the Department of Justice has said that "no single source exists that provides complete and up-to-date information about a person's criminal history."

And with so many copies in so many caches, it would be a Herculean task to right the records so many decision-makers rely upon as rough measures of character and worthiness.

Even when they are accurate, criminal records don't fade away: when a search result turns up a record, it will appear as recent and relevant today as it was ten years ago, and as it will be ten years in the future.

| PILING ON |

An endless morass of collateral sanctions—specific legal restrictions and generalized discrimination—attaches to criminal records. From housing to health, employment to education, immigration to adoption, and licensure to loans, civil and social punishments affect nearly every aspect of who we are and how we navigate the world. These "secondary" consequences can far exceed the direct punishment, swiftly and permanently relegating millions to second-class status. And one needn't be found guilty or take a plea; many people laboring under the legacy of an interaction with the criminal justice system were charged or arrested and never convicted, but that record lives on.

Criminal records can trigger sanctions that preclude licensure necessary to work in particular fields or facilities—from practicing law to emptying bedpans. Swiping a candy bar or a pair of jeans, throwing a punch, getting high, giving a cop your cousin's name, taking a car, or taking a life: from petty to profound, each can essentially lock you out of the job market for a lifetime. You may face restrictions on the government assistance you need. Rampant disenfranchisement can leave you without a political voice or the influence to change things that affect you.

Simply for having been taken into custody, you may lose your housing, your job, and your employment prospects. You may be barred from serving on a jury, in the military, or in public office. You may be denied loans, access to education, and licenses necessary not to just work, but volunteer, drive, or provide foster care. You may be deported. The American Bar Association (ABA) has begun to compile state and federal collateral sanctions in an online database, but the laws and regulations are too fish-slippery to grasp all of them. Woven into federal, state, and city codes are countless consequences: the ABA has identified more than 45,000 sanctions, but that number grows as new sanctions are found and created.

Legal scholar Margaret Colgate Love asks:

Why should someone convicted of possessing drugs be disqualified decades later from obtaining an electrician's license, from bidding on government contracts, or from obtaining a small business loan? There seems to be no logical connection between cheating on one's taxes and possessing a firearm, although in most states a tax conviction results in permanent loss of the right to bear arms.

Because these laws operate largely beyond public view, yet have severe consequences for those affected, sociologist Jeremy Travis refers to them as "invisible punishments."

Felony disenfranchisement, arguably one of the most pressing civil rights issues of our time, is moving into the public spotlight—and out of public favor. Voting is the bedrock of our country's identity and our democracy, and yet millions of Americans are precluded from the polls. Rates and laws vary by state: Maine and Vermont, for instance, do not restrict voting rights (even those currently serving time in prison or jail are able to cast a vote), while Kentucky, Florida, and Iowa impose lifetime disenfranchisement for all people with felony convictions. Citizens who have "done the time" must still receive a *gubernatorial pardon* before heading to the polls.

Unsurprisingly, racial disparities in the criminal justice system culminate in disproportionate disenfranchisement: African American adults are four times more likely to be disenfranchised than the rest of the country's voting age population. Put another way, nearly six million

Americans are locked out of the voting booth due to a felony conviction, 2.2 million of whom are African American. Two point two *million*. What's more, jurisdictional inconsistency and legal convolution too often result in eligible voters mistakenly believing they don't have the right to cast a ballot or being turned away by (at best, misinformed) election judges.

That number can swing presidential elections. For example, the 2000 presidential election was decided by fewer than 600 votes in Florida. Had the 600,000 Floridians who had served their time for a felony crime *and* who had completed probation or parole been able to vote, scholars have posited that Al Gore would likely have been this nation's 43rd president. Local elections matter too. The overwhelming majority of disenfranchised Americans are not in prison or jail, but living in the community, paying taxes, and driving over potholes on the way to the grocery store. Yet because of disenfranchisement, millions are left without a voice in choosing their political representatives—in Congress, in the state legislature, on the city commission, on the school board, or on the bench.

Criminologists have found that people who cast a ballot have lower recidivism rates than those who do not. A clear path to broader public and political engagement is one of the most important components of reentry, says prison justice organizer Kevin Reese. If

civic participation is taken away when one is in prison, arguably paying his or her debt to society, "restoration of that right should be the receipt upon return to the community—the acknowledgment of debt paid."

Because people experience collateral consequences as a suffocating and haphazard heap of restrictions and regulations, rather than individual curtailments, criminologists Christopher Uggen and Robert Stewart call it "piling on." They note that when sanctions are applied deliberately and appropriately, they can promote public safety. "When applied indiscriminately and unnecessarily, however, they can slow or prevent reintegration and impose great costs on individuals, their families, and their communities." Dr. Travis notes that in this brave new world, a debt to society is never paid: "these punishments have become instruments of 'social exclusion'; they create a permanent diminution in social status of convicted offenders, a distancing between 'us' and 'them.'"

As suffocating as the sanctions and broader practices may be, it's the paralyzing combination of legal sanctions on top of the expansive social proscription that creates internal exile.

For example, finding safe and affordable housing can be exceptionally difficult if one has anything from manufacturing methamphetamines to public intoxication on his or her record. In

some jurisdictions, public urination can bar access to subsidized housing (though there are few sanctions so preposterous, it seems, than barring a home with a toilet to someone who's had to pee in the streets). Private landlords frequently deny housing or inflate rent and security deposits for people with records. In spite of the Department of Housing and Urban Development's repeated calls to public and private landlords to view criminal record disqualifiers as the exception rather than the rule, housing remains a critical and elusive need for many individuals and families plagued with criminal records.

It's true that some employers are legally required to deny jobs to people with certain records, yet many more are not. Still, the vast majority of U.S. employers conduct background checks on job applicants. It's one thing to access a record, know that it is accurate, and then have the resources and savvy to reasonably, rationally, and equitably utilize such data in the hiring process. It's another—and far more familiar—thing to access inaccurate and incomplete data, rely upon gut in determining employability, and pay little mind to the severity or recency of the offense, the rehabilitation of the applicant, or even the nexus between the offense or alleged offense and the job at hand. Yet this is too often how hiring decisions are made.

EMPLOYMENT

The overwhelming majority of employers conduct criminal background checks on job applicants; many result in automatic denials, regardless of the severity, recency, or relevance of the offense or allegation to the job at hand.

 HOUSING

Finding housing (public or private) is extremely difficult with a criminal record. This results in increased homelessness and split families—where the person with a record (a parent, child, or other family member) is forced to find shelter elsewhere.

 LICENSURE

Criminal records (again, including mere arrests) can stymie or permanently bar people from thousands of jobs within licensed fields and facilities, from maintenance and cafeteria positions in schools and hospitals to practicing medicine or law.

 BENEFITS

Government assistance may be denied to individuals with certain criminal records (in particular, drug possession and sale).

 EDUCATION

The Common Application, used by more than 600 colleges and universities nationwide, asks the question that chills many would-be students: "Have you ever been adjudicated guilty or convicted of a misdemeanor, felony, or other crime?"

 IMMIGRATION

Crimes ranging from felonies to misdemeanors can affect one's ability to immigrate to the U.S. or naturalize; records can also prevent stable employment, making difficult the proof of solvency necessary for family green card petitions.

 TRAVEL

Criminal records can prevent people from traveling outside of the United States, from crossing the Canadian border to obtaining a travel visa.

 VOTING

An estimated 5.85 million Americans are prohibited from casting a ballot due to laws that disenfranchise people convicted of felony-level offenses.

Without a job or access to benefits, how does one put food in her belly or a roof over her head? Retired prosecutor Robert M.A. Johnson mused in our interview, "You don't need a resume to burglarize a home, you don't need to pass a background check to sell drugs at the corner. With few opportunities for work, how do we expect people to live?" That is, for some, living crime-free becomes increasingly difficult as avenues to earning a paycheck are continually blockaded.

The everlasting effects of criminal records are felt keenly in access to education. The Common Application—used by more than 600 colleges and universities to help determine the makeup of next year's incoming freshman class, asks: "Have you ever been adjudicated guilty or convicted of a misdemeanor, felony, or other crime?" Yes or no? Can you imagine your access (or your child's access) to education reduced to an x in a box? Schools may say that this is just one variable in a much longer algorithm used to determine who would be a "good fit" on campus. However, such an inquiry has a chilling effect upon potential applicants with criminal records. With education, as with rental housing applications, you have to pay to be denied: thirty, fifty, seventy dollars a pop, just to be told that you're not a suitable fit for that school.

Bear in mind, there is no empirical evidence showing students with criminal records pose a greater safety risk on campus, while there *is* evidence that education is one of the most successful and cost-effective methods of reducing recidivism, curtailing crime, and alleviating poverty. We should be doing everything we can to keep or push people into school, rather than locking them out.

But wait, there's more! Criminal records can seriously cramp your love life, too. When online dating profiles, professional network pages, social media's carefully curated photographs, and sports and academic accolades are eclipsed by a mugshot, getting a date—or approval from your beloved's family—can be an insurmountable challenge.

Criminal records can delay marriage licenses, hinder honeymoons for which checks are run or visas required, and stymie home and car loans. They can prevent you from coaching your daughter's sports team, chaperoning your son's field trip, or eating lunch with your grandchild in the school cafeteria. Records can lock you out of medical treatment, eldercare, and can bump you down or off an organ transplant list. You might be kicked out of a religious study group, book club, or social circle after a perceived slight inspires someone to Google your name.

"All it takes is one procrastinating person a few minutes, a passing curiosity, and an internet connection, and I'm done," said one woman describing the constant, dull hum of fear she experiences living with a criminal record. "Nothing else will matter."

This regime of relentless restrictions and stifling social stigma is disqualifying people from the very institutions we know help people create happy, healthy lives, lives as engaged citizens—sometimes, for those who have been incarcerated, just as they have been hustled through a well-meaning program of chemical dependency treatment, anger management, or education and job prep meant to set them on just those paths.

Once upon a time, you could outrun your past: cross a county or state line and start anew. In the history of chronicled criminality, it wasn't so long ago you could literally destroy a record—after all, it was a tangible, discrete document that could be burned, trashed, shredded, forgotten, forgiven. But this is the Information Age: our scarlet letters are both indelible and instantly, globally accessible.

Notably, while criminal records are harmful for some, they are catastrophic for others. For example, not everyone goes through a formal background check when job or apartment seeking: some have family or friend connections that allow bypass of the regular, and regulated, route. Even if histories are

discovered, many are caught by their social safety net: people who can vouch for or carry them until they get back on their feet. Not everyone has that safety net. For so many, that net is more like a thin thread, and a publicly accessible record can be the thing that cuts it.

| RACE AND RECORDS |

Dr. Pager studied the effects of criminal records and race on employability. She divided the study's job applicants into four groups: white and black applicants with and without a fictitious criminal record. Each applicant was provided with a comparable resume, sent to the same set of employers, and coached to behave similarly in the process. Dr. Pager then tracked the call-back rates for each group. At 34 percent, white applicants without a criminal record were most likely to be invited back for an interview and, at five percent, black applicants with a criminal record were the least. Perhaps most disturbing was that white applicants with a criminal record (who were already significantly disadvantaged—experiencing a halved call-back rate from white applicants with no record) were still more likely to get a phone call than black applicants without a criminal record. Dr. Pager writes that her findings suggest that, on the basis of race, black applicants are already seen as *criminals*: "[d]espite the lack of official conviction

record, their job candidacy is nevertheless suspected by virtue of membership in a group with high incarceration rates and pervasive images of criminality."

In her incredibly powerful and provocative book, *The New Jim Crow*, Michelle Alexander examines mass incarceration as a modern caste system, tracing its roots to racial segregation laws:

Today it is perfectly legal to discriminate against criminals in nearly all the ways that it was once legal to discriminate against African Americans. Once you're labeled a felon, the old forms of discrimination— employment discrimination, housing discrimination, denial of the right to vote, denial of educational opportunity, denial of food stamps and other public benefits, and exclusion from jury service—are suddenly legal. As a criminal, you have scarcely more rights, and arguably less respect, than a black man living in Alabama at the height of Jim Crow.

"We have not ended racial caste in America," Professor Alexander contends, "we have merely redesigned it."

GRADUATE STUDENT

INSURANCE FRAUD; POSSESSION AND SALE OF CONTROLLED SUBSTANCES; TRESPASSING; SHOPLIFTING

Pretty much every crime that I've committed is something that I morally justify to myself. Here's a small list.

There's drug use—buying and trying. I also have some sales (very small, maybe buying marijuana from one friend and selling it to another a few times). When I had surgery, I got as many painkillers as I could and sold those. Now that I think about it, when I was younger I tried growing marijuana but failed. It started coming up, but I think an animal came along and ate it. But had I been successful, I would have sold it!

I've trespassed over fences and into abandoned buildings. It's an urban explorer type of thing. Not so much the sewage stuff because that never really interested me. If it smells bad it takes away some of the excitement.

But most often, I've stolen from larger companies I don't care about and despise to some degree. Like at Walmart, I've purchased things and returned an older version in the package. Or if something was very expensive, I've ordered it online and then said it never arrived (there's no way to verify that in an apartment building).

Along those lines, I can tell you how I got my new MacBook. I had an old laptop that stopped working so I waited for a power surge in the neighborhood. Then I took it into the Apple store and they confirmed that it didn't work. The store gave me a write-up stating that the laptop was broken, but that they couldn't verify what caused it. So I scanned the form, Photoshopped that line out, and sent it to the rental insurance company. Failures under power surges are covered so I got a new computer.

There's nothing that I've done that I regret. And none of these things are so essential to me that if I knew I were to be punished for them, or if I knew I were to be caught, that I would have to continue doing them. I feel like I can be pretty reflective of these choices and decide whether I'd like to do them or not. I'm in a situation where I can choose which of these things I can do and I can do them in a safe manner.

Besides, I am not the person people are targeting or searching for. That's sad, but it's one of those things that knowing how the system works makes you depressed, but it also makes you more confident with your situation. Being a white educated person who doesn't have a record is a good thing.

So, yeah. That was the list that I came up with.

BANK TELLER

THEFT

It happened in college in the women's bathroom in the student union. I was washing my hands when a woman walked in, plopped her purse on the shelf next to the mirror in front of me, and disappeared into a stall. Before the toilet even flushed, I had plucked her wallet from the bag and was out the door.

I didn't need the money, but I wanted it. I think I bought beer, maybe peanut butter with it.

It was 80 bucks, but it didn't last long.

She had tickets to The Clash that night, good seats, too. I dumped them in a trash bin a few blocks away. I couldn't exactly bring them back to her or use them myself. I still feel bad about that.

I mailed her driver's license to the address listed—somewhere in Kentucky, probably her parents' home.

I work at a bank now. Down in Iowa, a man was fired from Wells Fargo because he stuffed a cardboard dime into a laundromat's washer 50 years ago. And I could have lost mine for some Jif and trashed tickets to a punk rock show.

I DIDN'T NEED THE MONEY, BUT I WANTED IT. I THINK I BOUGHT BEER, MAYBE PEANUT BUTTER WITH IT.

IN THE NEWS

In 2012, a 68-year-old man was fired from a bank for a crime he committed nearly five decades earlier.

Richard was 19 when he stuffed a cardboard cutout of a dime into a laundromat's washing machine in 1963. He was charged with operating a coin changing machine by false means and half a century later, he lost his job because of it.

In defending the termination, the bank says it was following new and stricter Federal Deposit Insurance Corporation regulations enacted after the mortgage lending crisis.

TEACHER

POSSESSION OF CONTROLLED SUBSTANCES; CRIMINAL NEGLECT

We were mid-field when I heard a crash. A van had busted through the school's fence, and several cop cars were directly behind him: it was a high-speed chase and the kids were all outside. The popsicles I had picked up for the students dropped from my hands in slow motion.

THEY CALLED ME A HERO. I DON'T SMOKE ANYMORE, AND WITHOUT A RECORD OR ANYTHING BLOCKING ME FROM WORKING IN THE FIELD, I'M IN A POSITION WHERE I CAN ACTUALLY BECOME ONE.

It was April 20th, and I had decided to get high before work to mark the day.

Fuuuuuuck. I couldn't think, I couldn't move. Kids came running towards me in a panic. I managed to line them up and pointed them toward the gym. I couldn't find the words; another teacher told them to *RUN! RUN!*

Later that day, everyone wanted to know what happened, so I told the story and told it in a way that made me feel good. I got a promotion and then another. I was called the "Safety Guru."

They called me a hero. I don't smoke anymore, and without a record or anything blocking me from working in the field, I'm in a position where I can actually become one.

GRADUATE STUDENT

BURGLARY

Oh man. There's so much. Here's one anecdote I remember:

One time we broke into a schoolmate's family's shed as retribution for ongoing disagreements. We thought we could find a spare key, but ended up smashing out a window instead.

It was one of those things where one kid says it out loud (*Let's break into their shed!*), so there's a greater chance of it happening. We figured there'd be steaks and beer inside—but really it was just some old tools and a pint of ice cream in the freezer. We took the ice cream.

I think getting caught for embracing that peer mentality would have hampered my career choices. But this was out in the middle of nowhere, so we were unlikely to be caught compared to kids our age doing similar things in the city.

Burglary with a
peer mentality.
Easier to get away
in the country.

DEACON, INSURANCE AGENT

PUBLIC INTOXICATION; RECKLESS DRIVING; DISORDERLY CONDUCT; DISORDERLY HOUSE; DISRUPTING THE PEACE; UNRULY ASSEMBLY

A while back I was taking the train; my headphones were in, but the sound was off. There were these two guys behind me, couldn't have been more than 18. Neither could find a job because of a felony. A *felony*? When I was their age, I was thinking about college, not a criminal record.

Our college was in a low-income neighborhood. We had a lot of contact with the police, but whether it was for driving infractions or frat parties, we were always told to *Keep a move on, Keep it down*. There were several all-out brawls. We were never ticketed, never arrested.

Every job I've held since graduation has been licensed, and I've never had to worry about my past. That's not true for so many others: I hear it time and again at different jobs, *We were gonna hire him, but he didn't pass a background check.*

And here's the thing: it's not just my day job but my church position that would be unlikely had I been caught.

> **EVERY JOB I'VE HELD SINCE GRADUATION HAS BEEN LICENSED, AND I'VE NEVER HAD TO WORRY ABOUT MY PAST. THAT'S NOT TRUE FOR SO MANY OTHERS: I HEAR IT TIME AND AGAIN AT DIFFERENT JOBS,** *WE WERE GONNA HIRE HIM, BUT HE DIDN'T PASS A BACKGROUND CHECK.*

PROGRAM DEVELOPER

THEFT; INDECENT EXPOSURE; MINOR CONSUMPTION; FALSE IDENTIFICATION; POSSESSION OF MARIJUANA

Generally, my offenses aren't that big of a deal.

I drank underage in high school and college. I went to bars with my sister's ID. I've smoked pot, but never bought it. I guess I've illegally downloaded music; that was huge in the dorms.

IT'S CRAZY. I'M HAVING TROUBLE REMEMBERING THINGS THAT I DID THAT WERE ILLEGAL, I JUST DON'T THINK ABOUT IT.

Let's see. There was a pizza-by-the-slice place on campus. You order your slice from one person, pay another, and get it from a third. At night, it was so busy you could definitely sneak around the second person so you wouldn't have to pay. You're not taking it from anyone—it's yours—you just didn't pay for it. I did that multiple times, and I definitely never did it when sober. I guess I didn't have the courage otherwise.

Oh, there's another thing, and telling you about this one is a little bit embarrassing. The college I went to was on a lake and skinny-dipping was kind of a thing. One day I went down to the private docks with this guy I had been dating. We started out in the lake and ended up on the dock. After we were done with it, we got dressed and headed back to the dorms. As we were walking up the hill, a police officer was walking down. Had we taken a little bit longer, he definitely would have seen us. That would have not been good.

It's crazy. I'm having trouble remembering things that I did that were illegal, I just don't think about it.

You know, with the college mindset, you do these things that in the morning are a funny story—nothing you think of as illegal.

Overall, I suppose I've done some pretty stupid things—but none of it defines who I am.

| PARALLEL STORY |

In 2003, he swiped two chicken wings from a salad bar on University Avenue. He was overworked, underpaid, and hungry. Besides, he shopped there all the time, so it was just like sampling.

He pleaded guilty to misdemeanor theft, lost his security job, and has struggled to find full-time, permanent employment ever since.

FINANCIAL COMPLIANCE MANAGER

AIDED AND ABETTED INSURANCE FRAUD; ARSON

I asked my husband, *What should I talk about?* I've done the normal things: drugs (used, participated in the sale of), theft, and so on. My husband said, *You musta forgotten about that arson and insurance fraud.* Oh yeah . . .

So this was before he and I met, when I was dating someone else. This guy knew this girl who had a car she couldn't sell. It was in rough shape. Someone told her, *You know you'd be better off if you just totaled it or if someone stole it.* So she asked the guy I was dating to stage a theft. This girl gave him the keys, but he pretended to break in and all that. He drove it out to the country, poured gasoline in the backseat, and lit a match.

He needed a ride back home, so I was there to give him one.

For the next few months, I watched the news incessantly. I was so terrified.

You know, if I'd been caught, I'd just be getting out. I wouldn't have this job now. I would not have met my husband.

Everything that I have in life, it's been since then. What if that were taken away from me? What if I never had it?

ARSON

HUMAN RIGHTS PROFESSIONAL

SHOPLIFTING; TRESPASSING; PUBLIC INDECENCY; PUBLIC URINATION; POSSESSION OF MARIJUANA; THEFT OF SERVICES; FAILURE TO OBEY BICYCLE REGULATIONS

You know, I've spent a lot of time thinking about this.

One thing that strikes me is how defensive I get when considering my own criminality; I don't think I'm usually like that. When you're told something is illegal, there's this assumption that it is also probably morally wrong, but my personal moral code conflicts with the law of the land. I don't tend to think things are wrong unless I think they hurt people. In abiding by my personal code more than abiding by the law of the land, I imply that I'm above the law of the land. Even if I happen to think that my moral code is better than the law of the land (which I do), this is a problem because (A) I can only get away with this because I'm white, which is unfair, and (B) if *everyone* did this it would be a *huge* problem.

So, that was unsettling.

RESTAURANT MANAGER

THEFT

I was 19 years old, and I had just dropped out of school. I had actually been working at a bank in collections, and I decided that I wanted to do something more fun, I guess. So I became a barista at a coffee shop—and I wasn't making a ton of money at my job.

We had a tip jar. We all pooled our tips, and there'd usually be five or six dollars in change and then a few $1 bills or whatnot, but throughout the day, we would cash in the change for dollar bills. So it started out,

I NEVER WANT TO BE SOMEONE THAT PEOPLE CAN'T TRUST, BECAUSE THAT WAS ONE OF THE LOWEST FEELINGS THAT I HAD.

I would just take an extra 50 cents and then, after a few weeks, I was taking an extra dollar every time, or a couple of dollars. We could sign our paychecks over if we just wrote "pay to the order of ___." We could take the cash out of the till and leave the paycheck in there. So I started taking an extra $5 or $10 when I would cash my check.

The owner pulled me aside and confronted me about it. They had been watching me. They had watched the last transaction that I did—and counted the till directly after. They'd counted it right before and after and knew that it was me who had been doing it.

So she said that if I signed my check over to her right then and there, which was probably around $150, that she wouldn't call the police. I'd obviously lose my job, but there'd be no other consequences. So that's what I did.

My mom and I had gotten a hotel room for us to celebrate kind of a coming-of-age thing—to show me that she was proud of me and she wanted to just have a kind of "vacation in the city." A mother and daughter thing. She popped a big garbage bag of popcorn, and we love popcorn, so it was a giant treat. She even rented a couple of movies.

And this thing with the till happened hours before we were to check in to the hotel. I just couldn't tell her . . . and I couldn't even eat the popcorn, you know? I was just sick to my stomach over it: she was showing me how proud of me she was, and I had just screwed up so, so badly.

I never want to be someone that people can't trust, because that was one of the lowest feelings that I had.

PERSONAL CARE ATTENDANT,
RECENT GRADUATE

POSSESSION OF CONTROLLED SUBSTANCES;
THEFT OF GOVERNMENT PROPERTY; UNDERAGE CONSUMPTION;
CRIMINAL INFRINGEMENT OF COPYRIGHT

I think about it often, the privilege I have. The privilege of driving like a hot mess. The privilege of not knowing where my insurance is, for example. The cops are always patient with me. I realize that isn't everyone's experience.

It's not just driving. This morning I had to submit to a background check for a PCA position. It's like they purposefully designed a burdensome process. I could only pay for the background check with a cashier's check or money order, the place was only open two days a week, and I walked in 20 minutes too late today in order to complete the check. Therefore I have to go back again. I was irritated at the inconvenience of it all when I realized: *I have nothing to worry about*. My record is clean.

GRADUATE STUDENT
DRIVING WHILE INTOXICATED

At closing, I didn't know which bar I was at; I didn't even know which side of town I was in. I remember puking out the car window as I was trying to find home.

It wasn't enough to make me *stop* stop—but I didn't go on any more twelve-hour benders.

Shortly after that, I got a job in the army that required a high level of security clearance; after that was college, and after that was graduate school. Perhaps none of that would have happened had I been caught.

But in some ways those are small costs. I could have killed somebody. Now that's way worse than any other consequences I could have felt.

SECURITY GUARD
DRIVING WHILE INTOXICATED

At the time, I was working for public safety, and driving was key to the job.

If I would have lost my license or been suspended, I would have lost my job. It could have had a domino effect, stopping me from being with you here today.

PROSECUTOR

SHOPLIFTING

I've always been a rule follower, but I could not stop stealing.

In school I worked hard to get good grades, and all I wanted as a reward was gum—Bubblicious, to be exact. But we grew up poor and on food stamps, and the answer was always no. No, no, no. So I took it.

Sometimes grape, more often strawberry. I stole what I wanted.

After high school, I went to college. I was the first person in my family to go to college, but I still found myself in a predicament: by sophomore year, I was pregnant. I had great social support, but no financial support. So I went back to stealing.

Baby need a new pacifier? Stick it in her mouth or in the diaper bag. So be it. I stole what I needed.

In my job now, my criminal history helps me be more empathetic. Yeah, it's still wrong— but I see the whole person. And I try to get my colleagues to see the same.

We are not the crimes we commit.

GRADUATE STUDENT
MINOR IN POSSESSION; PUBLIC INTOXICATION

My story is boring. Outside of religious ceremonies, I didn't drink until I was 18.

I went to a small, *very* liberal arts school where I was a lot tamer than many of my classmates.

My freshman year, we had a few dorm parties (all before my "No Shots" rule), and I competed in my first Tour de Franzia. That's right: 21 stages of drinking bagged wine. Go team! My sophomore year I moved into a duplex; a friendly drug cartel lived in the ground floor apartment, and I still get nostalgic any time I smell weed.

Mostly, we were white, upper-, upper-middle-class, and we were doing the same things that kids in town were doing and everyone knew it— but they were getting picked up and we weren't.

Now, I'm really looking forward to see where my classmates end up: undoubtedly in positions of power, unmarred by their criminal pasts.

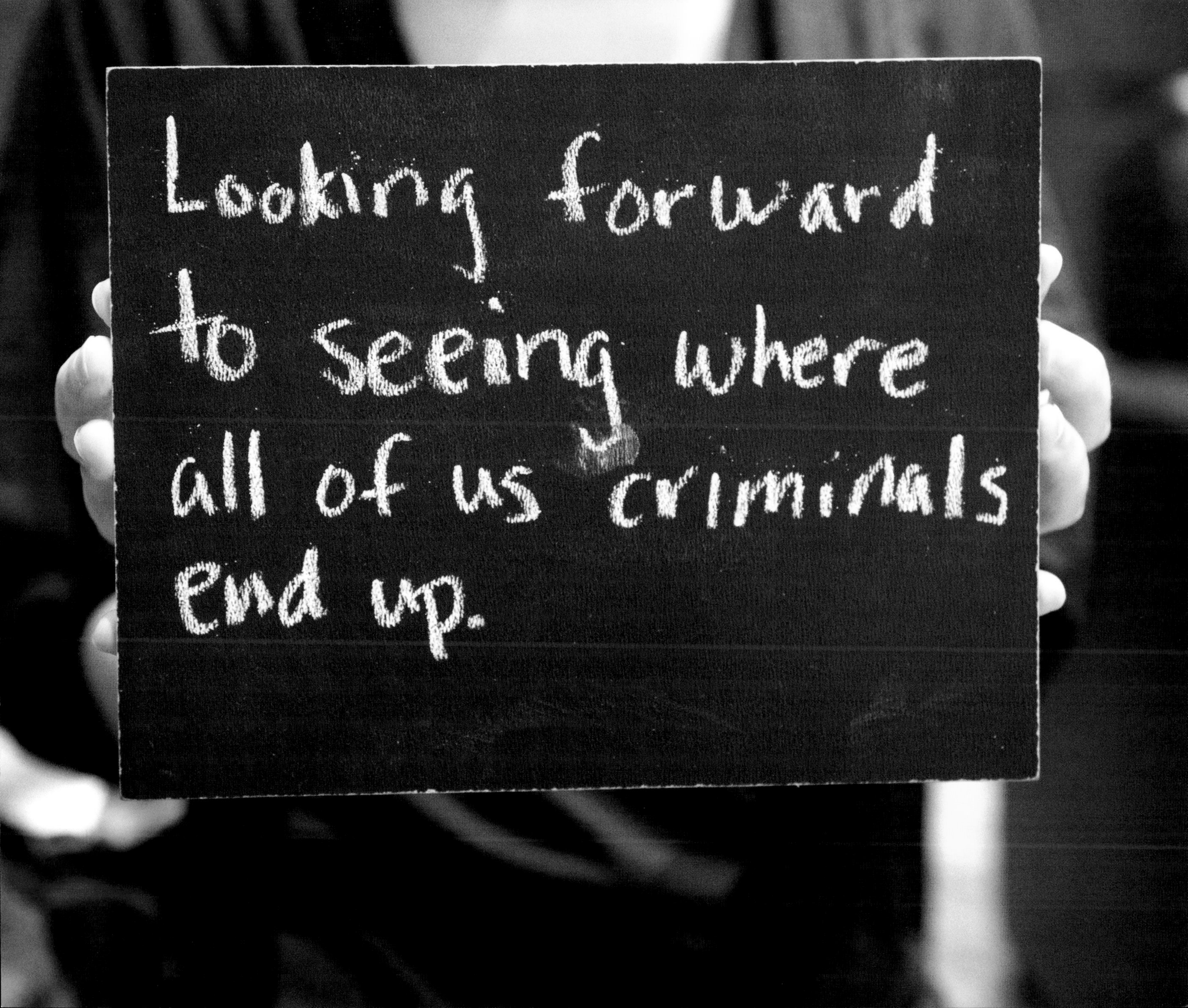
Looking forward
to seeing where
all of us criminals
end up.

STUDENT

I AM MORE THAN MY MUGSHOT

I don't really know how to start.

I feel like this might get a little emotional. Just sayin'.

I was the *three in four*; I'm now the *one in four*. It seems like society is telling me that I'm now a bad person, that I'm a statistic, and that I should question the value in my future. It hurts so much.

But I'm not going to let this one thing stop me from living my life.

I made a mistake. I learned from it. I'm ready to move on—I'm ready to live my life. My future is informed by my experiences—including my mistakes—but shouldn't be defined by them.

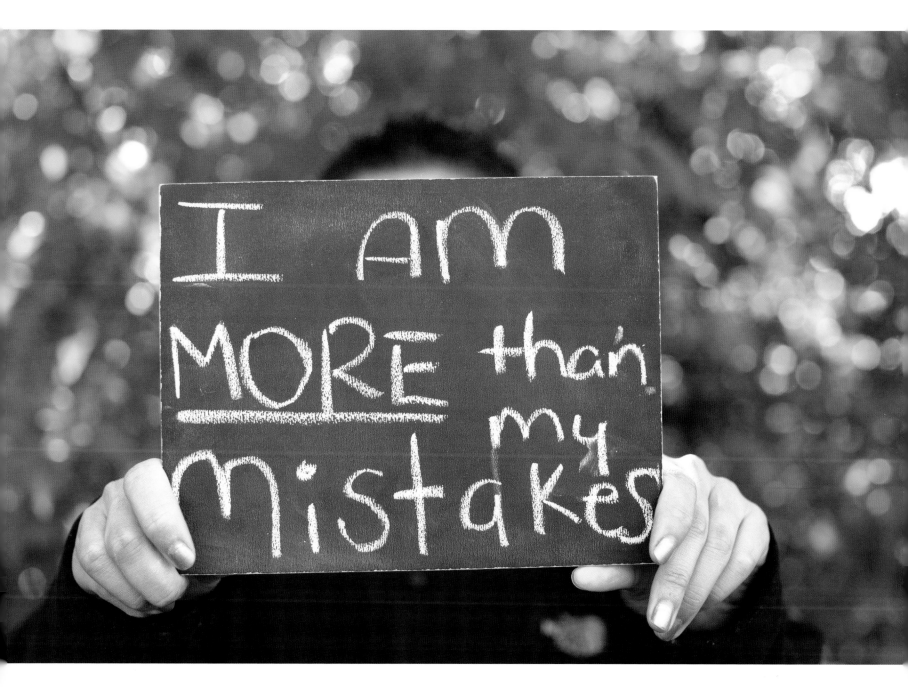

WAR ON DRUGS

In June of 1971, against the thick, velvety folds of the White House Briefing Room's dark drapery, President Richard Nixon addressed a roomful of reporters: "America's public enemy number one in the United States is drug abuse. In order to fight and defeat this enemy, it is necessary to wage a new, all-out offensive."

The path to mass incarceration was already set; Nixon built a superhighway on it.

In *The New Jim Crow*, a searing indictment of the U.S. criminal justice system, Professor Alexander traces the contemptible history of mass incarceration to the drug war, and the drug war back to the Civil War. After all, the abolition of slavery didn't suddenly erase centuries of perceived racial differences and the notion of white supremacy. The Black Codes came fast on emancipation's heels, soon followed by Jim Crow. Entire series of laws created by white southerners restricted black individuals' activity; public facilities were segregated while acts like "vagrancy," "mischief," and "insulting gestures" were aggressively enforced against African Americans. Punishment was often prison and forced labor.

In 1954, the Supreme Court decided *Brown v. Board of Education*, declaring racially segregated public schools unconstitutional and sparking the civil rights movement's push toward equal rights. In response, southern governors and law enforcement demanded greater "law and order," characterizing desegregation and civil rights supporters as criminals. The Civil Rights Act of 1964 may have formally dismantled the Jim Crow system by calling for an end to segregation in public accommodations, employment, and federally funded programs, but as Professor Alexander notes: "Any candid observer of American racial history must acknowledge that racism is highly adaptable."

The years in between the Civil Rights Act and the launch of the War on Drugs saw politicians clamoring for tough-on-crime policies and seeding fertile land with resentment and fear of black Americans.

Watching grainy footage from the news conference Nixon called to announce the War on Drugs, it is eerie how much the tall vertical folds of those draperies look like cell bars.

Decades after serving as White House Counsel to President Nixon, John Ehrlichman told a reporter that the Nixon camp "had two enemies: the antiwar left and black people," continuing:

> We knew we couldn't make it illegal to be either against the war or black, but by getting the public to associate the hippies with marijuana and blacks with heroin, and then criminalizing both heavily, we could disrupt those communities. We could arrest their leaders, raid their homes, break up their meetings, and vilify them night after night on the evening news. Did we know we were lying about the drugs? Of course we did.

It's not that the electorate was demanding battles. Even when President Ronald Reagan ran with the war baton a few years later, less than two percent of the American public considered drugs to be the most important issue facing the country. Nevertheless, punitive campaigns marched on. Few things in politics are as powerful as *othering*.

Soon came a deluge of zero-tolerance programs and mandatory minimum drug sentences. Once caught up in the tidal wave of criminalization, civil penalties kept people from coming up for air: public housing authorities evicted families, governments terminated assistance to caretakers, and students lost school loans due to drug activity and convictions. But that was just the beginning. Again, Professor Alexander:

> In the era of colorblindness, it is no longer socially permissible to use race, explicitly, as a justification for discrimination, exclusion, and social contempt. So we don't. Rather than rely on race, we use our criminal justice system to label people of color "criminals" and then engage in all the practices we supposedly left behind.

Real Estate Agent's story on following pages

REAL ESTATE AGENT
TRAFFICKING OF CONTROLLED SUBSTANCES

I was just finishing up my freshman year of college, and my roommate and I were listening to a lot of reggae, a lot of Bob Marley, Peter Tosh. That summer, we went to Jamaica. After hanging around a few days, someone came up and said, *Do you want to come up to see our ganja farm?* Everyone says they know Bob Marley, everyone says they've got a farm. But this was the real deal.

We rented a moped and drove up and down through fields and paths. There were no roads. The earth was packed soil, moist dirt, and rows of water. It was intense and lush and thick, and the plants were spotted amid all of this. The light glistened down on the full, mature plants. Buds 18 inches long, draped over one another. It was beautiful.

We paid the guy for a pound and the little tour and adventure. Back in the city, we bought a wooden carving of a head, a Rastaman, and sent it to another artist to hollow out. That guy did a rough and ugly job. *I can't take that back! I'm totally gonna get busted.*

Meanwhile, we bought hash oil—big goops of it and stuffed it into Crest toothpaste tubes. My roommate said he'd take that if I'd take the head.

We had one night left—and found a craftsman willing to carve new dreads and repaint the Rastaman. I did not have a restful last night. *I just kept thinking, Is this worth it? Is this insane?* But, you know, I was a 19-year-old knucklehead all over the whole Jamaican scene.

We flew into the U.S. and lined up for Customs. We were a mess. We ended up at the end of the line. It was getting shorter and shorter—and we were the last people there. We were sitting ducks, there was nothing left to do but bust us.

So where you two been?
-Oh, down to Jamaica.
First time?
-First time.
Welcome back to America.

I started walking and didn't look back.

Back home, we cracked it open and put the weed on a scale. We only got a quarter pound—and not the gorgeous buds, but some brown. To risk all of that for a QP?! I don't know what the laws were in my home state, but I can only imagine. Where would I have gone? Prison? I would have been a complete disaster. It would have affected everything. Everything would have been upside down.

I wasn't the only one, of course. I knew guys that were drug dealers. I learned more from conversations in their dorm rooms about market conditions, economics, supply and demand, than I did from any of the classes. And so many of these guys—none of whom were caught—turned out to be extremely financially successful individuals.

We were fortunate to have great weed, and extremely fortunate not to have it be our demise.

Now I'm much older. I have a kid who's a freshman in college. He's not like I was; he's a straight arrow.

I WASN'T THE ONLY ONE, OF COURSE. I KNEW GUYS THAT WERE DRUG DEALERS. I LEARNED MORE FROM CONVERSATIONS IN THEIR DORM ROOMS ABOUT MARKET CONDITIONS, ECONOMICS, SUPPLY AND DEMAND, THAN I DID FROM ANY OF THE CLASSES. AND SO MANY OF THESE GUYS—NONE OF WHOM WERE CAUGHT—TURNED OUT TO BE EXTREMELY FINANCIALLY SUCCESSFUL INDIVIDUALS.

| PARALLEL STORY |

It wasn't much—a few joints and a six-pack—but it was enough to get her booted from the dorm and lose her federal financial aid.

For the first few months following her guilty plea, friends would invite her to campus parties—where every other college kid seemed to be smoking or snorting something: still enrolled, still on track to graduate. She couldn't stomach it for long and was almost relieved when her boss moved her to night shifts at the gas station where she'd been working to pay down court and attorney's fees.

At first she was convinced she would fall right back into the college routine once the FAFSA bar had passed—but it turns out the college isn't as forgiving of academic disruptions as she had hoped.

She's lost the momentum and the clean record, and now in the moments between restocking the hot dog roller and announcing, *Pump Three, Please Prepay or Pay at the Pump* she wonders if she'll ever get back on track.

MONDAY SPECIAL

2PM - 7:30

HOT ROAST TURKEY SANDWICH

Cranberry Sauce,
Whipped Potatoes $5.95

TUESDAY SPECIAL

2PM - 7:30

BARBECUED PORK RIBS

(Served with Cole Slaw,
French Fried Potatoes &
Homemade Roll.)

$6.95

WEDNESDAY SPECIAL

EVENINGS ONLY
(Baked at Spring)

CHICKEN

Includes

CELERY DRESSING, CRANBERRY SAUCE
CABBAGE SALAD, WHIPPED POTATOES,
HOMEMADE ROLL

$5.95

ELECTED OFFICIAL

FELONY POSSESSION OF A CONTROLLED SUBSTANCE

I was 17, maybe 18. Not 19, because that's when I moved out of my parents' home. I was with a friend, Michael, dropping him off in my mother's car.

At his parents' house, Michael got out and stood by the driver's door. It was July and my window was rolled down. He had a joint in his hand and I had one in mine. Mine was lit. We passed it back and forth, inhaling summer with the smoke.

All of a sudden, a cop was at my friend's side. Michael must have swallowed his joint, but it was too late for me to do anything except snuff the roach in the ashtray.

The cop looked past Michael to me.

Can I search your trunk?
-Sure, but why?
To be quite honest, I smelled marijuana as I was driving by, and again now.

Marijuana in those days was a felony.

I can't quite say how I was feeling or what I was thinking other than, *Thank God he's asking about the trunk and not the ashtray.*

I still wanted to head off the cop, so I said, *Michael, are you wearing that patchouli oil?* Then I looked at the cop and said, *Officer, my mother is always complaining it smells like marijuana.* It's true, she was.

The cop looked at Michael. Michael, with all sincerity, told him he was wearing the oil and pointed to the patch of skin between his brows. He bent toward the cop, offering his forehead as proof.

The cop hesitated before leaning in, his nose almost brushing Michael's skin. The cop inhaled, and I held my breath.

Okay, he said. *I'll buy it.*

The cop drove off, and then I exhaled.

| PARALLEL STORY |

It seems like the cops singled her out: she was the only African American in a group of teens outside of a friend's house. She was scared out of her mind, so when they asked to search her purse, she handed it over. They found two joints and took her name and address. She missed the court summons—her mom and mom's boyfriend had gotten into it, and they had to leave quick.

After a while, she was stopped for a broken taillight. She was arrested on the possession warrant and spent the weekend in jail. Three missed shifts cost her a job. The car—broken taillight and all—sat in impound until she could find the money to get it out.

Once her hearing arrived, she paid a fine and it was "over," but she still gets asked about it on job applications. Maybe it's not a surprise she hasn't had an interview in a long time.

FEDERAL OFFICER

AIDING AND ABETTING SALE OF CONTROLLED SUBSTANCES

I had been the straight kid who enjoyed the company of delinquents. But I knew my limits: anytime cocaine showed up at a party, I would leave, or, if it was my place, I'd kick everyone out. But pot isn't the end of the world.

In high school and college, my friends and I would pack into my car and hit up the Grateful Dead concert tour. I preferred to be the designated driver (tame by comparison, with the occasional toke of pot). But on more than one occasion, there were hundreds of dollars of hallucinogenic mushrooms, LSD, hash, and weed on the persons of my passengers—some of it intended for sale.

There was one very close call: coming back from a concert in Canada, the border patrol

IRONICALLY—EIGHTY PERCENT OF MY CASELOAD WAS DRUG DEALERS.

found a wooden pipe with THC resin in my boyfriend's tackle box. They ripped my car apart, searching for more. When they couldn't find anything else, they let us go.

A few years later, I was appointed to a position in the federal court system working in the very district where I was stopped. Ironically—eighty percent of my caseload was drug dealers.

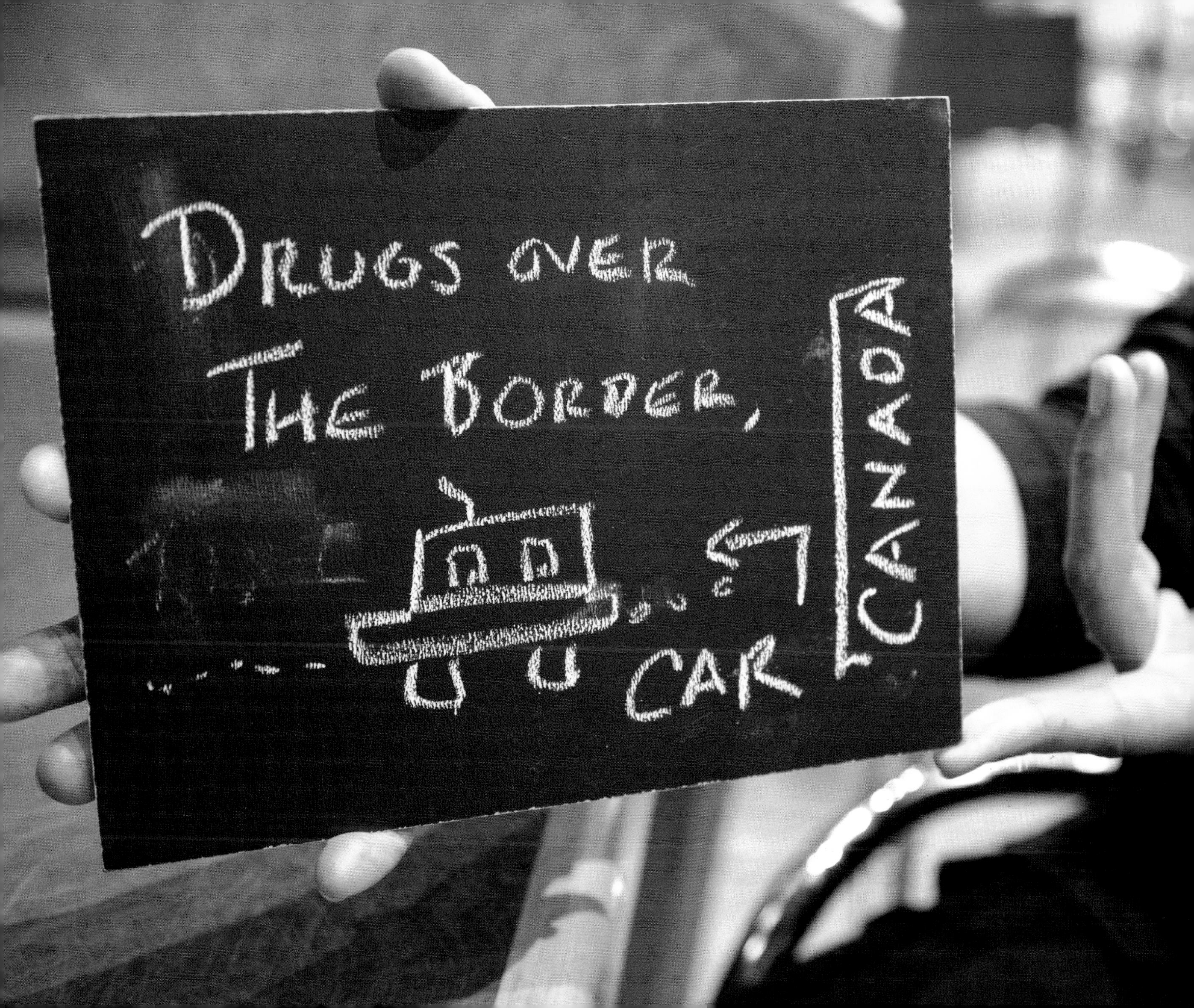
DRUGS OVER
THE BORDER,
CAR
CANADA

BUSINESS OWNER

SALE OF CONTROLLED SUBSTANCES

I grew up on one side of the lake but crossed it to go to college at a private school freshman year. Sophomore year, I transferred back home, moving in with my old high school friends. It didn't take long to figure out that they were no longer just smoking pot; now they were selling it. Now I'm no angel, but they took it to another level.

VERY FEW OF US HAVE WALKED THE PERFECT PATH. WE ALL MAKE ERRORS IN LIFE. HOPEFULLY, AS WE GET OLDER WE MAKE LESS.

It was soon decided that I was the ideal conduit to the untapped market across the lake.

I wouldn't say that my participation was key to the entire operation, but it helped. After they trained me in, I answered phones. I determined who was a genuine smoker and who might be a snitch, and I sometimes took money, too.

Did I profit? Sure.

Very few of us have walked the perfect path. We all make errors in life. Hopefully, as we get older we make less.

Now I coach my sons' hockey teams. Every year, I breeze through the applications: "Have you ever been convicted of," and then it lists ten or twelve offenses. I check no, no, no, no. If it asked, instead, "Have you ever committed," I don't know how I would answer.

I've been in sales for 20-plus years, and I can draw a straight line from my first internship out of college to where I'm at now. I've been lucky that nothing threw me off course.

| PARALLEL STORY |

I don't have a good reason for why I did it. I've been asked about it enough, you'd think I'd have a better excuse now. I did it because it seemed like everyone else was, so why wouldn't I? But not everyone gets caught. I was the only one of the four of us who did—and while I didn't do any jail time, I did have probation and I now have a record.

It's been eleven goddamn years, and I'm still paying for it: every time I fill out a job application, go for a promotion, move apartments, or work up the nerve to ask someone out, I know I'm going to be judged by what I did back then.

SOCIAL ENTERPRISE ENTREPRENEUR, FORMER MAYOR

POSSESSION AND SALE OF CONTROLLED SUBSTANCES

Anything was better than watching my family disintegrate. I couldn't hold us together, I couldn't keep my brother alive, but I could control my high. I could laugh and forget about what was happening at home; this was a new and welcome reality.

Oh, the luxuries to forget. I did such stupid, stupid things.

My girlfriend and I were driving along, and, in the spur of the moment, we decided to go to Canada. I had a roach clip hanging from the visor and pot in the trunk, divided into baggies and ready to sell.

Customs took one look at the clip and asked me to step out. After finding the bags of pot, he looked me over: I was a white kid and didn't look like "trouble." He said if I paid a fine, I could go on my way. I didn't have any money on me—so he told me to go down to a nearby corner store to see if they could help.

I explained the situation to the shop owner, and he asked if I had anything he could hold as collateral.

I showed him this chain. **This very chain.** It's gold, it's from Italy, and my mother had it blessed by the Pope.

He loaned me $500. I handed it over to the patrol, and I got my car back. You want to know the worst part? I lit up as I was pulling away.

People talk about "mission." I live my mission. My past has made me who I am.

Being able to tell this story is important: it's helped me understand—if you're a minority in this city, people have a radar out for you. No one had a radar out for me. If I would have been black, if I had been caught, I don't think I'd be here today.

But it's not just work for me: those experiences prepared me for life. When my daughter turned six, she began having seizures. Twenty, thirty a day. A couple of years after that, she developed diabetes—the same disease that killed my brother.

Here I was, back to where I had been before: someone I love, burdened with something I can't fix.

But I had seen what living with a sick child did to my parents and to me—and I wasn't going to let that happen again. I have so many more coping skills now than I or my parents once had. My wife and I are determined and driven and unwavering parents in this, and my daughter is a beautiful, hopeful, grounded soul.

That girl has taught me more in life than anyone else—and if I hadn't gone through my own experiences, I don't think I would have been able to hear it.

SMALL BUSINESS OWNER
SALE AND POSSESSION OF CONTROLLED SUBSTANCES

I was no baller. We just sold to friends.

A lot of the stuff we did then wasn't illegal. But now? We'd be in prison now.

TEACHER

AIDING AND ABETTING SALE
OF CONTROLLED SUBSTANCES

In the late '60s, I was a junior high teacher by day and a dope dealer's assistant by night.

Because of the war in Vietnam, there was a feeling among us that society had come unglued. Society wasn't going to work if it allowed guys my age to get drafted and sent to fight in Vietnam for no good reason. So if society wasn't working anyway, why shouldn't my roommate sell a little dope and why *shouldn't* I help him put it in little bags? As long as you weren't actively hurting people, there was no good reason to follow the law.

We were never paid, but my friends and I liked to smoke the free dope that was always sitting around. Eventually, we had a falling out over some of his drug dealings. He moved out, and within a few months he got busted and went to prison.

But I never got caught. I just kept on teaching.

TECHNICIAN

CONSPIRACY TO SELL
CONTROLLED SUBSTANCES

It was pretty informal. I'd wait outside while James met with his supplier. After a while, James would let me know it was time and we'd stuff the car with garbage bags of freshly cut grass from across the border and head back.

I never got any of the cash, but James let me smoke as much as I wanted. That was enough for me.

Within the year, James died of a heroin overdose.

I think about him a lot and about what might have happened to me if I had been caught. I wouldn't have graduated, gotten my job, married my wife, or be here today. I'd probably be drinking hooch in prison rather than being alcohol-free for the past four years.

And all for a friendship and a free high.

WIDENING NET

[N]o one has ever lost an election by being too tough on crime or too hard on inmates.

—*Jeff Smith, former Missouri State Senator and formerly incarcerated*

After the national anthem, a prayer, and a few remarks shared by a vice president on crutches, President Bill Clinton took the mic. It was the fall of 1994, planes were flying overhead and the wind occasionally picked at the American flags lining the stands. "There must be no doubt about whose side we're on," the president said as the crowd squinted in the sun.

People who commit crimes should be caught, convicted, and punished. This bill puts Government on the side of those who abide by the law, not those who break it; on the side of the victims, not their attackers; on the side of the brave men and women who put their lives on the line for us every day, not the criminals or those who would turn away from law enforcement. . . .

My fellow Americans, this is about freedom. Without responsibility, without order, without lawfulness, there is no freedom.

Then, flanked by liberals and conservatives alike, Clinton signed the largest crime bill in American history. The War on Drugs was well underway, crime rates were high, and states were already rapidly adopting "tough-on-crime" policies. According to a Vera Institute of Justice report, the 1994 Crime Bill rode "the crest of a national tide": money that would have gone to education is going to incarceration, state budgets are strapped, millions of children are growing up with parents behind bars, and the effects on poor communities and communities of color are profound. Moreover, corrosive collateral consequences reduce educational, employment, and civic opportunities.

In 2016, Clinton reflected on the bill with a group of mayors and law enforcement officials gathered in his presidential library: "We basically took a shotgun to a problem that needed a .22," noting, however ineptly, the unnecessary destruction caused by the expansive legislation. "We took a shotgun to it and just sent everybody to jail for too long."

| THE SWELLING CRIMINAL CODE |

Encompassing and outlawing far more than just drug activity, our laws have become so convoluted and voluminous that policy-makers—as well as police, prosecutors, and other criminal justice professionals—may understandably feel they're drowning. And if the federal criminal code is twisting, redundant, and contradictory, it is compounded as state legislatures pump out more and more laws. Each year, a crushing new wave of sanctions brings the nation's restriction watermark to untold heights.

As the net is cast increasingly wider, it's also fishing deeper. Listening to policymakers rationalize yet another round of criminal legislation, it seems our logic is caught in a dangerous and flawed binary: if we don't criminalize something (and criminalize it to the most punitive degree), we must be condoning it. We fail to entertain the notion that the criminal justice system may not be the answer to all that ails—or irritates—us. In fact, it can make some things far, far worse. Mass incarceration is the result of mass criminalization.

Reflecting upon the more than 4,000 federal offenses carrying criminal penalties, Right on Crime's Marc Levin echoes the warnings of psychologist Abraham Maslow: "if one only has a hammer, every problem is a nail."

| SEVERITY |

One oft-overlooked aspect of—and entry point into—our criminal justice system is the extraordinary number of non-imprisonable offenses that dominate the docket. That is, courts' calendars are jammed with misdemeanors, minor crimes that often do not result in lock-up.

Shoplifting, disorderly conduct, public intoxication, public urination, public indecency, underage consumption, driving under the influence, driving with a suspended license, trespassing, loitering, littering, and paraphernalia offenses are all common misdemeanors. There's also turnstile jumping, putting your feet on a subway seat, driving with a cracked windshield, sleeping in a park or in a cardboard box, begging alms or stopping to give them. Give a man a fish, it's a misdemeanor. Teach him how to fish and he fishes without a license, it's also a misdemeanor.

The exponential rise in zero-tolerance policies and aggressive enforcement have led to far greater misdemeanor convictions—and that's no minor matter. These "docket-cloggers" impose lifelong consequences for individuals and their families.

For immigrants, a misdemeanor conviction may lead to automatic deportation, Professor Jenny Roberts notes, regardless of work ties, time spent in the U.S., and family connections.

Low-level offenses can mean everyday people "may lose or be unable to get public housing and benefits, their driver's license, or access to student loans. If convicted of certain misdemeanor sexual offenses, they will be required to register as a sex offender, with severe restrictions on where they can live and work." Misdemeanors lock millions out of jobs, school, scholarships, loans, licensure, and more.

Meanwhile, the time devoted to fighting an average misdemeanor case belies the real consequences of conviction. Many defendants plead guilty at first appearance, without the help of an attorney. Those who do have representation may find that "counsel" is but a hurried conversation in a holding room, hallway, or through bulletproof glass in a courtroom's corner.

Despite being staffed with adept and dedicated attorneys, many public defense systems labor under the unrelenting strain of crushing caseloads and abominably inadequate funding and resources. The time you spend sitting in court or in a holding room waiting for your case to be called likely vastly exceeds the amount of time spent reading the charge against you, talking—if at all—to an attorney, or arguing the case (in those rare situations

where an argument is made). In the world of misdemeanor McJustice, your day in court might last a few minutes.

Just as disturbingly, many former misdemeanor offenses are reconfigured as felonies, carrying with them greater fine and time penalties. As legal scholars and countless public defenders have put it, we're moving toward a world where everything's a felony—it just depends on who's enforcing it.

Typically, more time is devoted to defending a felony case than a misdemeanor, but there is no guaranteed protection against the assembly line. The two-week trials of television are rare. Prosecutors wield incredible leverage over defendants: they dictate the charge, the plea negotiation process, and the potential exposure to mandatory minimum sentences. Misdemeanor or felony, perhaps it's no surprise that 90 to 97 percent of cases result in a plea bargain.

And after a first conviction, the next one is far more likely: you're seen as a criminal. A constant criminal, in all situations, for all time.

Trespassing
Felony Burglary
Theft of Services
Disorderly Conduct

ATTORNEY

TRESPASSING; FELONY BURGLARY; DISORDERLY CONDUCT; THEFT OF SERVICES

Recently, a client came into my office. He had been charged with a laundry list of offenses— for crashing a wedding.

This guy ate and he drank and he was arrested. Trespassing, Felony Burglary, Disorderly Conduct, and Theft of Services—aggravated by false pretenses.

Here's the thing: nothing got out of hand. Nothing was stolen, nothing was broken, no voices were even raised. He just appropriated an overpriced plate of mediocre food and

NOW I'M JUST WAITING FOR THE NEXT CLIENT TO REMIND ME OF MORE CRIMES I FORGOT.

now has a felony. Years later and this was still profoundly affecting him.

Here's this black man with a college degree, his only offense is crashing a wedding, and he can't get a job.

Holy crap.

A while back, I went to a baseball game with my delinquent brother. A few innings and shots of tequila in, and he was bored. I was a beer beyond my capacity and actually went along with his plan to get better seats.

We walked into the sports writers' box, but got kicked out before we could finish our first bucket of stolen popcorn.

So we went to the luxury suite instead. It was packed with execs; the waitress took our order—more food, more booze. A couple

more innings, and I locked myself in the private bathroom—where I spent the remainder of the game vomiting.

I'm sure the one reason no one asked us why we were there was because we were white. We were wearing t-shirts and, by our clothes alone, clearly didn't belong. But we were folded right into the crowd; people didn't care.

If I had to wager a guess, if I were any other color I would not have been allowed in; if I would have sneaked in, I would have been kicked out—or arrested, like my client.

I remember thinking: *Ha! What's the worst that could happen?*

Now I'm just waiting for the next client to remind me of more crimes I forgot.

GOVERNMENT EMPLOYEE

PUBLIC URINATION; UNDERAGE CONSUMPTION; PROVIDING ALCOHOL TO A MINOR

I celebrated my graduations in style. At the end of my senior year of college, my friend and I went bar-hopping and got pretty drunk. On our way home, we made a pit stop to pee right in the middle of the main quad.

Three years later, I finished grad school and visited a friend to celebrate. We got drunk visiting all the bars in the town where he lived, and then we staggered back to his house. Our route took us through a public park and across a river. We stopped on the bridge and peed into the water.

Two months ago, I was on a run on the single-track trails at a city park. I had to go, so I stopped and peed in the woods.

Convicted of all of these, my record would make me out to be a serial urinator. Add convictions for a few months' worth of underage drinking, along with providing alcohol to a minor (I once gave a beer or two to my 20-year-old sister), and my record would suggest chemical dependency issues. I am lucky to think of my criminal acts as fun nights with friends, not the incidents that ruined my job prospects.

TEACHER

DRIVING WHILE INTOXICATED

Looking back, I think the town would have tarred and feathered me
—all of us—if they had known and if they had the same standards
then as they do now.

With the passing of time and increasing of maturity, this kind of
activity lost its attraction. Thankfully, I saw the light before the
flashing lights saw me.

TEACHER

INCITING A RIOT

It was that realization *Holy shit, what did I just do?* I was super drunk,
and now suddenly I'm not. I'm not drunk.

Next thing I know, it's just dust and people falling all over each other.

TEACHER

FURNISHING ALCOHOL TO A MINOR

Here's what happened: I purchased alcohol once for a family friend. I was 30 and teaching at the time. She was underage and in search of a drink. She was also depressed. I don't know if I knew then that she was drinking quite as much as she was.

But I was old enough to know better. I was jeopardizing my job—and my career for life. If I had been caught, I would have lost my job and likely would not have received a teacher's license ever again.

Why did I do it? I think in part because I was shocked: no one had ever asked me to do anything like that before. A friend once said that my greatest fault was wanting everyone to like me. So maybe that's why I did it.

My friend killed herself a few years after that. The bigger significance here was that the one thing I did to help her was to get alcohol; I've always wondered what more positive thing could I have done.

That's been hanging over my head for many, many years. I'd like to think of myself as a person who tries to help people, but in this situation I didn't. I understand that on a rational level I'm not responsible, that I didn't hurt her—but the dots still connect on an emotional level.

ADVOCATE

UNLAWFUL POSSESSION OF EXPLOSIVE DEVICES

I love to light stuff on fire and watch it burn. I understand the morbid fascination with fire and explosives when people say, *I just wanted to see what it was like.* Yeah, I completely get that. Especially with fireworks.

I'M SHOOTING AN AERIAL AT A SPEEDING CAR, IT'S GOT A GAS TANK, AND I'M LITERALLY CONCERNED ABOUT A SPLINTER.

One year we hotwired all the fireworks together, duct-taping the fuses of bottle rockets, aerials with spray, mortars, and roman candles into one enormous and flammable mess. It went up like the Hindenburg, beautiful and frightening.

But we didn't light all of them that night. We kept several hundred bottle rockets in our cars for the days when we all got bored. Now, this was a stupid, stupid, stupid, stupid thing. My friends and I would drive in tandem along the highway, speeding and launching rockets into each others' cars.

As I was shooting at another car, I distinctly remember thinking that it would really suck if I got a splinter from the wooden stick at the end of the bottle rocket. I can't believe that was my only concern.

I'm shooting an aerial at a speeding car, it's got a gas tank, and I'm literally concerned about a splinter.

There was other stuff, too, although most of it was related to fire and explosives. At 16, I financed my sister's attempt to build a bomb out of kerosene, cleaner, and tin foil. Some were misdemeanors, some felonies, but I was young and suppose that even if I had really thought about what I was doing, the benefit of how cool it was outweighed the danger.

| PARALLEL STORY |

He was 15 and liked explosions. What 15-year-old boy doesn't? Anyway, my brother blew up the neighbor's mailbox with some concoction he made in our garage. He was arrested, stuck in detention, fell behind in school, and didn't get into the science club. He was a nerd, I know—but science club was everything to him. Now, his grades are down and mom can hardly get him to go to school. He just doesn't care anymore.

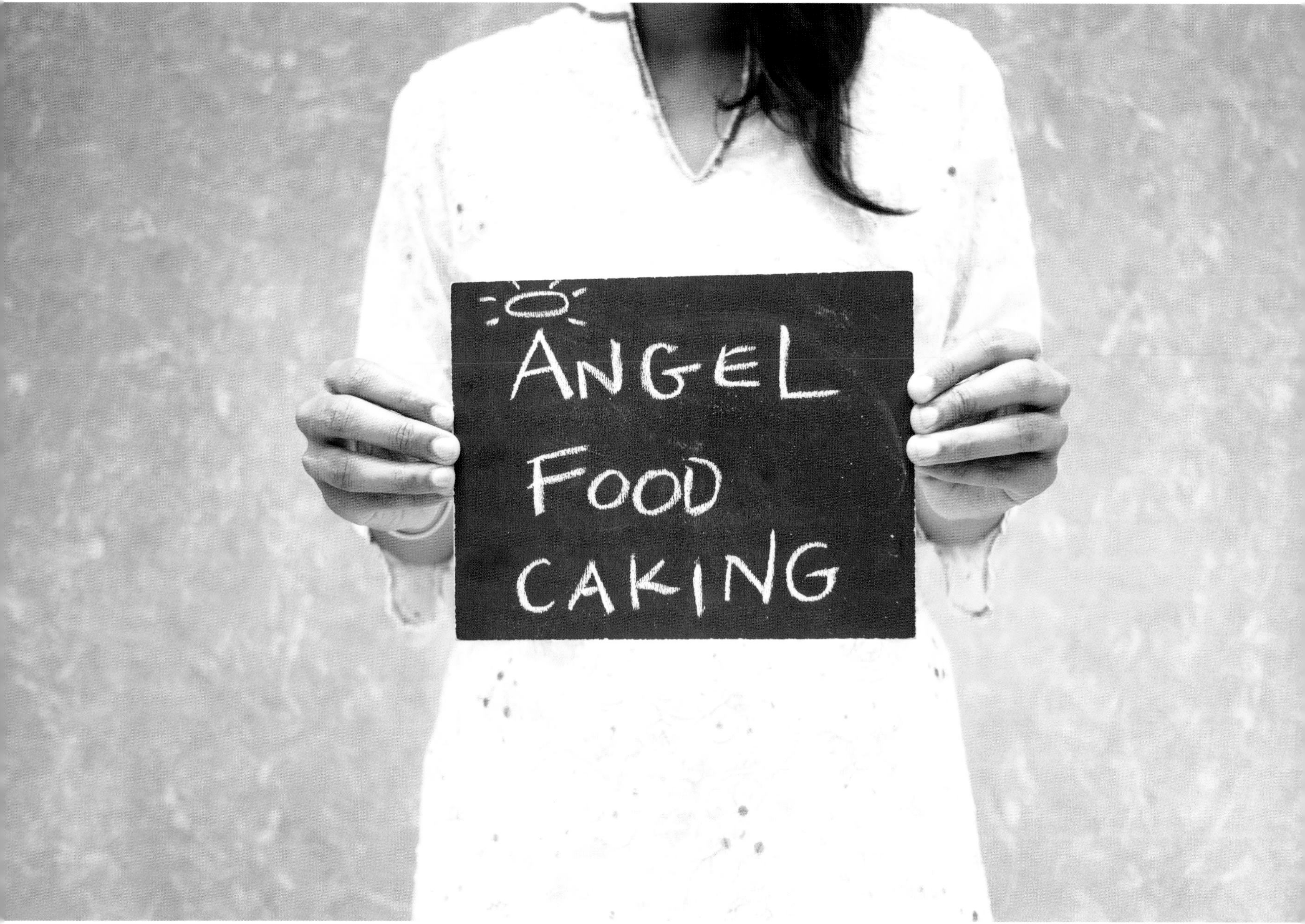
ANGEL
FOOD
CAKING

PRIMARY CARE PHYSICIAN
DESTRUCTION OF PROPERTY

This is a story of privilege and a little insanity. And as a Hindu child of immigrants who grew up in a vegetarian household, my story—it turns out—isn't just mine.

When I was eleven, I took the vegetarianism that I grew up with at home and kicked it up another notch: I turned into a label-reading Nazi vegetarian who would call up food manufacturers at their 800 numbers to find out exactly what ingredients were vegetarian and which were not.

This was the '80s and everything contained gelatin or beef fat: AKA, tallow, animal fat, shortening. Once I realized what those things were, it really put a damper on my relationship with all things Hostess and Little Debbie.

So began an exercise based in hope and ending in futility: I'd go into a store, pick up one of those plastic packages filled with bright pink Sno Balls dusted with coconut flakes, or cream-filled chocolate cupcakes with white icing, or oatmeal crème pies. I'd scan the ingredients, hoping to not see the offending ingredients listed, wishing that maybe they had changed the recipe and no longer put beef fat in that golden Twinkie this time round. I'd scan the ingredients, confirm that I couldn't eat it, and then I would surreptitiously squish the food inside the package on the shelf. Getting out my anger with each soft, gleeful squish.

Scan. Confirm. Squish. Scan. Confirm. Squish.

This went on for years. Each time, I'd think, *Just one last time.*

Look to the left, look to the right. Scan. Confirm. Squish.

Though I was pissed that someone thought that you needed to put a cow in a cupcake, I was also old enough to know what I was doing was wrong.

Years later, I befriended a Hindu woman who also grew up vegetarian and I discovered that she and her sister had also done the same thing when they were kids. They even gave it a name: Angel Food Caking. Finally, I had found a kindred spirit and no longer felt like such a freak of nature.

MORE THAN MY MUGSHOT

I don't remember what we were arguing about, because I don't remember arguing. I don't remember anything past that third pitcher: we were celebrating the end of college and the beginning of a lucrative career in the medical field.

Next thing, I'm getting arrested for assault and attempted theft because I grabbed a guy by his backpack.

I missed graduation and lost my job. It wasn't just that I couldn't use my degree—I was denied fast food jobs because of my record.

I don't want my whole identity wrapped up in the mistakes I made.

THE LUXURY TO FORGET

So once, I'd have to say about three or four years ago, I was in a bar and this guy was just being a real jerk to one of my friends. My friend was talking to one of his friends when they were interrupted. Apparently, the jerk wanted to leave. So he said, *Hey, stop talking to that cow,* meaning one of my best girlfriends.

I couldn't believe it. *Excuse me, what did you say?*

I told my friend to stop talking to the cow. And then he mooed at her.

At this point, I may have had too much to drink. I railed up and punched him as hard as I possibly could in the ear. He stood there stunned.

My friend grabbed my hand and said *RUN!* and we ran out of the bar as fast as we could.

MEDICAL EXAMINER
VANDALISM

Now when I look back on it, it was a time of teen angst. If I were born into a different socioeconomic status, it might have been the thing that broke the camel's back, the thing that got me going in the wrong direction.

| PARALLEL STORY |

He was caught poking holes in the back of a bus seat.

The whole seat's gonna hafta be replaced, said the administrator.

That's a felony, said the prosecutor.

That's messed up, said the kid.

That's bullshit, said the public defender.

That's the law, said the judge.

RETAILER

CRIMINAL DAMAGE TO PROPERTY;
TERRORISTIC THREATS

I was working at a retail shop in the mall and saving up for my summer wedding. My boss asked me to work overtime, and my fiancé and I were happy to have the extra cash.

With double shifts, the days were long. I cut out early one day in need of a break. My fiancé was not expecting me, and I knew as soon as I opened the door and saw my bitch-ass neighbor's shoes that the bum was cheating on me.

I could hear them going at it in the other room, so I slipped into the kitchen and grabbed one of those stupid Cutco knives (the ones he spent way too much money on) and headed out to our driveway.

One stab per tire and he was on flats.

At this point, I was no longer trying to be quiet. I wanted them to come out. But I guess they were too busy going at it to hear me. So I crossed the yard to her house and slashed her tires, too. Still nothing. I started calling and texting telling them to come outside so I could kick their asses, but got no response.

After a while, my friend picked me up and calmed me down. It took me longer than it should have to forget about him, but even a minute would have been too long for that bum.

| PARALLEL STORY |

A few years ago, she came home to find her husband in bed with a coworker. She packed up her three-year-old daughter and left, deliberately keying his new truck on the way out.

He called her in.

Now with felony damage to property on her record, she's been denied housing at every turn. She and her little girl are currently living in a shelter, unable to find a place that will rent to a "felon."

ATTORNEY

INDECENT EXPOSURE;
UNLICENSED USE OF A MOTORCYCLE

I'd say sex in cars, but that's lame—who hasn't done that?

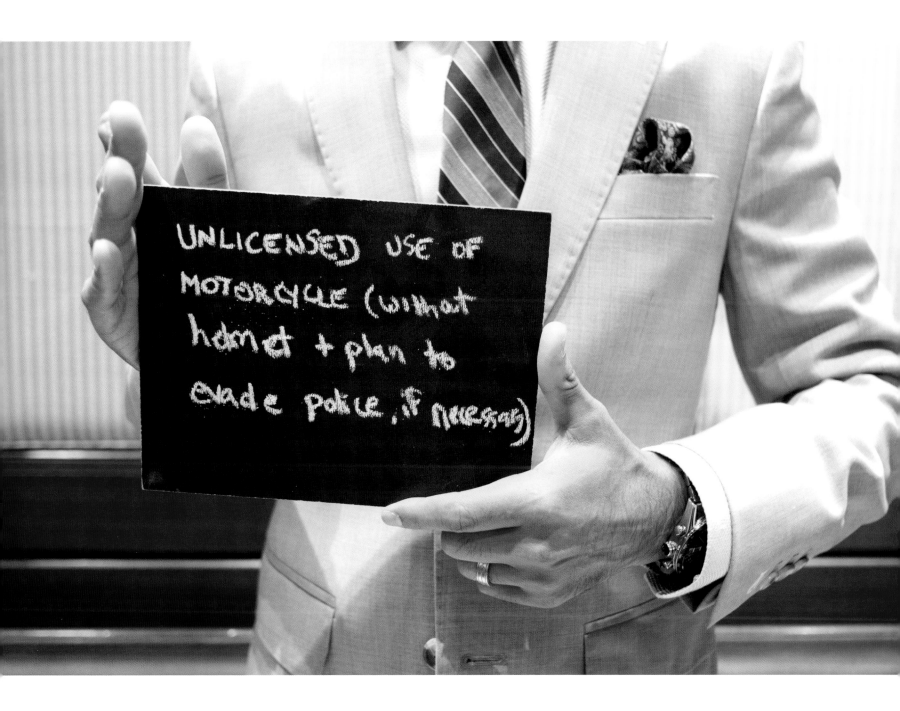

RESEARCH SCIENTIST

THEFT

It was a warm summer night, sometime between 1999 and 2001. I don't remember exactly when. The good people at the city were changing the fire hydrants in my neighborhood. They had left the job half-finished for the night, leaving detached fire hydrants on the boulevard near my apartment.

My roommates and I had been drinking, and through this haze—where many brilliant ideas were born—it was suggested we steal one. Alleviate the city the hassle of disposal, if you will.

We scurried down the street until we found one. It easily weighed 200 pounds, so the three of us huddled together to carry it, tripping over each other on the way home. We finally got it into our apartment and promptly and prominently displayed it in the living room. At some point, our neighbors—a few art students—painted it to look like a sunbathing beauty.

When we moved out, no one wanted it, so it went with me. I've moved it to two other homes now, and I think I'll keep her.

I suppose the fire hydrant wasn't the only thing I pilfered over the years. Salt and pepper shakers from restaurants, silverware from bars, mugs, pint glasses, and a carafe, road signs (*Yield, No Dumping, Highway 69*), banners from light posts like the big, canvas *"Welcome to Our Town"* banner that I shimmied up the pole to take, a surveyor's wheel from the back of a truck to measure my walk home.

Inspiration would usually strike on the walk home from a bar. I would bet that there are things I've forgotten, picked up at one point, and left behind in the bushes.

I haven't taken anything in a couple of years (well, except for one thing two weeks ago, but that was an exception). It just got less and less enjoyable. When you start to think of the consequences, the embarrassment of getting caught, it's no longer funny, just dumb.

I don't really think of them as crimes, though. I mean, really. Do people get convicted for stuff like this?

| PARALLEL STORY |

We were young, bored, and drunk. The night ended with the six of us clustered around a USPS mailbox, nearly pissing ourselves with laughter trying to pry it loose.

We were charged with theft and destruction of property. With a year of good behavior, no contact with my buddies, some community service, restitution, and an alcohol information class, I can have the case dismissed. It could have been a lot worse.

Still, I spend a lot of time mad at myself and worrying about the future.

I'm going to college, and I know I won't be able to let loose like the other dorm kids without records. Every time I apply for an internship, part-time job, or volunteer opportunity, they'll be able to see the statutory remnants of that stupid night. Who knows what that'll cost me?

THE WAR
WAGES ON

Well into its fourth decade, the War on Drugs has been one of the greatest contributors to our current carceral crisis. The casualties of this crusade are countless—from entire communities disenfranchised, to eviscerated civil rights and constitutional protections, to warped state and federal budgets, and beyond.

Nationwide, law enforcement made more than 1,561,000 arrests for drug abuse violations in 2014. In 2016, one in five incarcerated people was locked up for a drug offense. According to the American Civil Liberties Union (ACLU), more than half of all drug arrests were for marijuana in 2010: that year, cops made a pot arrest every 37 seconds and states spent over $3.6 billion enforcing possession laws. Between 1980 and 2015, there were six times as many arrests for drug possession as for sale. And the arrests for sales almost never take down kingpins. If the purpose of the War on Drugs has been to target the masterminds behind the illicit trade, we've failed.

While neither use nor dependency necessarily results in additional illegal activity, many crimes may be rooted in addiction; individuals serving time for a property or person crime can often trace acts back to chemical dependence. As Paul Butler notes in *Let's Get Free: A Hip-Hop Theory of Justice*, the high cost of illegal drugs contributes to about half of robberies, burglaries, and property crimes. And by criminalizing usage instead of treating addiction as a public health concern, we've pushed people to the edges of society. For many, it's safer to hide an addiction than seek help.

Neuropsychopharmacologist Dr. Carl Hart argues that society's response to drug use shouldn't be a dichotomy: jail or treatment. After all, most people who consume drugs do so without any problems. Many would benefit, he argues, from simple education (*e.g.*, if you're using heroin, don't drink). And for those who are addicted, Dr. Hart's research shows that when people are given access to better options, they can drastically decrease or even abstain from drug use. Meaningful employment is one of the most attractive alternative reinforcers, he says, and providing viable economic opportunities will go a long way in decreasing drug abuse in the United States. In the meantime, crime will persist: even if you took drugs out of the equation, poverty would still be there. The perpetual punishments heaped on as a consequence of criminal records prevent many from accessing the very alternatives that might actually cause decreased drug use and crime. The human cost of the misguided and unrealistic war, Dr. Hart believes—particularly among marginalized people—is incalculable.

Within this drug-war dragnet, the racial disparities are as staggering as they are unconscionable. Black and white people use and sell drugs at roughly comparable rates, but their punishments couldn't be more different. Consider marijuana: while both black and white people use it at similar rates, on average, a black person is 3.73 times more likely to be arrested for possession than a white person. Those disparities continue through criminal charging, conviction, and incarceration too. As Professor Alexander notes, the majority of illegal drug users and dealers are white, but three-fourths of people imprisoned for drug offenses have been black or Latino.

And all of this for what? The War on Drugs has been ineffective in treating addiction, reducing use, or making America a safer place to live. There are too few effective chemical dependency programs inside jails and prisons, leaving, for many, root causes of criminological acts just as present upon release as upon arrest.

Professor Butler notes that twice as many people die from using drugs now than did before we launched the War: "The day that we bring the troops—the police and the prosecutors—home from the War on Drugs, the United States will be a safer, and more free, country."

Some states are moving toward decriminalizing or legalizing marijuana, but many more jurisdictions—including the federal government—are not. In fact, some states and the new U.S. Attorney General, Jeff Sessions, have actually stepped up enforcement. Everything else beyond pot is still punished to the fullest: for instance, possessing a single pill of someone else's prescription medication is not only unlawful, it can be felonious.

At least three former presidents seem to be proof of Dr. Hart's assertion that many people can get high *and* still live a full and fruitful life: Bill Clinton, George W. Bush, and Barack Obama each admitted or refused to deny illegal drug use, and each rose to our country's highest office. If they'd been caught and incarcerated—whether for dabbling or dependence—that dream would have been over. Look on stage and on the practice field; look at the boardroom, the classroom, the state capitol; look at your colleagues, your faith group, your neighbors. Look in the mirror. Among us, there are people who have consumed controlled substances and yet are nevertheless healthy, productive members of society.

The stories that follow concern the use, abuse, and sale of drugs (including alcohol); several touch upon themes of race, class, privilege, addiction, and mental health.

JAIL STAFF
POSSESSION OF CONTROLLED SUBSTANCES

In high school it was weed, college mostly mushrooms. I loved mushrooms. I'd buy mushrooms today if I knew someone who could get them—it's just I've severed those ties.

I credit Adderall for my undergrad graduation, though. My friends and I were fuck-ups. Smart fuck-ups but fuck-ups nonetheless. Three days before graduation, we were all past due on our final papers. Our professors had been lenient, but there's a limit to that, right? So we set up shop outside at a picnic table, chain smoked and pounded away at our keyboards. Every three hours, a friend would dole out the pills: *Two for you, two for you, two for me.* We were united, in it together. We didn't eat or sleep or blink for three days. I remember looking up from the monitor to see people on morning walks with their dogs; a hot second later they'd be on their evening walk. Time had collapsed.

I don't know what I wrote—but it was good enough to graduate. We celebrated the occasion with ecstasy, but because I'd been on uppers for three days straight, I didn't feel a thing. I was searching the trees' leaves for something different, something beautiful. Nothing. I didn't need ecstasy; I needed sleep.

A while later I interviewed for a job at a jail. Without a record, I only had to worry about self-disclosure during the psych eval. I was terrified; I practiced *"No, never" "Not for me"* over and over. A few weeks later, they called: I got the job.

Then there I was, on one side of the bars for doing something a lot of guys on the other side had gotten caught for. I knew it was a matter of privilege. *Are you bullshitting me?* I thought. I felt like a hypocrite, so I stopped.

Mostly.

THEN THERE I WAS, ON ONE SIDE OF THE BARS FOR DOING SOMETHING A LOT OF GUYS ON THE OTHER SIDE HAD GOTTEN CAUGHT FOR. I KNEW IT WAS A MATTER OF PRIVILEGE. *ARE YOU BULLSHITTING ME?* I THOUGHT. I FELT LIKE A HYPOCRITE, SO I STOPPED.

ATTORNEY

UNDERAGE DRINKING; FURNISHING ALCOHOL TO A MINOR; POSSESSION AND CONSPIRACY TO SELL CONTROLLED SUBSTANCES; ASSAULT; DRIVING WHILE INTOXICATED; CHILD ENDANGERMENT

Freshman year, I started drinking.

Sophomore year, I was a go-between for a dope-dealing friend and the football team. He sold more than just pot—ecstasy, sheets and sheets of acid—but I never ran more than marijuana.

Junior year, I spent Tuesday nights loading up my bloodstream with drinks and my car with pounds of marijuana for a friend from a nearby town. It's amazing I was never pulled over on the long drive back.

Senior year, my friends and I made a lot of money selling keg beer and jungle juice to underage kids.

In law school, I got into a drunken street fight. My friend pulled me out of the middle just as the cops were closing in.

Up until a few years ago, I was still driving drunk. I knew what I was doing was wrong and how stupid it was. For example, one night after four tallboys, I drove my little girl home in a car with a broken taillight, right through an area heavy with police presence. Two weeks later on the same stretch, I was pulled over for the taillight—but this time, I was sober.

I still mind-trip over that: it's just pure luck that I wasn't stopped the night I'd been drinking. If I had been, they probably would have taken my daughter from me.

How would my life be different had I been caught? In college, I probably would have gotten wrapped up in the system. I was an angsty alcoholic—angry and with a bad attitude. I could see how that, if coupled with police interaction, could have ended poorly.

If I had been caught for some of the later activities, I don't know where I'd be. Once you reach a certain point, once you're a certain age, people are no longer willing to forgive.

D was at work when his sister called: his grandfather had passed and the funeral would be the next week, near his mother's hometown in Canada. He got ahold of his boss, covered his shifts, packed a few bags with clothes, and then picked up his wife from work and son from the elementary school. Just south of the Canadian border, they bought sandwiches and sodas, but the quiet sadness in the car made it difficult to eat.

At the border, patrol asked for his license and his wife's, while their son slept in the backseat. The officer returned after a short while, explaining that a routine background check revealed a DWI conviction on D's record from eight years ago. Even though he had paid his fine, finished probation, and hadn't had a drink since the arrest, he was prohibited from entering Canada.

Arguing and pleading got them nowhere. On the way back home, D asked his wife to pull over to the side of the road. He stumbled out of the car, vomited in the ditch and on his shoes, and finally wept.

VOLUNTEER COORDINATOR

DRIVING WHILE INTOXICATED;
POSSESSION OF CONTROLLED SUBSTANCES;
UNDERAGE DRINKING

We drank a lot then, it was the culture: probably *four weeks out of the night* we were drinking.

We lived by a Taco John's my sophomore year, literally right across the street. We'd be drinking at our house until two, three in the morning when we'd get hungry. Taco John's restaurant closes early, but their drive-thru stays open. Now, they don't let you just walk through a drive-thru. So we'd get into our cars and drive through to get food, turn around, and go the few feet back home.

I never drank a drop of alcohol in high school. But once I got to college, I started drinking and smoking pot. That was our lifestyle.

After I graduated—thank god I graduated—I moved away from the college town, got a job, and got on with my life.

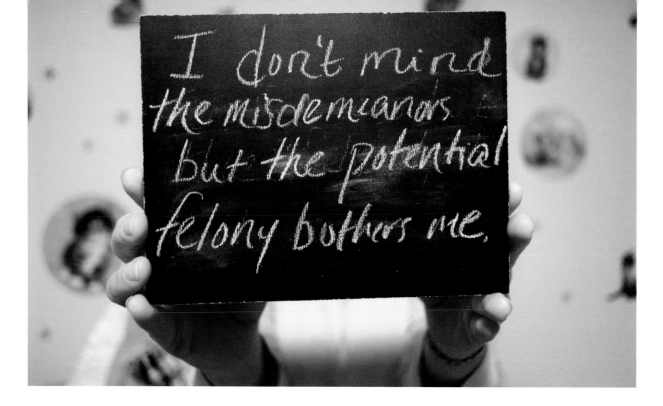

I don't mind the misdemeanors but the potential felony bothers me,

LICENSED COUNSELOR

CRIMINAL DAMAGE TO PROPERTY; DRIVING UNDER THE INFLUENCE; UNAUTHORIZED DISTRIBUTION OF A CONTROLLED SUBSTANCE

What have I gotten away with? At first, all I could recall was underage drinking, although not a lot of it. But then I thought about it some more, and as I continued to think about it, everything got bigger and bigger.

Reckless driving? Yes. A lot. Marijuana? Yes. Damage to property? Yes. (I drove the getaway car when my friends sawed down the local truck-stop sign.) Did I drink and drive? Well, yes. I don't think I can come up with exactly how many times, but I'd say somewhere around ten.

Kids do stupid things, and I was no exception.

I come from a poor family, where expectations of me weren't that high. Had I been put in the juvenile system at any point, I may have decided not to have high expectations of myself.

Perhaps most frightening, though, was some-thing that happened the year after I became a licensed counselor. I had leftover Klonopin and a friend who had difficulty sleeping. I brought the pills over to her house in a little baggie—not even considering that it might be illegal.

I can't imagine I'd be where I'm at now if I had been caught. I don't think I'd be here, with this job, with these beautiful daughters, with this beautiful life.

PROFESSOR

UNAUTHORIZED DISTRIBUTION OF A CONTROLLED SUBSTANCE

Several years ago, I was a bridesmaid in my sister's wedding. I was pregnant at the time and taking prescription medication to ease severe nausea. But that day I wasn't the only one feeling sick—my sister woke up with the stomach flu. Being the good big sister I am, I didn't hesitate to give her a pill before the wedding and a few to take on her honeymoon, too. The medicine worked like a charm: she was able to enjoy her day vomit-free.

Was my crime justified? I think so. But I also realize that my excuse is no better—and probably less compelling—than that of a single mother who sells drugs to pay the rent.

| PARALLEL STORY |

Three pills—that's it. Three pills in a Ziploc, in a car with a cracked windshield. I got pulled over on my way home from work, again.

After I started working the late shift, it seemed more nights than not I was stopped. Windshield, drifting lanes, failure to signal (I did signal!).

I didn't think anything of it when the cop asked to search the car. What do I have to hide, right?

Turns out the painkillers from my mom, left over from a surgery, were something to hide. She'd given them to me back in November when my bad back had me doubled over the dinner table. I had popped a few then and kept the rest in the car for an emergency. I'd completely forgotten about them.

I lost my job and it's been hell finding another. I'm not even thinking about school anymore.

My mom feels horrible, but she didn't know it would go like this—how could she?

YOUTH COUNSELOR

POSSESSION AND UNLAWFUL DISTRIBUTION OF CONTROLLED SUBSTANCES; TRESPASSING; UNDERAGE CONSUMPTION; PUBLIC INTOXICATION; FURNISHING ALCOHOL TO A MINOR; DRIVING UNDER THE INFLUENCE

I was thinking about all of the things that I had done—*Have I done that?* Yeah, I've done that. Yeah, I've done that. Yeah, I've done that too.

I hadn't really thought about any of it much until I started writing it all down. Once I started tabulating everything, it turned out to be kind of a long list. Would you like to see it?

First, there's "use, distribution, sale, and possession of marijuana—under two grams."

I WAS READING THE STORIES OF PEOPLE WHO WERE CAUGHT—AND THE CONSEQUENCES THEY'VE HAD TO DEAL WITH—AND WOW. I AM SO SO SO LUCKY.

That was me using it, of course. But I'd also sometimes buy it on behalf of my friends and then sell it to them.

Then there was the same basic thing, but with prescription medication; that happened more than once.

There was trespassing and breaking and entering (I was exploring abandoned buildings); petty theft; being in a bar under age; underage drinking; public intoxication; buying alcohol for a minor; speeding (who doesn't?); driving under the influence (tipsy once, high another time); open bottle in a car.

What is that? Fifteen? Twenty? Twenty-two crimes?

I was reading the stories of people who were caught—and the consequences they've had to deal with—and wow. I am so so so lucky.

petty misdemeanor

use, distribution, sale and possession
of weed   ≤2g

use, distribution, sale and possession
felony   of prescription drugs w/o
                a prescription

vandalism

petty theft   possesion of stolen property

misdemeanor
~ tresspassing
breaking and entering
attempted breaking and entering

underage drinking
being drunk in a bar underage
    public intoxication
    public urination
contributing to the delinquency of a
            minor
speeding
driving drunk   22
driving high

furnishing alcohol to a minor

STUDENT

SALE OF CONTROLLED SUBSTANCES; EXPLOSIVE DEVICES; SHOPLIFTING

For me, I was in a place. I wasn't lost: I was floating.

There was nothing holding me, there was no stability. One of my parents had a few interesting mental conditions, and I didn't leave home unscathed. During my formative years, a normal day was a great day—and I didn't have many great days. I was really pissed off most of the time.

People thought I would do things without thinking, but that's not true: I mapped out all of the possibilities and consequences, but the last point in my internal flowchart was always *Fuck it.*

There wasn't one isolated incident; it was a medley of acts.

Some of it was profitable. I sold painkillers and, at one point, a re-up was four figures, easy. We started making edibles, because you can double your profit. Now I don't know if there's such thing as a "moral drug dealer"—but if someone wanted a huge quantity, I would say no. I didn't want to wake up the next morning to find that some guy had offed himself. But sometimes you'd forget, and I do regret the immoral acts.

Some of it was chaos. We threw a half stick of dynamite in a parking garage to set off car alarms. Vandalism, destruction: just pure fun.

EVERYONE HAS DONE SOME SHIT, MAYBE NOT THIS INTENSE—BUT EVERYONE'S DONE SOMETHING. SOME PEOPLE GET CAUGHT, AND IT'S NOT THE GREATEST SYSTEM FOR THEM— ESPECIALLY WHEN THEY DESERVE THIS OPPORTUNITY AS MUCH AS I DO. OR MAYBE, I *DON'T* DESERVE THIS OPPORTUNITY AS MUCH AS THEY DON'T. WE ARE EQUIVALENT. WE DID THE SAME THINGS, WE JUST DID THEM IN DIFFERENT WAYS, AND I HAD BETTER LUCK.

Some of it was for the rush. I didn't buy any clothes for an entire year. I liked having things that weren't mine; getting something out of the store was a challenge.

People assume your quality of life decreases if you're caught—but I never expected good things to come out of my life. Though, I didn't expect bad things either.

Four years ago, I changed the way I was acting and the way I was interacting with the world around me. It didn't change overnight, but that was the start of it.

Everyone has done some shit, maybe not this intense—but everyone's done something. Some people get caught, and it's not the greatest system for them—especially when they deserve this opportunity as much as I do. Or maybe, I *don't* deserve this opportunity as much as they don't. We are equivalent. We did the same things, we just did them in different ways, and I had better luck.

Distribution
of illicit
substances

THE LUXURY TO FORGET

MORE THAN MY MUGSHOT

Before my husband died, when the pain and cramping was so bad he couldn't shampoo his own hair or grip a pencil, I baked. I have asthma, so we couldn't smoke—so the marijuana went in the butter, and the butter in the brownies. He probably did it ten or eleven times, four times I joined him. Solidarity, I suppose. I guess I justified it: it was an herb, it helped, his mother knew about it.

After he died, there was some of it left over in the house. I think it got used, but not by me. Maybe I threw it away.

But look at me. I'm white, a scholar, a woman. No one's going to search my house. I'm aware of that privilege.

I would do it again: it was such an obvious and correct decision.

My husband, a Marine who couldn't untwist his hand to hold mine, for a short while felt a little bit better. In that context, it was okay; it wasn't drug use, it was something else.

He may have been in his forties, but he was still her baby. And when the pain seized and contorted her son's body, he would smoke. She never touched it, but was thankful that something—anything—would help him.

Some time after cancer took his life, police executed a search warrant, citing an anonymous tip that she'd been warehousing drugs. They found ziplocked baggies of marijuana in the freezer—untouched since her son passed. In fact, she hadn't been able to move anything: his toothbrush by the bathroom mirror, his boots by the back door, his illegal pain medication in the freezer.

She was arrested, charged, and pleaded to felony drug possession. The drug offense resulted in lost housing; her court fines, fees, and mandated treatment sapped whatever she could have put toward the inflated deposits required by private landlords. She thought about moving back to the Reservation to stay with her sister, but there really isn't room right now.

At 72 years old, she's left with a felony record, no home, and no son.

YOUTH COUNSELOR

POSSESSION AND SALE OF CONTROLLED SUBSTANCES; VANDALISM

It wasn't just the color of my skin—it was the neighborhood, too. If I'd grown up in downtown, I'd have been in and out of juvie. There was only one cop car for the whole neighborhood.

We never got caught, and we were never worried about getting caught.

| PARALLEL STORY |

I was five and my friend and I were waiting outside the convenience store for my brother to get my mom groceries. There was a dog tied up to a street sign, and the owner had said we could pet him while we waited.

A cop pulled up to the curb and got out. He started asking after guys in the neighborhood.

Next thing I know, my brother's coming out of the store and this cop is launching at him. The milk hits the pavement and just explodes. The cop yells at my brother for getting his uniform messy and slams him on the sidewalk. My brother's blood is mixing with the milk and dirt and I'm screaming and the dog is going wild and the cop is saying *Stop or I'll tase you* and I don't know if he's talking to my brother, me, or the dog.

My brother yelled at me and my friend to go home; I could tell he was scared and confused and angry as hell, but my feet were stuck. I just stood there, my tears and snot and piss mixing with his blood and the milk and the dirt.

When the cop cuffed my brother, he found a joint and some papers in his pocket. He spent the next two weeks in jail. Years later, I found out my brother had been charged with possession, assaulting an officer with fluids, and obstruction. It wasn't long before I was that black kid on the pavement, before I was the one spilling blood, and before another five-year-old was screaming for a cop to leave me alone.

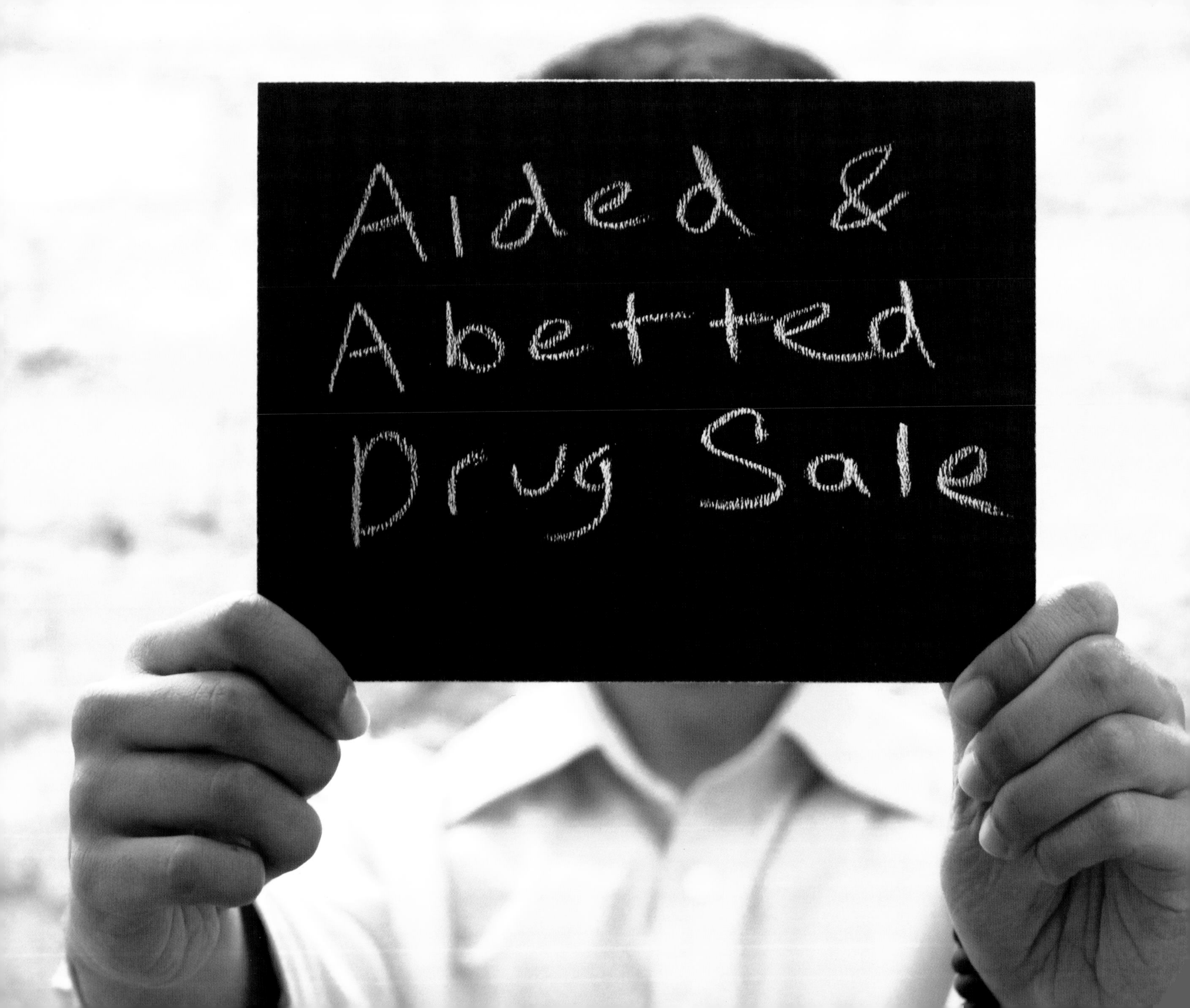
Aided &
Abetted
Drug Sale

ATTORNEY

AIDED AND ABETTED SALE OF CONTROLLED SUBSTANCES

I was shy in college. Painfully shy.

When I left home for college, I left behind the few comforts that in high school seemed to keep me grounded.

But that feeling of being cast adrift changed when two things happened: 1) my student loan check came and 2) I met Luke. Luke was a sophomore living in the same dorm, one floor up. He was an entrepreneur in need of fast cash to finance collegiate drug runs, and I had the means to help him. Along with a percentage of the profits came a built-in social life, complete with friends and (more importantly) girlfriends.

After a while I started smoking as enthusiastically as Luke was selling. It took some time, but eventually I was able to walk away and sober up.

After college I went to law school. Now I'm an attorney working at one firm and applying at others.

I can't tell you how many background checks my name has been run through in the last year, but I can tell you how very relieved I am knowing that each time it will come back clean.

STUDENT

POSSESSION AND SALE OF CONTROLLED SUBSTANCES

When I got to college, I was one of the few freshmen who both smoked and knew someone who sold weed. I started buying for friends, and then friends of friends. A few months in, I was buying ounces at a time, and then expanded to acid.

I'm not really in the demographic associated with dealers, and my customers were people I wouldn't have interacted with normally: footballers and frat bros. I guess that's a lot of why I did it—that and breaking whatever stereotypes.

By junior year, it became less about having weed conveniently for my friends and myself and more about keeping up with what people expected of me.

After the last batch, I began redirecting my customers to another person. I miss them more than I thought I would.

PUBLIC EDUCATOR
I AM MORE THAN MY MUGSHOT

I was the gay kid everyone beat up on, until I was the gay kid that could get you high. Suddenly, I was invited to all the parties; I got hugs in the hallway, the most popular kids started blowing up my phone. They loved me—or they loved what I supplied. Back then, it didn't matter. I took any kind of friendship I could get.

Eventually, I was caught. I'm nearly 30 now and wondering if was worth it. I still can't find decent housing; every job interview makes me relive those years, explain and apologize for what I did. Some employers have been okay with it, but kept me at entry-level jobs; other are like, *We don't hire felons*. I'd like to go back and tell the 16-year-old me not to do it—but then again, I wouldn't spend another second in those years for all the money in the world.

I'm damn smart, dedicated, and driven. I've worked on shoestring budgets and helped manage massive federal grants. If you could see what I'm capable of, you'd want me on your team. You'd want me to *lead* your team.

NOTE:

LGBTQI youth and adults, especially LGBTQI people of color, experience increased criminalization and abuse by law enforcement, vulnerability and violence in lock-up, and too few resources upon release. This is particularly true for transgender women of color who are far more likely to be targeted, harassed, arrested, and detained by police than is the general population. Or, as both the Center for American Progress and the Movement Advancement Project note, the American criminal justice system not only fails transgender people, it targets them.

LEGAL ADVOCATE

SALE OF CONTROLLED SUBSTANCES; FLEEING POLICE; HARBORING A FUGITIVE; CONTRIBUTING TO THE DELINQUENCY OF A MINOR; DISPENSING DRUGS THAT RESULT IN DEATH

When I was 14, I picked up a fast food job working with older kids. One night, they thought it would be funny to get me, the weird nerdy kid, high. Soon I went from occasionally to enthusiastically smoking, then to selling. By my sophomore year in college, I had more than $20,000 in savings and a shared brick of cocaine in the dorm room.

There are a million incidental stories in between that I can only kind of remember now. I ran from police. I was held at gunpoint. I helped a juvenile who'd sold on my behalf leave the state to flee an arrest warrant. Someone I knew died after taking drugs that came from me. I OD'd a few times and came back, and I never had to worry about the medical bills. I was questioned by a DEA representative in the hospital after one, and then I was promptly forgotten about as the investigation moved on.

I've had so many lucky breaks, you know?

Like, I'll never forget this one time. I brought in Adderall and Xanax into the projects—a pretty gritty neighborhood—and left with half a pound of weed, 6 grams of coke, some acid, some ecstasy, and some mushrooms. Several felony amounts.

It was 2:30 in the morning and I was two blocks out of this guy's apartment when this cop pulls me over. He looks in and takes one look at me and—I will remember this to the day I die— goes, *What are you doing in this part of town?*

If I had been black, I *know* he never would have asked me that question.

I was like, *I don't know. I turned off the interstate to get some gas. I just got out of a concert? I think I got lost. I don't think I'm supposed to be here—this looks like a bad neighborhood.* He gave me the fastest route to the interstate, didn't even ask for my driver's license or registration.

I guess I thought this would all be fun and exciting. It was just depressing and terrifying. And I hurt a lot of people in a lot of ways. I watched a people get hurt and hurt themselves, and I never did anything to stop it. That still bugs me.

You wonder why I'm motivated to do the work I do today? I kinda feel like I owe it to someone at this point. I didn't earn this second chance, but I can put it to good use.

FILMMAKER

POSSESSION OF CONTROLLED SUBSTANCES

I'd say the majority of my crimes were motivated by getting fucked up when I was young and stupid and didn't have legal access to anything.

Actually, I can pull up a list of all of the drugs I've done. Hold on . . . Okay. Shall I list them?

Tobacco, alcohol, marijuana, shrooms, LSD, cocaine, Dilaudid, Robitussin, hydrocodone, hash, Adderall and other ADHD meds (for academic purposes), Klonopin, ketamine, MDMA/ecstasy, Methylone (my personal favorite: it's like ecstasy, where you feel all the love, but you don't feel compelled to tell everyone; you're a little bit more self-actualizing), and DMT. That's all I can remember, at least.

The cops near where I went to high school had better things to do than bust little white idiots. It was a predominantly black, inner-city public school and we just seemed to slip under the radar. Never really got hassled. Never really felt threatened. No one looked at us twice and we didn't have to deal with the consequences.

Even if I had been caught, I think it would have been okay. I'm in a stratosphere where one arrest probably wouldn't kill me. I'm well-connected, white, and upper-middle-class, I would have been able to work something out.

As Louis CK said, *I'm not saying white people are better. I'm saying* being *white is clearly better.*

FATHER, POET, CRISIS MANAGER
I AM MORE THAN MY MUGSHOT

In college, I was surrounded by kids living their lives like they had never been away from their parents before: keg parties, weed, coke, chaos. I had left a mostly black and poor neighborhood for the mostly white campus bubble. It was unreal.

That was before moving back home, before the bubble dissolved, before I had a cop's knee in my back, another's boot on my neck, another's gun inches from my face, before the humiliations and dehumanization that comes with cuffs, sleeping forty to a cell—packed like sweaty, distressed sardines—and before the years of denials that come with a drug offense.

I can't recreate the bubble, but I can create community and a safe, healthy home for my kids.

I'm a good dad. I'm a great dad. (I think I earned a secondary degree in Dora the Explorer.)

I'm a writer. My closet is filled with shoeboxes filled with poems and prose. Writing is my escape, my ventilation.

You want me on your team. I can calm a roomful of people in crisis in moments—at work, at church, at home.

But you'd miss all of that if all you saw was my record.

GRADUATE STUDENT

POSSESSION OF CONTROLLED SUBSTANCES;
THEFT OF GOVERNMENT PROPERTY;
FALSE IDENTIFICATION; PUBLIC URINATION;
OPEN CONTAINER; PUBLIC INDECENCY

Should I tell you about the drug offenses? There's marijuana, coke, LSD, Molly, study drugs. Sorry, this is really weird.

Oh, I stole a traffic cone.

I used a fake ID, peed in public, had an open container.

I have never been arrested, much less convicted.

Oh, I had sex on an international flight. I'm sorry—I was 18.

I'm nervous talking about it. It's a little uncomfortable, you know? Wow. I am a criminal.

I know that my affluence, race, and gender play a role in this. I'm so fortunate to still be where I am today.

Most of it happened in college, and I don't regret it. It's a part of my life—of who I am. Those mistakes? I learned from them. I wouldn't trade that.

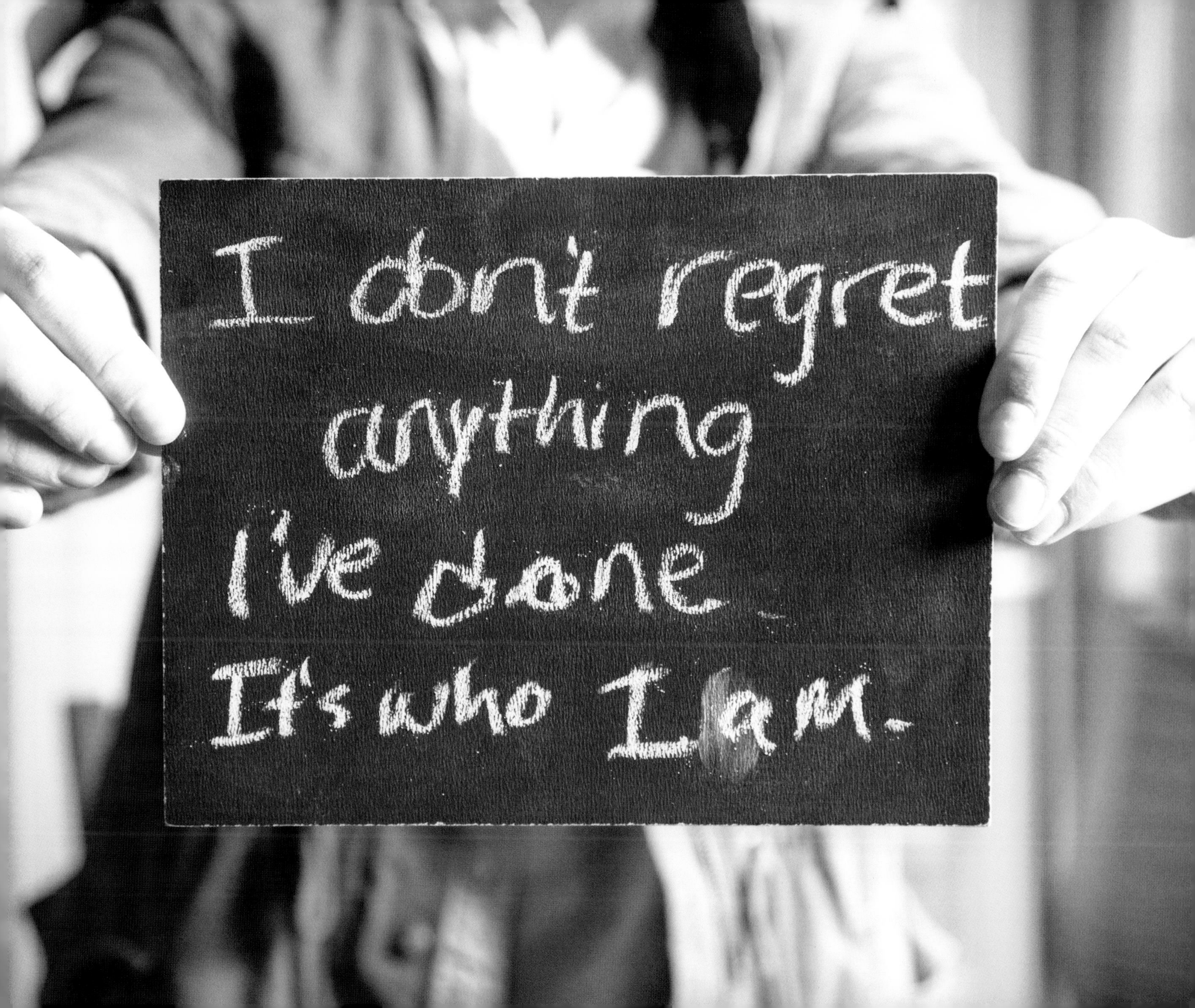

INTERNATIONAL SALES

UNDERAGE DRINKING; DRIVING WHILE INTOXICATED; PUBLIC INTOXICATION; DISORDERLY CONDUCT

I definitely benefited from my white male privilege. Time and again we were told to *Sleep it off, You better get yourself home, Oh, you kids,* (seriously) and *Boys will be boys* by police.

I went to rehab. I relapsed. I went to rehab again—all on company health insurance.

My rebound was very easy. I have a clear narrative: *I went through a tough time, now I'm better.* People respond well: *He's heroic! Look at what he's done, how he's improved himself!*

But I see their reactions to black men who have gone through the same experience: *He's an addict. What a waste on society.*

WHO GETS TREATMENT AND WHO GETS JAIL

In dollars, in collateral damage, and in human dignity, when it comes to substance abuse, treatment costs less than incarceration.

Our nation's recent response to a rise in heroin abuse stands as testimony to that: policymakers, conservative presidential candidates, and police all speak with compassion and humanitarian urgency about the friends and family swallowed whole by addiction. It wasn't always like this. For decades, the (wanted) poster children for the War on Drugs have been young, faceless black males—wearing bandanas and sagging jeans, notes law professor Ekow Yankah. Super predators, thugs, criminals. "Back then, when addiction was a black problem, there was no wave of national compassion," says Yankah. Today, nearly ninety percent of new heroin users are white; most are middle-class people and living outside of the inner city. The corresponding response by police chiefs, Professor Yankah notes, is not an attempt to invoke war, but to save lives:

Suddenly, crime is understood as a sign of underlying addiction, rather than a scourge to be eradicated.

One former narcotics officer said: "These are people. They have a purpose in life, and we can't look at it any other way."

But he couldn't quite put his finger on just what had changed. His words reflect our collective self-denial. It is hard to describe how bittersweet many African-Americans feel witnessing this. Glad to be rid of a failed war on drugs? Yes, but also weary and embittered. When the faces of addiction had dark skin, the police didn't see sons and daughters, sisters and brothers. They saw brothas, young thugs to be locked up, not people with a purpose in life.

No one laments the violence the crack bomb set off more than African-Americans. But how we respond to the crimes accompanying addiction depends on how much we care about those affected. White heroin addicts get overdose treatment, rehabilitation and reincorporation. Black drug users got jail cells and just say no.

It would be perverse to want to go back, and this is not just about racial guilt. The hope is that we really can learn from our meanest moments. This stark moment gives us the opportunity to quit our dedication to ignoring racism.

Next time we or even you are faced with an indictment of institutionalized racism, maybe we can swallow the knee-jerk dismissal or the condescending finger-wagging, and imagine if you would accept such treatment of your own. We don't have to wait until a problem has a white face to answer with humanity.

CORRECTIONS PROFESSIONAL
SALE OF CONTROLLED SUBSTANCES

Hopefully I'm not wasting your time; everyone thinks their history is more dramatic than it is.

I got into trouble constantly as a kid.

In high school I started experimenting with alcohol, marijuana, whatever I could get my hands on. I was still in school when I started living out of my car, sleeping in Walmart parking lots and dodging cops.

After about a year, I moved into a house with two college gentlemen and started dating a girl who kinda lived in the basement. I picked up a job at a gas station, but it was just a cover. What I really did to make money was sell blotter (LSD). I'd buy a sheet with 100 hits for $150 and sell each hit for five dollars. It was more than enough money to support myself, but eventually just went to buy meth—my drug of choice. A lot of crime comes from that: people trying to sustain a drug addiction.

These two older guys, Odysseus and The General, would come over and we'd spend the night partying. They were incredibly resourceful: we'd steal swing sets from Menards and music equipment from neighboring venues, returning and pawning everything for cash and then hitting up the sellers downtown.

I wonder if the color of my skin didn't save me from serious problems.

More than once, I'd get pulled over by a cop and—no matter how out of my mind I was—I'd be told to *have a nice day*.

I don't know where O and The General are now. I know a lot of it was drug induced—"I love you, brother" and everything, but I did care for them. For a while, O was pimping. There was a deep internal screening going on, everything was so muffled in regards to your morals. Now I would have nothing to do with anyone selling women for money, but then, we all just looked the other way.

When my first kid was born, I cut off everything. I haven't had anything for twelve years; my wife could tell you the exact date. According to my therapist, incidents of abuse caused me to spin out. But I think I just liked feeling different. I lacked any confidence, but when I altered my mind, it was bearable.

I'm careful. I don't take Nyquil because I like feeling different, and I know I'll want to feel different again tomorrow.

| PARALLEL STORY |

The best and worst moment of my life was my first hit of meth. I had been through a rough childhood, with the physical and emotional scars to prove it. I never thought I could feel so good in this skin.

At that time, I didn't have much: a graveyard shift at a gas station, a few false starts on a GED, a couple of applications pending at nearby shops. My car constantly broke down.

Looking back, I can't believe how much of what little I had I've lost. I lived in that busted car to where I didn't think I could ever really unfold myself again. I still don't have my GED. I started partying and lost my job after not showing up for a couple of days. At last count, I had 17 or 18 petty thefts on my record for stealing stupid stuff to keep up the high.

These days, I can't get too far into any store before I'm escorted out. I get it. But you know, I've worked hard to sober up. I just want to know if it'll always be like this.

MEDIA MANAGER

CRIMINAL DAMAGE TO PROPERTY

It happened over a decade ago. I was in grad school in a small town. The people were predictable, and I was bored. Most days, I would leave school by five and be at the bar by six. Sometimes I talked to people, sometimes I brought them home. But largely, nothing really interesting happened. I was stuck.

I had drunk a pitcher by myself that night, leaving sometime before close. Walking through the parking lot, I suddenly needed to know what it would sound like to pop a tire. I had to know if it would really *pop* or just *swoosh*. I took my Swiss army knife—I always had it on me those days—and jammed it into the driver's tire of a beat-up '70s Chevy. It was disappointing. Just a *pfffft* and it was over. So

I thought maybe it was an anomaly—the next one would be better. One led to two which led to three which turned to four and the car just went *plop*. Of course I shouldn't have expected anything more than a slow leak in that town.

The next morning I realized what I had done. I felt so bad. It was just some beater car, some guy just trying to get by. I made it all the worse.

In life, I did okay. I have a good job, I own my own home, and I volunteer in the community. But that night still causes me guilt.

I'm not a bad person, even though I did something bad. It's just not who I am.

LAW ENFORCEMENT OFFICER
DRIVING WHILE INTOXICATED

I got married young and, even then, I knew it wouldn't work. I had very low self-esteem and low self-worth. He only hit me once, but he was very controlling: I had to be home at a certain time, the car's mileage had to match his calculations.

So I drank. That's what you do when you're 21 and trying to get out of your own life.

I had a million excuses for driving drunk: *I'm good. I've done this before. I live close by. I don't want to pay for a cab. I don't have time to come back tomorrow morning to get the car.* I'd find the reason to get behind the wheel and get home.

Shortly after the divorce, a friend turned my life around. He helped me regain confidence. I worked hard, I stopped acting recklessly, I stopped drinking and driving. I eventually went back to school, began a career in law enforcement, and remarried.

Then, a few years back, everything changed.

I had just been offered a Secret Service position. It was the most grueling selection process of my life: a four-hour polygraph, a two-day physical, and a lifetime of inquiries. But this was the career opportunity that I had been working toward.

Shortly after receiving the news, my husband and I were driving home from a work function when a drunk driver hit us head-on. We collided at 60 miles per hour: a crush of headlights, engines, airbags, and bones.

The other driver blew a .23 two hours after the accident; he walked away unscathed. My husband was airlifted to the hospital with a fifty percent chance of survival; even now his memory is shot, his brain injured. I had significant nerve damage—but more than that, this guy cost me my dreams.

The week after the accident, the Secret Service rescinded their offer. They had accepted me in one condition, and I came to them in another. *Thanks, but no thanks.*

I spent the next four months in an absolute rage. I was bound and determined to find that kid. Thank God I didn't.

I kept thinking about how I live my life now—rather than how I lived at his age. Every single excuse I used then (*I live close by, I've done this before*), I saw a counter excuse now: there was no reason good enough for him to get behind the wheel.

The anger consumed me. I couldn't eat, I couldn't sleep. It was the focal point of my existence—and a coworker noticed. She suggested I try to write down how I felt. I dismissed her at first, but after she left, I found myself at the computer.

YOUR PROJECT MADE ME REALIZE THAT IT COULD HAVE BEEN ME. IT IS DIFFICULT TO LOOK AT YOURSELF IN A FLAWED WAY, YOU KNOW?

I vomited all over the screen in a stream of writing rage. Every vulgarity, every poisonous thought. And things slowly started to get better.

When you work in this environment long enough, you become calloused. You have a tendency to look at everyone else except yourself.

Your project made me realize that it could have been me. It is difficult to look at yourself in a flawed way, you know?

I can honestly say that I haven't forgiven him—yet. But I'm close. Now, I really believe that I could walk up to him and say, *Dude, I hope you've got everything else together—because this is going to follow you for a while.*

ARTIST, FATHER, SON

I AM MORE THAN MY MUGSHOT

Getting home was like a game of chess. It was never a straight line.

You had to know which stores stayed open late, which alleys were lit. I'd usually get off the bus a few stops early, cutting through buildings and trying to stay out of sight.

I attended an arts school outside of my neighborhood, and wasn't exactly welcomed home each evening. But even if it meant switching up my two-hour commute so I wasn't predictable, running for my life once the bus pulled away, and hiding until dawn in abandoned buildings with rats crawling over me, it was worth it. I wasn't going to end up like everyone else.

But one mistake . . .

I picked up a criminal record the day I attempted suicide. My girlfriend and I had lost our child; it was a miscarriage. Just a few years before that, my dad had died. I couldn't handle this much loss, this much heartache.

I drank to forget about it and I drank to remember. I drank to escape and I drank to be able to talk about it. I drank and I drank and I drank.

I hopped out of a moving car and was arrested after climbing over an airport fence. After I got out of jail, I chased 36 Tylenol PMs with a half bottle of Smirnoff. The landlady found me before my heart stopped.

My scholarship was revoked; on the job market with no degree is hard enough—with a record, not a chance.

Here's the thing: I'm good. I don't want to sound pompous—but I have the ability and capability to work in marketing, to work in design, to work. To work.

But if all you see is a criminal, you'll never see what I really am.

DRUG COUNSELOR

I AM MORE THAN MY MUGSHOT

UNITED STATES VS ME. That's what the sign outside of the courtroom said: the whole United States against me. I'd never been arrested before, I had no idea what was going on. I had recently started selling drugs to support my own habit. I was charged, I was released, I relapsed. I was arrested, I was released, I went to treatment. The U.S. Marshals delivered me to the treatment center in leg chains, belly chains, and a black box over my handcuffs. I was told I would fail at recovery—so I became hell-bent on succeeding.

Months go by, and I stop relapsing. I start volunteering. When I finally go back before the judge for sentencing, I've got loads of letters from the community and organizations talking about how I've turned my life around. My attorney is telling me to prepare myself; I think: *I got this*. The judge says he's read all of the letters and he's gonna give me a break: he'll only sentence me to 87 months.

Eighty-seven months was a break? Who does this to people?

Six weeks later, two of my best friends and their dog drove me to the federal prison. I said goodbye and walked through a set of sliding glass doors. It wasn't what I had imagined: there was a receptionist, flowers—it was almost inviting. She directed me through a second set of doors … and *that*. That was horrible. When those doors close behind you, you know they're not opening again for a long, long time.

When I was finally released, finding a job was hard. I got one; they told me it was too much unsupervised traveling while I was on supervised release. Another job, same thing. I ended up in telemarketing—along with all the other felons. Turns out we're really good at sales. Seriously, all of the top guys were from prison.

I know because I'm white and educated and upper-middle-class that I faced fewer barriers than others face. Tell me: how? How do others do this? How are they expected to succeed?

I often look with wonder at my life. I'm married, I'm a drug counselor, I volunteer on several boards, testify in legislative hearings, and sit at head tables with the sheriff and his wife. I even grow pumpkins. Like blue-ribbon-winning, 384-pound pumpkins. Best in Show.

And I'm a felon.

I wear this shirt to start conversations. To show people that "felons" are humans, too. There's a saying in recovery: You can only keep what you have by giving it away. Goofy, but true. I keep my hope by sharing it with everyone.

STUDENT, SINGER, CHANGEMAKER

I AM MORE THAN MY MUGSHOT

I did not wake up one morning and decide I want to be a drug addict and an alcoholic, and I didn't go to sleep one night hoping I'd wake up with with bipolar disorder. But life can be unkind.

T was a bad boy, but with his blue eyes and blonde hair, he was the most beautiful human being I had ever seen. Our lives consisted of sex, fighting, and getting messed up.

We used and abused until finally we got caught. And caught again.

Being in lock-up was a horrible experience. Someone screaming an inch away, spit flying onto your lips, steel doors slamming behind you, an audience every time you use the bathroom.

Even after T and I split, I was in and out of custody. It wasn't until I was really working at sobriety that I met JD.

JD could see that I had issues. He told me that I was still unhealthy and needed to work on myself first. I relapsed again before I was able to right my world.

I'm two years sober and the last year has been the best of my life. I joined a choir, mentored others in recovery, and I've built a relationship with God.

I'm a student now, and my goal is to dig deeper into fixing our juvenile justice system, with a special focus on the treatment of girls.

You know, every person has a story and reason for them being exactly where they are. We all have gifts and strengths and things to offer to our community—even those girls, even me. Right now, we don't care about those whom we don't know. I'm going to help change that.

DIRECTOR OF MARKETING AND SALES
CONSPIRACY TO MANUFACTURE, POSSESS, IMPORT, AND DISTRIBUTE CONTROLLED SUBSTANCES

Well, it's kind of crazy. I've never told anybody about this.

I was 18, living in a city close to the Canadian border, and dating a Canadian. I had a fake ID that said I was 19—the legal drinking age in Canada. So on weekends we'd cross the border to go to bars, and soon we were going to raves. It was the '90s, you know? We dabbled in drugs—pot, mushrooms, ecstasy—the whole rave scene. I would tell myself that because I wasn't doing the "addictive drugs" that we had been warned of in school like crack, coke, or heroin, I wasn't *really* doing anything *that* bad.

We knew a guy who knew a chemist—and, as it turns out, a manufacturer of pure-grade MDMA. This stuff was *amazing*. We thought: *Why aren't we bringing this back with us?*

So my boyfriend and I stuffed condoms with ecstasy and put them in our underwear. We'd pass through border security without issue.

My boyfriend would sell it; I got a $1,000 cut each time—as an 18-year-old, it was all the money I needed for the month. We did it four to five times, maybe. I don't even remember.

I almost thought I was doing a good thing: people were going to use, we were just helping them use pure.

I was a white young lady from the suburbs; there were so few "red flags." If I had been black, I think I would have been treated differently. We probably would have been stopped. Can you imagine if I'd been caught? Oh my god, what would I do?

After a while, we split up. My new boyfriend said that if I wanted to be with him, I couldn't use. So I stopped. I turned my life around, went to college, and now I'm trying to help kids not make the same stupid decisions I did.

I think about it all the time—especially as a mom. Please, for the love of god, let my children be better than me!

So, what do you think? Is it what you thought?

I suppose if I had guessed, I would have said you swiped a pair of jeans.

Oh yeah, I did that, too.

FATHER, SON, LEADER, AND MORE

I AM MORE THAN MY MUGSHOT

I carry them with me. The things I've done and got away with, the things I didn't do and was accused of.

I was in a gang, a brotherhood. I was rebellious and reckless and, for one night, I was kind of a ringleader. Actually, I *was* the ringleader.

We took some things from someone who had taken even more from our neighborhood; I got on the first bus out of town before he could figure out who did it. I needed the distance and I needed the sun.

On the Greyhound, two time zones away, a cop came on board. *These your bags?* He asked, pointing to the duffels without the drugs. *Yep. Just those.*

He emptied them out on the seat behind me: socks, t-shirts, and a PS2, but not much else. He seemed disappointed; I was beside myself with relief.

In the desert, I got perspective. My life had flashed before my eyes on that bus, with that cop. I wouldn't be here today if he had checked the other bag, that I know. I didn't even think about what could have happened until it almost did.

So when I came back home, I decided I wanted to improve my community, and the day my oldest daughter was born, I knew I wanted to build a legacy for her.

I could do better. We could do better. I took every organizing and leadership class I could get into; for three years, I volunteered in every program that would take me.

When my youngest was born, I was ready to buckle down.

I started my own program mentoring youth. Helping them recognize their unique value, arming them with critical thinking skills necessary to question the world.

It was incredible—the rush you get from creating something. By being successful at something you love.

And I almost lost it all. I was accused of assaulting a friend of a friend and spent a week in jail. The deal was tempting: plead to this little thing you didn't do, and we'll drop the bigger thing you also didn't do. I wanted to be done with it, so I took it. When I got home, I was so hurt, so upset. Here I was trying to figure out my life, do something better—and this could take it all away.

Once you get that first mark, it's easier to get a second one. I was driving with my dad and daughter when the cop pulled us over. He yanked me out of the passenger's seat by my collar, slamming me into a telephone pole—you know, the ones covered in old nails and staples? So these nails are piercing my skin and my daughter's screaming and my dad is saying *What the hell is going on?*

I was back in jail. Eventually, the charges were dropped, but it sticks with me. **Having to define myself by what I'm not. And if I'm always just responding to what I'm not, you're not going to hear what I am.**

I'm a father.

I'm a son.

I'm a leader.

I'm a dreamer.

I'm a community organizer.

I'm a natural problem solver.

I've mentored more than 300 youth in the city.

I was recognized by the mayor; I was lauded by the governor.

And I'm working every day to build that legacy for my kids, to make this country and this world a better place.

**People enter the system disadvantaged
and leave even more so.**

While African Americans, Latino Americans, and Native Americans—and in particular, those in poor communities—are disproportionately affected at every stage in our criminal and juvenile justice systems, perhaps no point is quite so poignant as prison. The disparities in who we lock up are indefensible: the lifetime likelihood of imprisonment for white men is one in 17; for Latino men, it's one in six.

For black men, it's one in three.

One in three.

Fathers, brothers, sons, husbands, partners, friends, mentors, scholars, leaders, lenders, artists, activists, advocates, providers, and more are devoured by the criminal justice system. Their absence in the home, in the community, and in the economy cannot be overstated.

And while most people in prison are men, women's imprisonment rate increased by more than 700 percent between 1980 and 2014 (nearly 1.5 times the increase for men). According to The Sentencing Project, the racial disparities in lifetime likelihood of spending time in state or federal prison is one in 18 for black women, one in 45 for Latina women, and one in 111 for white women.

Native Americans are likewise disproportionately punished. One out of three women incarcerated in Montana, for example, is Native American.

Many people in prison struggle with chemical dependency, mental illness, and cognitive disabilities. And the rates of poverty are staggering. For example, two-thirds of people in jail report annual incomes under $12,000 a year prior to arrest. The significant and enduring economic repercussions accompanying incarceration not only affect the person who is locked up, but his or her children, too.

We do little to address these issues once someone is in the system. In fact, we do a lot to exacerbate the problems. Prison is a brutal, degrading, dehumanizing place— where unfathomable boredom and isolation are punctuated by inexpressible fear and violence. It's warehousing with trauma. With too few exceptions, meaningful educational and treatment opportunities are non-existent: saddled with criminal records, real chances to move on and move up are exceedingly rare.

People enter the system disadvantaged and leave even more so.

In his book, *Race to Incarcerate*, Marc Mauer explains that "[w]e may try to comfort ourselves by calling prisons 'correctional institutions,' but it is clear that . . . we as a nation still cage the least fortunate among us" in an attempt to solve our problems—or at least claim we're trying.

| CUSTODY |

The U.S. is the world's warden: we claim about five percent of the global general population, but nearly 25 percent of its incarcerated population.

Surprisingly, perhaps, mass incarceration is relatively new: between 1925 and the early 1970s, imprisonment rates were fairly steady (controlling for general population growth), hovering around or below a couple hundred thousand people in state and federal prisons. In 2014, that number was more than 1.5 million.

With an additional 731,000 in jail, it's like locking up every man, woman, and child in Houston, Texas. This, in the land of the free.

The federal prison population swelled by nearly 800 percent in 33 years, and states are by no means immune to the epidemic. During a 21-year stretch, states joined the feds in constructing a new adult facility nearly every week. Even still, our lock-ups are bursting at the seams.

Intake room at Alcatraz Federal Penitentiary. This maximum security prison on San Francisco Bay's Alcatraz Island closed in 1963; photographic access to operating prisons is far more difficult, underscoring the "out of sight, out of mind" mentality that accompanies the warehousing of more than a million people. Alcatraz is neither out of sight nor mind: it is now a National Historic Landmark, visited by more than a million people each year.

Throughout this book are photographs of Alcatraz and Philadelphia's Eastern State Penitentiary (1829–1971), another National Historic Landmark. For many more examples of reclaiming prison spaces into parks, landmarks, entrepreneurial hubs and more, see YesInMyBackyard.org.

For example, California's penchant for incarceration led to a class action lawsuit and, ultimately, to a mandate from the U.S. Supreme Court to drastically reduce the number of people behind bars. Justice Anthony Kennedy, noting that people in prison "retain the essence of human dignity inherent in all," wrote: "Prisoners are crammed into spaces neither designed nor intended to house inmates. As many as 200 prisoners may live in a gymnasium, monitored by as few as two or three correctional officers. . . . As many as 54 prisoners may share a single toilet."

In addition to overcrowding, abuse, and other ills that plague prisons, there are missed opportunities. For example, prior to the early 1990s, people behind bars could use federal Pell Grants to access postsecondary education. Then, in 1994, Congress passed legislation denying those grants to prisoners despite evidence that education helped reduce recidivism and improve carceral order. Even today, some states are disbanding those few prison-based post-secondary and liberal arts education programs that have survived the cuts. With notable and inspiring exceptions, there are too few meaningful opportunities for the incarcerated to learn. Those classes that are offered reach capacity long before fulfilling demand.

Central to the initial decision denying education on the inside was the cleaving of *us* and *them*. Sociologist Joshua Page studied the public discourse surrounding the 1994 debates and found a veritable "legislative penal drama," complete with heroes and villains. Politicians pitted people behind bars and "undeserving street criminals" against crime victims and law-abiding students from working families. It was a zero-sum—and disturbingly familiar—game, in which for the "good" to win, the "bad" must lose.

And so the "othering" arguments continued. Those behind bars had little support, much less voice, as they were demonized, as rights and opportunities were stripped away.

Meanwhile, the overwhelming majority of people behind bars return to the community. To put it bluntly: our most marginalized citizens and neighbors are devoured by a system that offers few chances of rehabilitation, education, or treatment. They serve their time and are spat out on the streets, branded with a criminal record, even more disadvantaged than when they went in.

| JAILS |

State and federal prisons only tell a small part of our lockdown's tragic story. A Prison Policy Initiative report finds that while 641,000 people leave prison each year, *at least 9 million* cycle through jail. What's more, the Vera Institute of Justice notes that three out of five people in jail are legally presumed innocent—they're simply too poor to post even the lowest bail amount. Even a short stay, the report explains, is more than an inconvenience:

Just a few days in jail can increase the likelihood of a sentence of incarceration and the harshness of that sentence, reduce economic viability, promote future criminal behavior, and worsen the health of those who enter—making jail a gateway to deeper and more lasting involvement in the criminal justice system at considerable costs to the people involved and to society at large.

Many people, unable to post bail, plead guilty in exchange for time served. Essentially, *say you did it and you can go home—with probation and a record.* As Vichal Kumar with the Neighborhood Defender Service of Harlem says, "Not only does this offend basic norms of human rights and personal dignity, it cuts against the spirit of fairness and equality under the law." For millions, this means going to court is little more than a costly charade, a performance in which the protagonist doesn't understand the plot, has few lines, and has little agency to improvise or question.

To these enormous counts, add 41,000 more people locked up on immigration holds, 13,000 in territorial prisons, 1,400 in military prisons, 2,500 in Indian Country jails, and 6,400 in civil commitment. And that's just adults.

An island on the East River; a single wing of a building in Los Angeles; a subterranean labyrinth in Chicago. Each has been called our nation's largest mental health institution. And each is a jail.

It wasn't always like this, though that's not to say it was better. People diagnosed with mental health concerns were once placed in overcrowded, squalid psychiatric institutions—or insane asylums. In the 1970s, a social movement to deinstitutionalize people with mental illnesses—coupled with strained budgets—gained traction, and eventually the asylums were shut down.

Communities were ill-equipped to handle the transition. Patients spilled out of the facilities, equipped with few resources and almost no mental health programming or treatment to support them. Many became homeless, embroiled in the criminal justice system, or both.

Individuals suffering a mental health crisis are more likely to encounter the police than get medical help. Acts of violence, survival, addiction and inconvenience result in lock-up: two million people with mental health concerns are booked into our county jails each year. One Bureau of Justice Statistics study found that nearly three-fourths of women and more than one-half of men in prison and jail reported a diagnosis, treatment, or symptoms of a mental health disorder in the last year.

The population has shifted from one form of warehousing to another.

Jails and prisons are now *de facto* health care providers for many underprivileged people, and it's hard to assess the quantity and quality of care across these institutions. Police and corrections officers may serve as front-line psychiatric workers, but too often without appropriate training or support. The lack of resources can be stressful and dangerous for the officer and horrifying for the civilian. Violent and inhumane conditions in jails and prisons can further traumatize an already vulnerable population, and abuses behind bars may aggravate symptoms of disorders, making future treatment more difficult. What's more, people with mental illnesses tend to be held longer in lock-up and, upon release, are at a higher risk of returning to jail than those without mental health concerns.

Rates of self-medication and chemical dependency run high: the National Research Council notes that, in jails, seventy percent of those with a serious mental illness have a co-occurring substance abuse disorder.

I didn't need jail, I needed a doctor. It's a lamentably common refrain. Take, for instance, one gentleman who, drunk and deeply depressed, had tried to take his own life three years before. Now saddled with a criminal record, he has difficulty finding employment, a place to live, and even a place to get help: the last two treatment facilities denied him a bed due to his criminal conviction.

Some don't make it to jail, much less come home. According to the Washington Post, a quarter of the 498 people shot and killed by police nationwide between January 1st and July 3rd in 2017 showed signs of mental illness.

Surveys suggest that police may perceive mental health related calls as unpredictable and dangerous; without adequate training, that perception can inadvertently escalate the situation. And while some jurisdictions are investing in efforts that train officers to deescalate situations safely and without force and encourage officers to build meaningful rapport with community members and community-based mental health resources, we need more. More training, more rapport, more resources.

Without change, millions of people will continue the costly cycle through the criminal justice system, resulting in tragic outcomes, missed treatment opportunities, and a failure to improve public safety. The National Alliance on Mental Illness calls the criminalization of mental health a "tragedy of national proportions" and a crisis of both our criminal justice and broader health care systems: "It is a trend that is expensive, ineffective and inhumane."

At any given time, thousands of incarcerated women are pregnant. For many, this will mean limited prenatal care, shackling and belly chains during transport to hospitals for check-ups, continued restraints during labor, families absent and correctional guards present for birthing. Shortly after giving birth, the mothers will be once again handcuffed. Stories of women receiving postpartum care amounting to little more than a handful of sanitary pads are common.

Most of these newborns are taken from their mothers immediately or within hours of their birth. Some are allowed to stay for a few days and, in rare cases, a year or more with their mothers in custody. The eventual separation is as inevitable as it is heartrending.

At the other end of the life course, prisons are in need of geriatric units. People serve more and more time behind bars due to a confluence of implacable codes: mandatory minimums (which remove judicial discretion in determining severity of punishment), three strikes laws (which significantly increase sentence lengths—often to life— for a third violent crime or serious felony), truth-in-sentencing (reducing potential parole time and requiring people to "sit the time sentenced") and trend towards longer sentences. Criminologists, meanwhile, will point you to the "age-crime" curve, which depicts a lopsided arc of life-course criminality, rapidly peaking in adolescence and then for most quickly declining—with a few burps—as they mature.

Nevertheless, in 2010 there were 26,200 people aged 65 or older in prison. Experts project that by 2030, one-third of all those incarcerated—more than 400,000 people—will be over 55.

There are nearly 160,000 lifers behind American bars, about 10,000 of whom are serving time for nonviolent offenses. This population has more than quadrupled since 1984; nearly half are African American and one in six is Latino.

Some may be paroled, but for tens of thousands, there's no chance of getting out. Picture this: right now in the U.S., there are at least 41,000 people serving life sentences without the possibility of parole; England has just 41.

Kidney failure, dementia, and strokes. Elderly men and women unable to climb into upper bunks, take showers without assistance, or stand for count.

Says Families Against Mandatory Minimums' Julie Stewart, "Our federal prisons are starting to resemble nursing homes surrounded with razor wire."

Living on probation is like living in a netherworld.
—Jason Sole, author and activist

Recently, the U.S. prison population began to show signs of downsizing. Though the reduction has been small—state prison populations declined by just over three percent between 2009 and 2013—it marks a notable reversal in a four-decade-long upward trend. Sociologist Michelle Phelps notes the decarceration is spurred in part by local budget crises and a shift in the politics of punishment: there's an increasing appeal to probation over prison. There's also an appeal to supervision in general, driven in part by the expansion of misdemeanor convictions. The Robina Institute calls this another example of American exceptionalism: the United States' probation rate is more than five times that of European countries—despite roughly comparable crime rates for many common offenses.

With more than two million people in prison or jail and nearly *four million* on probation, it's no longer just a matter of mass incarceration, Dr. Phelps observes: we've got a mass probation problem, too.

Along with probation comes a flood of court-ordered conditions intended to regulate the defendant. In addition to directives from the judge, conditions often include requirements to comply with more nebulous mandates from the probation officer. For some, it's navigable, either because of their own means or because of their assigned probation officer. Probation officers can help negotiate the choppy waters of "reentry" and few in the system better understand how difficult it is to live with a criminal record. For others on probation, they're caught in a whirlpool of regulations and restrictions, without land or lifeboat in sight.

Some refer to being on probation as being half-free: with one foot in jail, the other can't go far. Others call it the "installment plan": chipping away at the longer suspended sentence with days or months in lock-up for violating conditions of release. And violations come easy.

From breaking a law to falling behind on fees and fines, people on probation can quickly find themselves in custody. Generally, people "on paper" must submit to a search of their home, car, and person at any time; not consume or be in the presence of others consuming alcohol or drugs; meet regularly with their probation officer; and, upon demand, pee in a cup in front of a witness. Some are required to submit a DNA sample; others to share email and social media passwords with their probation officers. Working or going to school are central to many conditions of release.

Legal scholar Fiona Doherty enumerates other typical conditions such as supporting dependents, working diligently at a lawful occupation, and avoiding injurious and vicious habits as well as persons and places of disreputable character. The result is "an almost farcical level of control over people's lives," she explains, while diverging "radically from the conceptual and jurisprudential underpinnings that are invoked to justify them." In short: "probationers must be *good people*, in addition to being law-abiding people" (emphasis added).

Many are ordered to undergo and pay for medical, psychiatric, and psychological assessments—including drug and alcohol dependency and sex offender evaluations. They must comply with, pay for, and complete all recommendations that result from such assessments. The bills for these tests and treatments rapidly reach into the thousands. Then there's restitution, and probationers are frequently required to pay for nights spent in jail, check-in and check-out fees, court clerk fees, public defender fees, public safety fees, and, of course, fees for the privilege of being on probation itself. The list goes on.

Given that eight or nine out of ten probationers are so poor as to qualify for public defense, these conditions, in particular, seem to prime people for failure. Some turn to selling drugs or stolen goods to pay the state; others, homeless and jobless, are instructed by probation officers to sell plasma to pay for treatment.

Supervision stretches from a year to two to ten to twenty and beyond; it is often longer than even the suspended sentence (that is, the total months or years a person would spend behind bars if their probation were revoked). With so many demands and restrictions, and so few resources and opportunities, some people who could get out on probation willingly forgo the "privilege" and "sit their time" behind bars instead.

FORECLOSED

FUTURES

One-third of all U.S. young adults have been arrested for an offense other than a minor traffic violation by the time they reach the age of 23. An increase in arrests for drug-related offenses, zero-tolerance policies in schools, and a more aggressive and punitive justice system have resulted in countless youth and young adults cuffed, caged, shackled, and paraded in county courthouses across our country.

The disparities and the destruction of the justice system start early. Crowded classrooms, overwhelmed teachers, and draconian disciplinary policies have created a school-to-prison pipeline that is woefully well-oiled. Some schools even look like jails: metal detectors, bulletproof glass, surveillance cameras, drug tests and drug-sniffing dogs, locked and crammed classrooms, and police liaisons lining the hallways. Students have become inmates-in-training.

With suspensions and expulsions alarmingly commonplace, it can be hard to stay in school. Kids are arrested, detained, adjudicated, and expelled for acts ranging from throwing peanuts to punches, from carrying nail clippers to knives on school grounds.

While white youth are more likely to be suspended or expelled than black youth for objective violations like bringing drugs or guns onto campus, black youth bear the brunt of suspensions and expulsions where administrators have discretion—say, when a child is deemed disrespectful or to have violated a dress code. Bias—implicit and otherwise—clearly plays a role in how these subjective punishments are applied at the early stages of life in social institutions.

In total, black and Native American students are suspended and expelled at wildly disproportionate rates. And while boys receive the majority of suspensions, black girls are suspended at greater rates than girls of any other race or ethnicity—and most boys.

Following expulsion, youth are more likely to have future interactions with the justice system.

It's no small number of kids caught in the criminal-case quicksand: in a single year, more than one million delinquency cases (children ages 6–17) cycled through U.S. courts. Not all of these kids end up in custody: with innovative efforts from the Juvenile Detention Alternatives Initiative and others, we've reduced the number of kids we're caging. Still, there are tens of thousands in adult prisons and jails, juvenile detention, and out-of-home residential facilities.

Even pretrial detention—before anyone has been found guilty—isn't harmless; like adults, kids locked up pending a court hearing are more likely to be charged, adjudicated, and committed than similarly situated youth who were granted the ability to remain at home. And just as in every other stage in the justice system, African American, Latino, and Native American youth are disproportionately affected: they are far more likely to be detained than white youth—even after controlling for seriousness of offense and criminal history.

Detention can have profound and deleterious effects on a child's mental health, physical health, education, employment prospects, and ability to live a jail-free life in the future. Even more heart-wrenchingly, it can kill.

Horror stories abound of kids held for weeks, months, and *years* in pretrial detention. Take Kalief Browder, a 16-year-old sent to Rikers Island because someone said he stole a backpack. He spent nearly three years in lock-up, almost two in solitary confinement. He was starved, he was beaten, he was never found guilty.

Soon after his release, Kalief took his own life.

Among the 34,000 in juvenile detention, thousands are there for technical violations (failure to comply with probation) and hundreds for offenses that would not be considered unlawful if they were older (such as running away, truancy, liquor and curfew violations, and ungovernability).

How is this possible? Some of it lies in the language we use—and the language we don't.

Law professor Perry Moriearty and her co-author William Carson note that in the case of the "super-predator" war, mental associations, as well as dissociations, were critical to the mass criminalization mania:

At the same time the "super-predator" war amplified the American public's predisposition to associate adolescents of color, and in particular young black males, with violence and moral depravity, it also led the public to dissociate young black males from the one trait that should not have been up for debate: their youth. The result was a veritable feedback loop whose cognitive output, the mental imprint of "morally impoverished" "super-predators," continually fed its input. Thus, even as crime rates among black youth have dropped steadily since the mid-1990s, these self-reinforcing associations and dissociations have prompted lawmakers and their constituents to continue to support laws and policies that they know disproportionately punish and incapacitate young black males.

Super-predator vs. youth. At-risk vs. at-promise. Kid vs. thug. Criminal vs. clean. Our children vs. their children. Think of the effects such *otherings* have had.

Consider the kids who languish in custody after admitting guilt: eating, sleeping, waiting in trapped air, thick with the stench of wet feet, rotting milk, and despair. Missing school, the big tournament, and the pick-up game down the street. Missing grandma's funeral, family barbecues, county fairs with cousins, and a movie with the friend that would have turned to a crush. Missing sibling rivalries, a burger with a mentor, and flipping a tassel-topped mortar board into the air. Missing, as former President Obama said, the margin of error afforded to the rest of us.

Consider the kids kept in solitary confinement, a cell no larger than a parking space, looking out a scuffed window at a grey-painted brick wall. Consider the thousands of individuals sentenced to die in adult prison for crimes committed while underage.

Consider the thousands each year that leave lock-up, only to be saddled with a scarlet letter—their futures foreclosed before their brains are even fully developed.

And consider the words of Dr. Karl Menninger: "I suspect that all the crimes committed by all the jailed criminals do not equal in total social damage that of the crimes committed against them."

PARK

PRISON

Kids as young as ten are pulled out of school, jeans and tees swapped for orange jumpsuits, chains at the wrists, waist, and ankles for staring, shouting, scribbling on desks, and forging excuse notes.

Teens walking home from school, friends' homes, or work find themselves pushed against a wall and frisked, bent over a squad car's hood, slammed into the pavement with a knee in their backs, detained, stripped, and searched for looking *suspicious*.

Far too many young adults outside of the campus bubble spend their formative years—years invaluable to career and family prospects—in jail, for engaging in the same behavior other kids get away with or are punished for by parents and teachers rather than police or courts.

And while more youth and young adults are caught up in the system, it's important to note that the arrest, charging, conviction or adjudication, detention, jail, and probation are just the beginning of the entanglement.

Official and unofficial chronicles of those interactions (juvenile records, criminal records, mugshots, news articles, and more) can plague the child as she or he works to navigate the already choppy waters of youth and adulthood.

Yet we've learned a lot about brain development in the last few decades. We know that our brains grow, rewiring themselves throughout childhood and adolescence and reaching maturation only in our mid-20s. We know that trauma can delay that progress. We know that youth and young adults are impulsive, hormone-driven, and susceptible to peer pressure. We know that testing boundaries, taking risks, and making mistakes are a part of growing up.

We understand how labeling a child can lead to external stigmatization as well as internal limitations. We know that criminal activity for many is fleeting—and we know that records are not.

Consider the benefits of forgetting. The bliss of ignorance. Many of us are able to mythologize our pasts, to recall ourselves as kinder, wiser, and less culpable than we may have truly been. But those who carry a criminal or juvenile record are forever reminded of their mistakes, forever introduced to the larger society by their pasts.

Forgetting, it seems, is a necessary part of the human experience. It allows us to move on. But in this data age—for those who were caught—the luxury to forget is a distant memory.

In this section, we'll take a look at crimes that occurred before the participants' brains were fully developed.

The deck is stacked in my favor

STUDENT

ASSAULT; DISTRIBUTION AND POSSESSION OF CONTROLLED SUBSTANCES; UNDERAGE CONSUMPTION; PROVIDING ALCOHOL TO A MINOR

I see kids in court all the time for stuff that my friends and I did. Chucking water bottles, playground fights—I used to get yelled at by the Vice Principal; they're charged with assault. At twelve. That's absurd.

It's crazy to think about the stuff I've gotten away with: drug possession, distribution, underage consumption, purchasing alcohol for a minor. Pretty proud of the fact that I haven't driven drunk.

(whispers) *I've done other things too.*

Through my family, through my jobs, I'm connected. I've seen that click when a cop sees me. *Oh hey, it's you. Go on home.* I'm not a threat.

WHEN YOU THINK ABOUT IT, WE'RE ALL JUST ONE ACT AWAY FROM LOSING IT ALL.

When you think about it, we're all just one act away from losing it all. One cop away. One charge away. One juror away. It's unsettling, the amount of chance in the criminal justice system.

I'm a white woman; chance has been in my favor. Statistically, I'm not where they're looking. The cops, the courts, are focused on someone else.

BUSINESS
OWNER

THEFT

It was the perfect crime for a 12-year-old.

FRAUD INVESTIGATOR

BURGLARY

When you're 14, you're not thinking of the consequences. We just wanted to have fun and get away with it. And we did.

Look at where we're at now: Carl is a cop, Mike's an engineer, Joey manages a textile company, and Mark runs his own business. If we would have been caught, who knows?

TEACHER

THEFT; TRESPASSING; POSSESSION OF CONTROLLED SUBSTANCES; DRIVING WHILE INTOXICATED

I was a nice boy—and then sometimes I wasn't. We stole little things: *candy, trinkets, stuff you could hide in your pocket.* And big things: *auto parts from a nearby junkyard (we called it the "midnight auto supply"); the steering wheel of a parked car at a filling station (we used it in building a Frankenstein go-cart); a stop sign (which we unbolted and installed in our college dorm room).*

We'd throw snowballs at cars, sling-shot rocks and BBs at moving freight trains. We'd drive after drinking and inhale when smoking pot. We'd sneak into garages and barns just to have a look and climb out onto the roofs of office buildings.

We did it for the moment, for the thrill. But I never thought "I'm a bad guy." If you come to think of yourself as criminal, you've passed a threshold. You get onto a trajectory that's a bad path. Thankfully, I wasn't caught, and I didn't consider myself bad—nor did others.

Experimenting with delinquency is normal—and so is giving it up. How many kids get a police record, or a longer record, for the same or even fewer criminal acts my friends and I did?

I have that story. Everybody has that story. If you find someone who claims they've never committed a crime, either they're lying, they have a poor memory, or they're very abnormal.

NOTE:

Examining the criminalization spiral that begins with trivial labels *(he's at-risk)* and grows to something more detrimental *(he's a risk)*, sociologist Victor Rios notes, "In the era of mass incarceration, labeling not only generates criminality; it also perpetuates criminalization."

LIBRARIAN

BURGLARY; INTERFERENCE WITH TRANSIT OPERATOR

In my growing up, the whole social attitude toward juvenile behavior was very different than it seems to be now. I mean, I'm confident that some of the stunts that we pulled as kids— if we did the same things now, we would be in the court system and probably incarcerated faster than we could blink.

It's interesting that we're here, because the site of probably the most devilish—I was pretty straight-arrow when I was growing up, but our favorite Halloween stunt was enacted one block over from where we're living right now. The hill going up Pascal was the streetcar line when I was growing up.

So the stunt on Halloween was always to get a five-pound can of lard from somebody's pantry and grease the streetcar tracks. The streetcar—you know, he'd come down Como, turn onto Pascal, and go down the hill to Midway Parkway, and then start up the hill and get about halfway up the hill, and the wheels would start spinning. We were all, of course, sitting in the bushes, laughing ourselves sick,

but I mean, as I say, if that sort of thing—if you did that today and a cop came by, you would be in deep, deep trouble.

In terms of most of my involvements in school—I was in the Library Club, which was the most prestigious organization in the whole school, and I think I still have my Library Club pin . . .

This crazy jewelry box is so dusty. You can tell I never go into it. I think it's in here.

Here it is. Isn't that wild? Being a member of the Library Club was the impetus that launched my entire career in libraries. The 66 kids in the Library Club ran the whole library. At least, we thought we did.

I would think that the rules for participating in something like Library Club would have been strict enough that, if you got out of line, you would be ineligible in today's world, if not suspended from school for who knows how long. Or worse.

CRIME IS AN EVENT IN A LIFE COURSE

Crime is an event in a life course; it is not a static characteristic of a person.

We commit crimes, we stop committing crimes. (Or perhaps, more accurately, given the over-breadth of our criminal code: the number of crimes we intend to commit decreases over time.) Criminologists point to employment, marriage, education, and simply growing up as factors in our reduced criminality. They have a word for it: desistance—the cessation of offending.

Professor of Criminology and Social Work Fergus McNeill and colleagues say studying desistance forces us away from fixed models of people as criminals and encourages an understanding of changes in personal identities. We move from offender to *father, student, husband, leader*: "it implies valuing people for who they are and for what they could become, rather than judging, rejecting or containing them for what they have done."

HEALTH CARE CONSULTANT

SHOPLIFTING

When I was 15, my mother died. I thought that didn't have much effect on me. As a 15-year-old, I couldn't let it. But what I found myself doing was leaving school, from where I had no friends or acquaintances really, going over to the shopping mall that was across the street, trying on clothes, and stealing them.

I remember in particular a white tennis dress. I did not play tennis. It was cute. I took it home, I showed it to my sisters. I didn't tell them right then that I had stolen it. I stole a lot of other stuff, but sort of more of the adolescent variety, you know: nail polish, bangles, records even sometimes—which are kind of hard to steal.

That was a period of six months or so where that was a release, frankly. (I realize now.) At the time I don't know what I thought I was doing. I think I just didn't think.

And fortunately I was never caught. It could have been the beginning of a whole different life.

I'm happily married, I have two brilliant kids, I work as a health care consultant, and work as a neighborhood activist.

| PARALLEL STORY |

I think I shoplifted because I was bored. For the thrill. Because my friends were doing it. Because I just really wanted a pair of jeans that I couldn't afford as a broke college student. It didn't seem like a big deal until, unlike my friends, I got caught.

Anyway, it turns out that it is sort of a big deal.

It's been years, and I still haven't told my family (even though we're close). Recently, I opened up to a friend; I guess I expected her to laugh, or more likely, one-up me with yet another story about her wild youth.

Instead, her whole demeanor changed. She actually said she wasn't sure she could look at me the same now that she knew I was a "thief."

It really hurt.

I suppose I'll be paying for these jeans for a long time.

01010111 01101001 01110010 01100101 00100000
01100110 01110010 01100001 01110101 01100100

and

01000001 01110100 01110100 01100101 01101101
01110000 01110100 01100101 01100100 00100000
01100011 01110010 01100101 01100100 01101001
01110100 00100000 01100011 01100001 01110010
01100100 00100000 01100110 01110010 01100001
01110101 01100100 00100000

IT SYSTEMS ADMINISTRATOR

WIRE FRAUD; CONSPIRACY TO COMMIT CREDIT CARD FRAUD

I should preface by saying, technically, it wasn't illegal. Or, at least, all of it wasn't illegal—unethical, yes—but not illegal: I don't think law had caught up with technology at that point.

I was an awkward, overweight, pimply teenager who was into computers. In the old days, they had this thing called the BBS system, a precursor to the internet. On BBS, there were different boards, or chatrooms, for different interests. My brother and I got into a board for people into "phone phreaking."

Phone phreaking was when you built a machine that would mimic the dial sounds of a touch-tone phone, allowing us to prank friends and complete strangers anywhere for free. We soon bored of that and wanted to try something new. That's when we met this guy I'll call Harold.

Harold said he could show us how to do something really cool. We figured we weren't going to be sports stars, so we might as well be coding geeks.

So Harold sent a partially written program for us to finish. The program contained the first four numbers of all the major credit cards in the U.S. Our job was to create an algorithm that would generate random numbers in four digit spats to make up the rest of the card.

We were then to call a credit card clearinghouse and pump the numbers into the system. If the numbers were valid, our dot matrix printer would spit out the valid numbers with the expiration dates. Mind you, all of this is now covered by security—but back then . . .

It worked. We got 80 pages of these numbers, sent some to Harold and kept some for ourselves. We went to the local CD shop and tried to buy music with nameless credit card numbers scrawled on pieces of scratch paper. Needless to say, we were not successful.

Anyway, the clearinghouse was able to call the house phone and figure out that we were behind this. They yelled at us for a long time, but didn't do anything else.

After that, we got so paranoid and freaked out—we asked my parents to cancel the modem line and we never looked back.

I now work in IT systems administration: security and so forth. It goes without saying I wouldn't have this job—or likely many others, had I been caught for something stupid I did back then.

STUDENT

AGGRAVATED ROBBERY

I was 15; I was lost. All the worst things had happened at the worst possible time: the girl my foolish 15-year-old self thought I loved left for Europe, my best friend had come back from an extended vacation with a crippling addiction to cocaine. Life was not particularly fun.

At this time, my cousins lived across the street. We always hung together, doing random stuff. One day, one of them said, *Do you want to rob somebody?* It had never crossed my mind before.

Why not? It's not like I had anything better to do. Besides, it was a way to take my mind off all of these things. I wouldn't say they pressured me into it, but I wouldn't have come to that conclusion myself.

Later that night, we covered our faces with scarves and waited around a different neighborhood until we found someone who looked like a good target. We stopped this person, held them at knifepoint, and took the watch, money, and left the ID.

I never read anything about it, never heard anything about it. We split everything between us.

Months went by, and I couldn't spend the money. I kept it for so long . . . I eventually just put it in a charity jar and sent it on its way.

It never hit me. I never felt bad. Looking back, I regret it, but I don't feel bad about it.

I just wish I had made a different decision.

| PARALLEL STORY |

V had just gotten off the late shift and was walking home. He saw this guy coming toward him, smoking a cigarette. As the guy got closer, V asked to bum one.

Get lost, the guy told him, except not quite like that.

You know what, give me the whole pack, V said, except not quite like that either. V had two windshield wiper blades he was bringing home to put on his girlfriend's car, so maybe the guy saw those and thought V might do something; he tossed the pack at V and ran the other way. V picked it up even though he didn't even want them anymore; it seemed like a waste to just let them get all soggy on the street.

V hadn't finished the first smoke by the time the cops caught up with him. He pleaded guilty to Aggravated Robbery and was on probation for three years. That was seven years ago.

V will admit what he did was stupid and wrong. But last June, his girlfriend had twins. He's still working odd hours at the garage, and she needed help with the girls. Her mom stays at public housing, where there's grass and a playground and it seems like a safer place for them to be. The problem is, with V's record, he can't stay with them. He wonders, *Do I ask them to give that up so that I can come home to my family?*

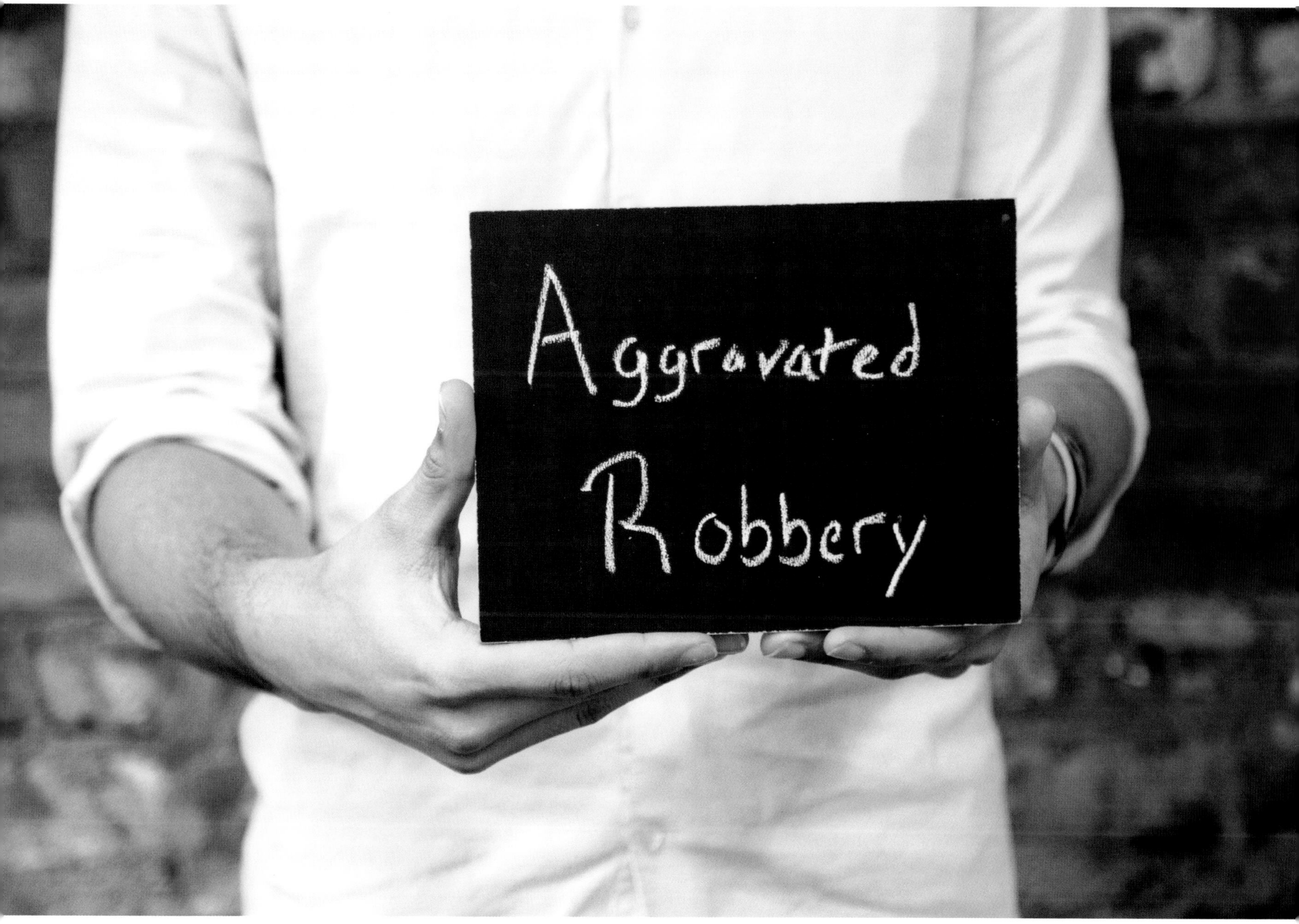
Aggravated
Robbery

BIOPHYSICIST

FIRST DEGREE ASSAULT FOR THE BENEFIT OF A GANG

He was 14 when his family moved to the neighborhood. The six-by-five block radius was rough, but not the roughest in town. That said, when J found himself befriended by two older guys from around the corner, things got noticeably better. There was Junior, a man who had dropped out of school when he was still a boy, and Deion, who was only 17 but walked with the authority of someone far older. There were others, too: Judge, Manny, and Bugs were three on J's side of the street, just two doors down. In some sense, if he really thought about it, J supposed he was in a gang.

The summer J turned 15 started off uneventfully. His parents worked double shifts and were rarely home, and there was little to do other than hang out and will the cool morning air to linger a little longer into the afternoon. It was on one of those ordinary mornings that everything changed.

There was a knock at the front door. Through the screen, J could see a boy cupping his eyes to block out the sun and peer through the mesh.

The boy asked if J's parents were home. He was selling magazines for a fundraiser. When J told him they wouldn't be back until dinner, the boy thanked him and said he'd stop by later.

Soon after, Junior stopped by on his morning rounds. When J offhandedly mentioned the magazine seller, Junior perked up. Apparently, there had been a rash of burglaries in the neighborhood. Rumor had it that a boy from another gang had been breaking into nearby garages, stealing tools and other pawnables in the middle of the day.

Within minutes, eight or nine of J's friends, including Deion and Manny, gathered in J's garage, smoking cigarettes and speaking sparingly. After what seemed like an hour, J heard someone walking along the rocks that lined the garage's south wall. A moment later, the magazine seller's face appeared at the window. It was too bright outside and too dark inside for him to see J and the others. He deftly jimmied the window open and began to crawl inside. The boy realized he was not alone when he got half-way through the window. He yelped

and tried squirming back out but Junior caught him by the neck and pulled him in.

J doesn't know where the lead pipe came from but he remembers that Junior swung first, hitting the boy in the stomach with such force that J staggered backward and into Manny.

One by one, everyone took a turn until it came to J. It wasn't a question. It was an ultimatum. *Do it, or you're next.*

J remembers the sound of the lead pipe hitting the boy—a soft, wet pop, like the sound canned jam makes when the vacuum seal is broken. He remembers the smell of sick and blood and piss, the stench of hate and fear and nothingness. He remembers the knots swelling up on the boy's face like midday suns threatening to explode.

Someone else—Deion?—dragged the boy away. J never saw him again.

PEDIATRICIAN

ARSON; CRIMINAL DAMAGE TO PROPERTY

I was a kid. Sixteen, maybe fifteen. It was the middle of summer, and I was bored out of my mind.

I was a dork and the slapdash summer group I hung out with was mostly harmless, too. Once or twice a week, we'd find ourselves in the house on the cul-de-sac, draped over basement sofas or stretched out on the floor, listening to a Tom Lehrer cassette on a boombox. We'd sing along, tripping over our own tongues in a struggle to keep up with "The Elements," a speedy recitation of the periodic table set to piano. See? Harmless. But even nerds get into trouble.

One of the boys first got the idea. We'd fill an apple cider bottle with a household chemical and some packing material. The two react to create a flammable gel. Then all we would need was a target and a spark.

I can't remember who suggested a state park Porta Potty. It was ideal—a smallish, enclosed structure outside of suburbia. Someone put the premixed mess in the trunk, wedging it against the side with a couple of thick textbooks. We piled into one car, driving five miles under the speed limit the entire way. The Porta Potty was at the edge of the parking lot. For some reason I had envisioned it beyond a hill or two, surrounded by trees and out of view.

Some of us stayed inside the car, petrified that at any moment the bottle would blow, taking eyes and fingers with it. We doused the inside of the toilet and walls with its sticky, noxious jelly. Standing a few feet back, we lit a gas-soaked tennis ball on fire. One of us held the door open while another tossed it in. Those outside the car ran for their lives, those inside curled up into tight balls and braced for the blast.

I can remember the heat more than the sight, and the sight more than the sound. It was beautiful and terrifying all at once. Carbon, oxygen, and hydrogen in a very specific and frightening form. Dazed, we drove back home in silence.

For months afterward, we'd see each other in the hall or parking lot, and I swear I could feel the heat embracing me again.

I suppose there are a few felonies in my history, if I really think about it. But blowing up a state toilet is arson, and arsonists can't work with kids. I'm a pediatrician now, and it's been a long journey to get here. This morning, I kept a three-month-old heart beating with my index finger. I'd say that's a much better use of my hands.

IN THE NEWS

A teenager in Florida was expelled from school and charged with a felony after experimenting with chemicals to test reactions.

Kids should learn *there are consequences to their actions*, said the school district.

SOCIAL WORKER

ASSAULT; POSSESSION OF CONTROLLED SUBSTANCES; FALSE REPORT OF A FIRE; TRUANCY; UNDERAGE CONSUMPTION

I have a rap sheet of uncaught crimes, most pretty insignificant. We were naughty kids—pulling fire alarms, smoking pot, and bolting from our private school to drink beer by the lake in our uniforms.

But I suppose the thing that I feel the worst about happened on senior skip day. We had been partying all night, hanging out at the lake. I don't think that we were too intoxicated, but certainly not clear-headed.

A classmate had gone into the park's Porta Potty. She was the type that would powder her nose, you know? Not like me, not like us. Once she was in the Porta Potty, a few of us shoved our weight against one side, tipping it over with her in it. It was just a reaction, a response to me being there and her being there.

Feces, urine—the waste covered her.

I don't know what I was thinking, but I wasn't expecting that. We ran as fast as we could. I saw her later. She was angry, but more than that, she was deeply embarrassed. I think she knew who did it, but she never said anything.

I left for college a few months later and eventually got a good paying job. I gave up drinking for Lent, pulled myself out of the social situation I was in, and started to work on me.

Looking back, I can contextualize it. I was lost and wanted to be accepted. I lacked self-confidence and self-worth. I was easily influenced by people around me. That person who tipped the Porta Potty, that wasn't me, but I didn't know that then.

I've always been interested in helping people. That's how I was made. It just took me a while to get there.

| PARALLEL STORY |

I don't really know why I did it. I know I should have some excuse for picking on him, but I can't really think of one.

Maybe I just wanted to be a part of the team, and to be a part of something means that there must be at least one person who's not a part of it, you know?

Anyway, I did it and it was wrong and I've said sorry to him, sorry to his parents, sorry to the principal, sorry to the judge, and sorry to my mom. Sometimes I feel like I'm sorry-ed out, that I've covered everyone I was supposed to cover, and then there's another person telling me I'm a jerk.

Yeah, it was a jerk move and I wish I could take it back because it's not all of who I am—but it's all that people see.

What luck ending the year in a Cap n Gown v.s. City Jail

VICTIMS' ADVOCATE

BURGLARY; UNDERAGE CONSUMPTION

I was a senior in high school and lived in a small town. A very small (and very white) town. Each class only had about 30 people in it, just to give you an idea. A one-stoplight kind of town.

Getting booze really wasn't a problem: my friends and I all had buyers. But we wanted more.

It was February, maybe March, when we started planning. There was a beverage company on the outskirts of town which functioned as the liquor distribution center for the region. It was a pole barn structure, you know, with tin siding over plywood. Nine of us would meet after school and on the weekends, concocting a very long and thoroughly thought-out plan of how we were going to break into the company during the middle of the night and take as much liquor as we could.

We studied the patrols of the two police cars on duty, watching their routes. We studied the layout of the building. Somehow, I don't remember how, we got a sketch of the interior, so we knew what liquor was where. We bought walkie-talkies, had a van and a decoy car, a designated meet-up, and set alibis.

My best friend and I were the ringleaders. We assigned everyone a duty, reserving the least culpable positions for ourselves, just in case. Chad had the worst job. He was a big guy who had the muscles to peel back the tin siding so he was in charge of actually breaking in. I was hunkered down in the woods, watching the squad car.

Once the cop headed out of town, I radioed in the okay to Chad. He pulled the siding back and used a handsaw to cut a hole in the plywood. Once he was in, the group of guys hiding in the woods ran up to create a chain to pass the cases of beer and bottles of liquor from the store to the van nearby in a vacant lot.

In 30 minutes, we got eight cases of beer (maybe more) and 20 bottles of liquor (with some Schnapps for the girls). It doesn't sound like a lot now, but it was a really big deal then. We all met up at an abandoned cabin and split up some of the loot, but stashed most of it for later.

We waited three months to throw a party. It was out in the field, everyone came. At the end of the night, we tossed all of the empty bottles in the bonfire.

You know what's interesting? These were transferable skills.

The plotting, attention to detail, execution, delayed gratification, and, hey, even an interest in criminology.

Maybe it's no surprise that we are now police chiefs, college professors, coaches, nurses, and victims' advocates.

| PARALLEL STORY |

When he was 18, he swiped a single bottle of 3.2 beer from a gas station refrigerator, in a failed and foolish attempt to impress a crush at a house party.

He was caught, charged with misdemeanor theft, and pleaded down to a petty misdemeanor. He paid Court Admin the fine with birthday money and thought he was done with it.

Fourteen years later, he applied to be a cop. The Board of Peace Officer Standards and Training told him he was permanently prohibited from becoming a peace officer due to his petty misdemeanor theft.

He wonders how the police chiefs can talk about the need for officers of color, "officers that reflect the communities they serve," and then adopt and fiercely protect policies that prevent that from happening, policies that benefit the applicants who are *not* from the community; applicants who have *not* grown up with police on the corner, police in the grocery store, police in school.

| PARALLEL STORY |

You wanna know where I see burglaries the most? It's in these subdevelopments where every house looks the same as the next as the next as the next. Ticky tacky houses.

I had this guy, just loaded after a game. Wakes up on his couch, and has no idea how he got home. And why everything is shifted, slightly off, like a parallel universe.

That was his ceiling light, his closet, and his front door. That was his carpet and his stairs. But that was not his mom and not his sister on those carpeted stairs. Whoever it was, they were terrified out of their minds. Ya know, can you blame them? The cop tells him he's gonna taze him unless he gets up and all he can think is *Who let you in? Who let any of you in?*

Bam. Felony burglary just like that.

—public defender

| PARALLEL STORY |

A car slammed into her car several years ago. She was in the hospital for a day before work granted her medical leave. She was back at the job soon enough—and on her feet for the eight-hour stretch. After the doctor started cutting back her pain meds, each shift felt like an eternity. So when a coworker started selling her pills, she was grateful. Then she was hooked.

Two years later, she was caught breaking into yet another store, pockets stuffed with pawnables and gift cards with no cash value.

Work kept her on as long as she was in treatment. But then the company was eventually bought out by another, and with new management came new rules: everyone had to go through a background check.

It was humiliating, losing her job like that. A good warm-up to how humiliating the job search is going now.

WHAT HAVE YOU HAD THE LUXURY TO FORGET?

WHAT WOULD YOUR LIFE BE LIKE WITH A
CRIMINAL RECORD?

After coming home from Iraq, he couldn't find a job, so he moved back in with his mom. They got along well enough, but once his younger brother joined them, the house got really crowded.

One night he and his brother were drinking and playing a video game when one cheap shot lead to another and the gaming console ended up out the window. The brothers spilled out into the driveway, cussing and swinging at each other. Eventually, the cops showed up. When the younger brother refused to comply with the officer's commands, the cop reached for his taser.

The older brother can't remember what happened next, but the report said he rushed the officer and grabbed the taser before it could deploy. The second cop tased and cuffed first the older brother, than the younger one while the mom cried out from the front stoop.

The older brother went through a vet diversion program, and eventually the case was dismissed. But the arrest record for disarming a peace officer resulted in rescinded offers for a full-time position with benefits working building security, a job delivering furniture to assisted living centers, and even a position bagging groceries at the supermarket.

FORMER LEGISLATOR
FELONY DISARMING A PEACE OFFICER

The summer before I left for college I worked as a lifeguard at a neighborhood park.

It was a poor park. Racially integrated, but pretty poor. It was crowded, the summer was hot, and every day there were fights.

There was a policeman that worked at the park, and he wasn't what you would call a really great guy. He had a billy club he named Old Glory.

When there were fights at the pool (and there were a lot), the officer would poke the kids' ribs or whack their shins with Old Glory to break it up. One day, two kids were shouting and shoving each other, and one pushed the cop. Angry, he cracked Old Glory across this boy's head, and the kid's eyes rolled back as he hit the ground unconscious.

A few days later, the policeman was in the locker room playing a dice game, craps maybe, with some of the other lifeguards. He had left his billy club near the shower a few feet away. He was distracted, so I took the opportunity to grab it. This guy is cracking people on top of the head with this thing, I thought. Maybe he shouldn't have it around for a while. So I swiped Old Glory.

I showed it to all my friends. It was an impressive thing. Eventually I returned it, pretending I had just come upon it one morning. Everyone thought some kid from the neighborhood had taken it. Then it was back to whacking as usual, but for at least a portion of the summer we were all spared Old Glory.

MECHANIC

THEFT AND DESTRUCTION OF GOVERNMENT PROPERTY; RECKLESS DISCHARGE OF A FIREARM

My uncle gave me a thirty-aught-six rifle, and he told me when he gave it to me that I'd have to get at least one deer with it, so I took the gun and didn't really think about it.

I went to school, and the house I lived at—we were kind of notorious for having a kegger a month during the school time. So I'd been at the house; my roommates left. They got a car for dirt cheap—500 bucks—and they were a little drunk and decided to go knock over some road signs. They came back to the house where I'm hosting this party. My roommate tells me to come down to his room, and he's like, *Hey, do you have any change on you?*

I go, *What?*

No, seriously, do you have any change on you?

Yeah, I've got, like, 50 cents.

Here, give it to me. We've got to pay the parking meter. As I go into his room, he's got a double-posted parking meter sitting on his bed.

So we got an even better idea after we put the change in it. The red light starts blinking, and we're pretty drunk and dumb, and we're like, *Oh, shit, they might be able to track this thing*, 'cause we stole it.

We're thinking there's probably at least 50 bucks worth of change in the thing, so we grabbed my uncle's rifle and went out to the country. From about 30 yards away, leaning back and forth 'cause I was pretty drunk, I took one shot at it and boom, right through the lock. The thing tips over, and about 40 bucks worth of change flies up.

We ended up ditching the parking meter, but I still have the lock—with a hole perfectly through the locking mechanism on it—in a box somewhere.

That's the story. It wasn't a 12-point buck. It was, I guess you could say, a 40-buck parking meter.

SCHOOL EMPLOYEE

ARSON; VANDALISM

Last night, I started thinking about all the things I've gotten away with, counting them off on my fingers. There was that, and that, and yep, that too. The one I wanted to tell you about was something my buddy and I started doing when we were in high school, and continued to do on summer breaks in college.

The elementary school in my hometown has a tall white wall separating it from the woods beyond. We'd mix up what he called "napalm" in a bucket—or whatever was on hand—and take it down to the school at night and "paint the wall."

I never struck the match—I was far too scared I'd hurt myself—so my buddy did. One time we painted an evil-looking smiley face. Just bizarre, I know. And once that napalm stuff lights up, it lights forever. So there we would be, with this face or whatever burning bright into the night, confident we wouldn't get

NOW I WORK AT A SCHOOL. CAN YOU IMAGINE? I WOULDN'T BE ALLOWED IN THE FRONT DOOR.

caught: you see, the chances of a cop coming by were slim to none.

Now I work at a school. Can you imagine? I wouldn't be allowed in the front door.

You know, I never really thought about it all. It's just kids being kids—normal behavior. But, yeah, it was exhilarating.

THE COLOR OF GUILT,
THE PRESUMPTION OF INNOCENCE

According to a study published in the *Crime and Delinquency* journal, one out of every two young African American males has been arrested by the time they reach the age of 23 for an offense other than a minor traffic violation. That's in comparison to a general population average of one in three. Said the study's author, "many males—especially black males—are navigating the transition from youth to adulthood with the baggage and difficulties from contact with the criminal justice system."

Who ends up in the juvenile justice system is "one of the most glaring examples of racial injustice our nation has to offer," Nell Bernstein notes in *Burning Down the House*. She adds:

Fully 80 to 90 percent of American teenagers have committed an illegal act that could qualify them for time behind bars, and one-third of all teens have committed a serious crime. Most, however, never see the inside of a cell, or even a police car.

That's not typically the case with black and brown youth, especially those from poor communities. Unlike their white counterparts, they are more likely to be arrested, charged, detained, sentenced to locked institutions, kept longer, and sent back more often—despite engaging in the same behavior.

For kids who get a pass, Bernstein notes, "the overwhelming majority simply grow out of it." They grow up. And they enter adulthood unimpeded by relentless reminders of past mistakes.

DOCTOR'S ASSISTANT

THEFT

Back in the day, we thought no one could touch us. We were just kids—what could anyone do to us?

And it wasn't that I didn't have money. I was a really spoiled kid. I could say, *Hey Dad, I'm going to the mall*. He'd say, *Here's some money*. But there was a thrill factor to taking something that wasn't mine.

It started with a girlfriend. She said, *Haven't you ever taken anything before? Let's go.*

That first time, I was terrified. The shop was dark though, and teenagers were working. They didn't notice, or probably care.

We took t-shirts, we took jewelry.

Gradually, we grew more intense. We wanted a bigger challenge.

We bought wire cutters—I still remember their green handle—I stuffed them into my big bag, and we hit up a new store. My friend distracted the staff while I sliced through the theft-prevention wires on a pair of shoes.

I think the workers were just noticing that something was off when we ran out of the store. That was the only time, besides the first time, that I was truly shaken.

I know I obviously shouldn't have done it—and really, I took less than most people I knew.

GRADUALLY, WE GREW MORE INTENSE. WE WANTED A BIGGER CHALLENGE.

But I think about what would have happened had I been caught. I was an upper-middle-class white girl. A friend of mine was caught, someone a lot like me; they didn't even call her parents—just told her not to do it again.

I work in a clinic now and handle the ordering. Yeah, I notice that there are plenty of expensive items just lying around, just going to waste. I know I could take stuff—but the thrill is gone. My conscience would eat me alive.

I've changed a lot since high school, and thankfully nothing has held that back.

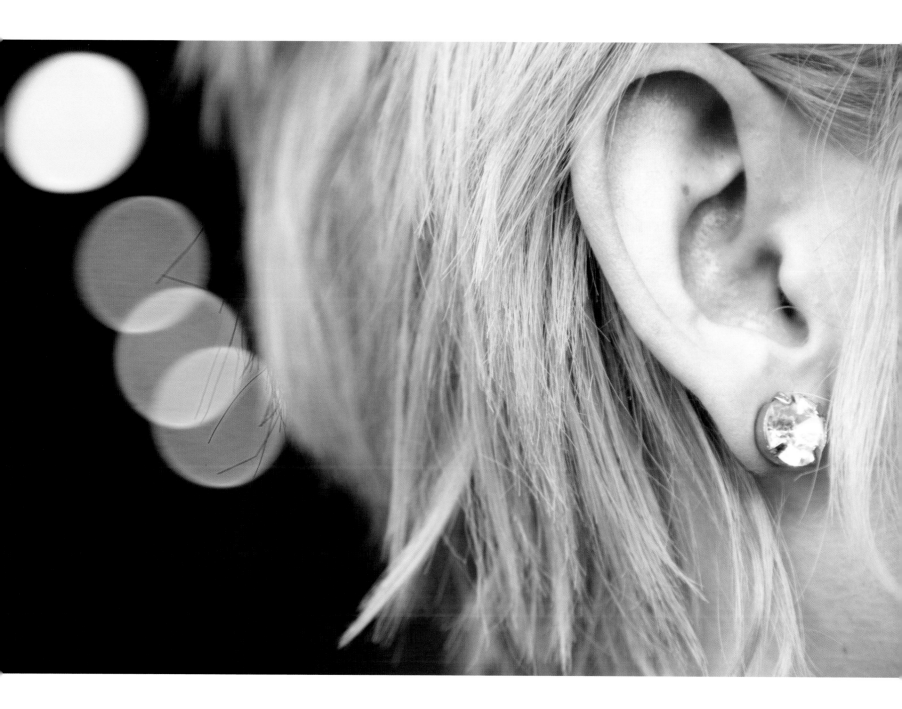

CHIEF FINANCIAL AND OPERATING OFFICER

BURGLARY; ARSON; POSSESSION OF CONTROLLED SUBSTANCES; SHOPLIFTING; CRIMINAL DAMAGE TO PROPERTY

Let's just say I'm never going to be president.

I was a horrid child. I'll list the types of offenses, and you can choose which you'd like to talk about. Alcohol? Marijuana? (Smoked, baked, and supplied.) LSD? Shoplifting? (Make-up, perfume, eyelash curlers, fake eyelashes.) By eighth grade, it was all routine.

Let's see. I stuffed a potato up a tailpipe and blew up a car. I blew up a mailbox. I torched a friend's AC. That one was a mistake.

I was particularly adept at breaking and entering—a career I continued until 10th grade. My friend and I would dress in all black, slinking around the neighborhood. A cop stopped us once. *Oh, we're out looking for our lost dog. Have you seen him?* Why would anyone scurry around in all black looking for a pet in the middle of the night? He didn't even question it, just let us go on with our night.

Sometimes we'd break into homes and just eat their ice cream. Other times we'd rifle through their stuff.

I still have some of it, such as a single, simple gold bracelet and a silver carafe (now tarnished) from another venture.

The bracelet I just took on our family vacation to Barbados. I often wear it when I travel. If it's stolen, oh well. I didn't spend anything on it.

So anyway, that's what I did growing up. Don't tell my son.

RESEARCHER

THEFT

My friend worked at the dorm's front desk. Over the course of the year, anytime someone would lose a student card—a card connected to a debit account—it would end up behind the desk.

The last week of classes, my friend grabbed all of the unclaimed cards, and, together, we hit the vending machines.

I kid you not: I did not think I was committing a crime. It was pop and candy—Wild Cherry Pepsi, to be exact. That's brain development for you.

My friend was a white woman, and I'm African American.

If I had been caught, I would not be where I am today. I'm not sure if my friend would have been so affected.

I would like to think that our criminal justice system isn't that blatantly racially biased, and I would like to think that I would have been treated less harshly than the mastermind behind the crime, but I've seen the system and I've studied the system and it likely wouldn't have been the case. Rather, it's like, "That's expected of you. You're a black female." And they likely would have treated her more leniently.

Years later, she could have told people it was a time in her life that she went down the wrong path with the African American.

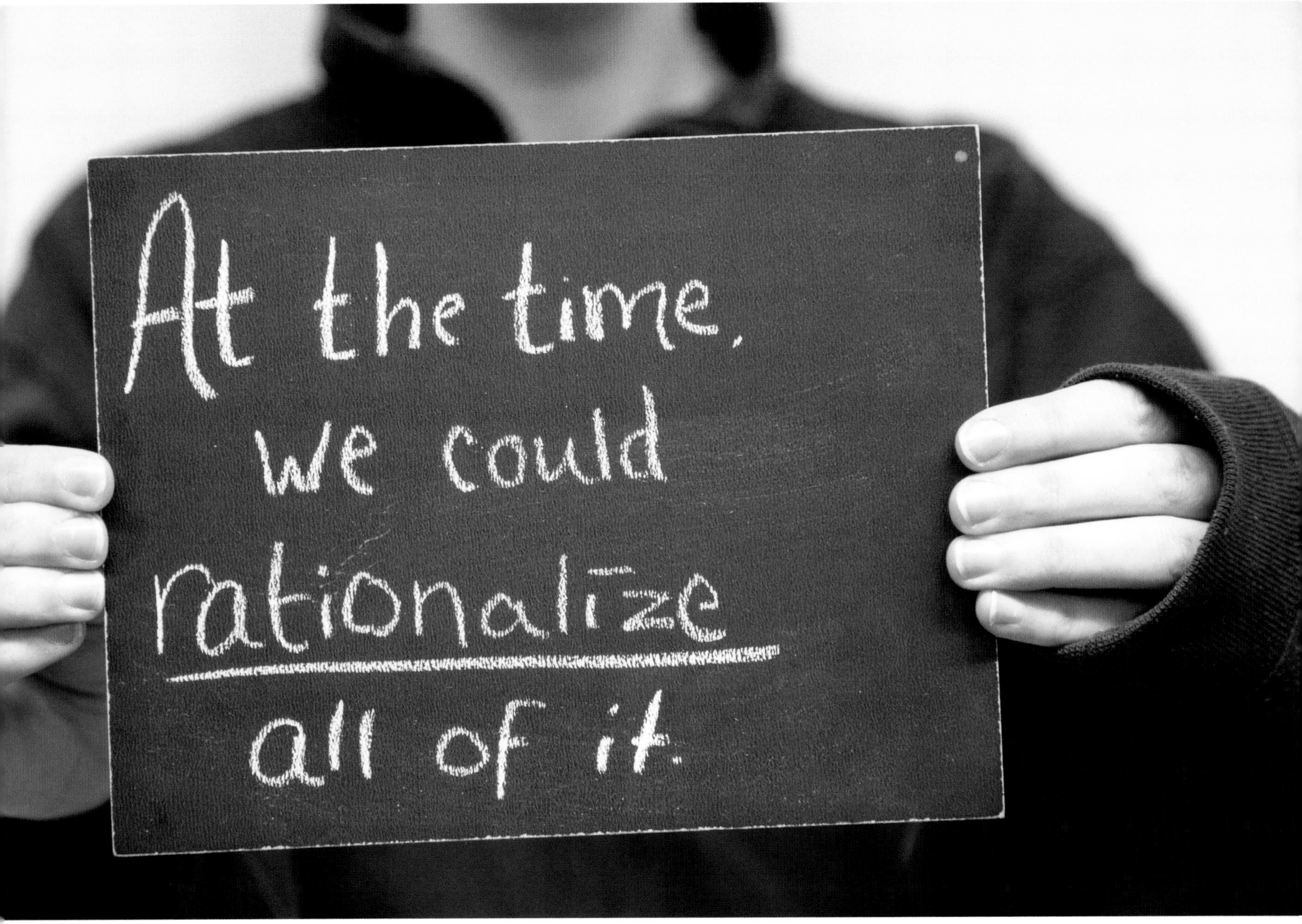
At the time,
we could
rationalize
all of it.

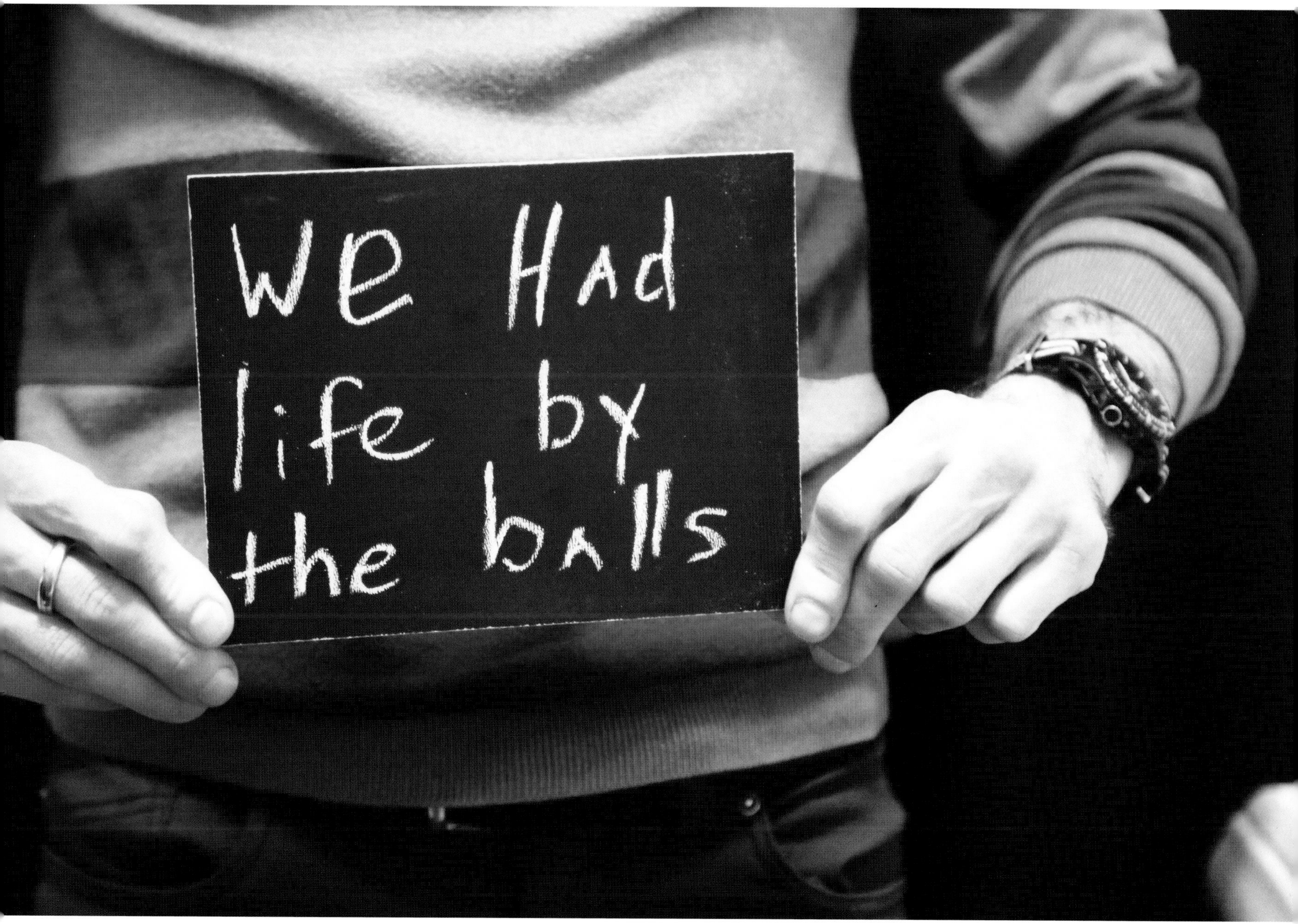
We Had
life by
the balls

AUTHOR

FINANCIAL FRAUD

When I was 20, I had a friend who worked at a local department store. His job was to preapprove applicants for credit, and I was "Harvey MacDonald" from Alabama.

I used the card a couple of times—bought some clothes and some other bullcrap.

On the third try, they asked for ID.

Oh—I left it in the car. Be right back!

And they didn't see me again.

If I had been caught, I wouldn't have gotten those student loans or been admitted into school, and I wouldn't have gotten my last several jobs. I would be a dude packing boxes right now. It would have become who I am, not what I did. That's how the world would see it.

I would have been contemplating something crazy to raise my kids.

And I wouldn't have been able to look my mother in the eye.

MANAGER

FELONY THEFT

I was a manager at a comics store in the mall, and I'd been there for a while.

My friends and I were working when the liquidators came in.

Congratulations! You're going out of business!

After a company has been liquidated, it tends to only stay open for a few months. *We want you to work for us through this process! Why hire and train an entire new staff?*

The next step in the process is taking an inventory of all the comics, games, and toys, the guy said over and over again as he was explaining the process to us. *Today is Monday, we're taking inventory on Thursday. The inventory on Thursday is the inventory that matters.*

Liquidators buy inventory based on estimates, so if the stuff is worth ten grand, they'll buy it for three and try to sell it for seven in a short turnaround. The rep made it very clear that our salary and bonuses would be based on how accurate their inventory was and how little they lost through what is called shrinkage. Shrinkage is the variance between what they're supposed to have and what they end up having.

These guys work on the same bases of commission. It's a bottom-ended business. Pennies on the dollar type of stuff. So whatever inventory was in the store on Thursday was the inventory that mattered. As for the inventory on Monday, Tuesday, or Wednesday . . .

He was all but giving us the keys to the store. They do the formula—it's cheaper to let these kids take armfuls of stuff than it would be to train temps. Or so they thought.

In the back room, there was a full-sized Dalek replica. It had come in on a late shipment and we had good reason to believe that neither the old company nor the new liquidators knew about the over-sized pepper shaker's existence.

Whovians pay serious money for Daleks.

By Monday night, it was listed on eBay. By Wednesday morning, we had built a crate and shipped that four-foot-six-inch cyborg to upstate New York where some nerd was very happy.

We split the three grand three ways and worked through the liquidation. I found a new job with little effort. On my resume from the comic shop? "Management team specializing in theft prevention."

| PARALLEL STORY |

I was working for a department store—you know, where employees get a monthly discount but aren't really paid well enough to always use it. So I had an agreement with a couple of servers from the restaurant next door: I'd extend my discount to them, they'd extend theirs to me. I didn't think I was hurting anybody. You know, I even thought I was *helping* business: the savings weren't that great which meant the store was still making bank, and these guys weren't gonna shop there without some money off. Management didn't agree. I was shown the video and the receipts while my boss called the cops.

I don't think what I did was right. I was young, stupid, and I'm so sorry. But it's been *years*. When do I get to say I'm not a thief anymore?

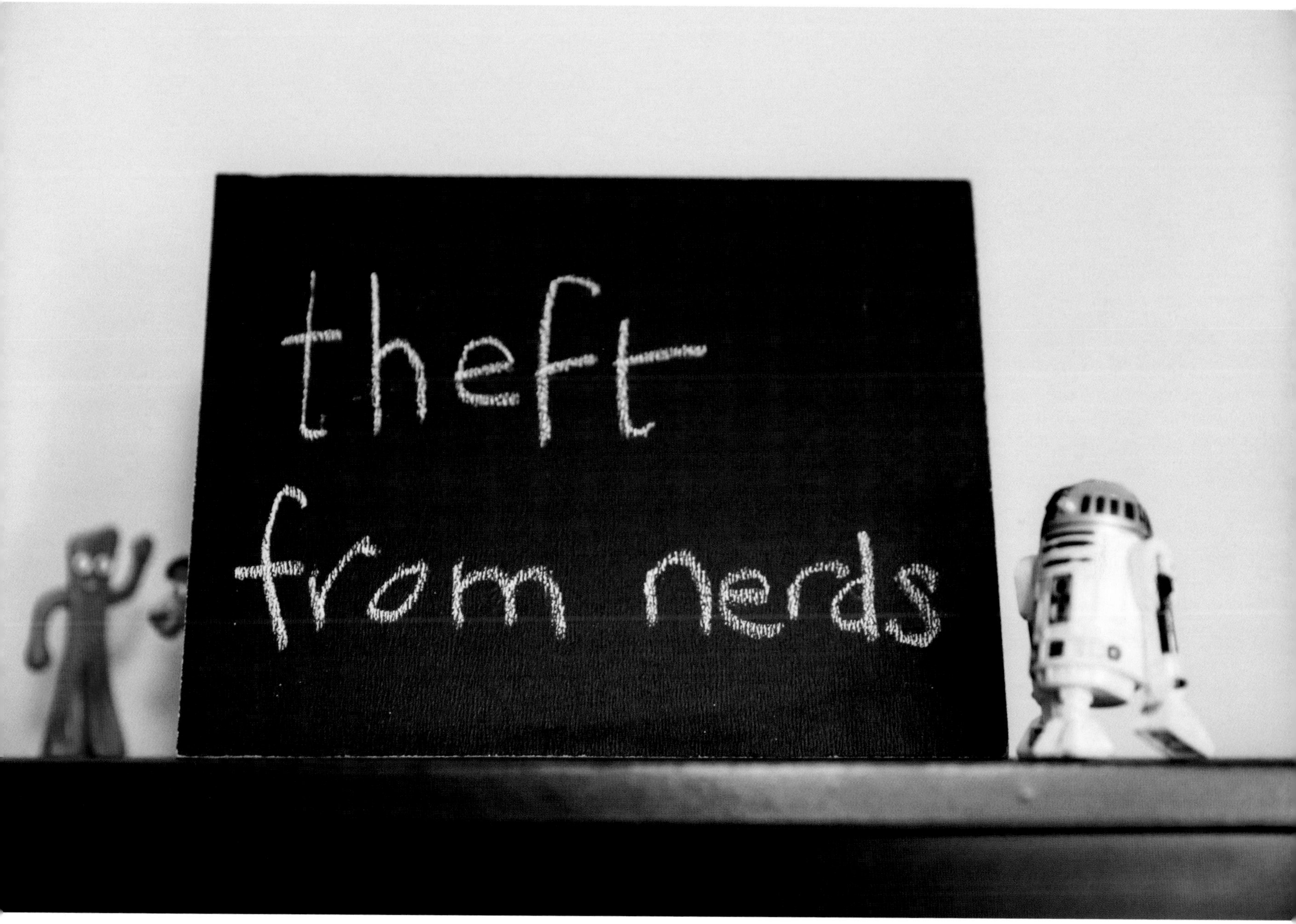
theft
from nerds

COLLEGE STUDENTS

CRIMINAL INFRINGEMENT OF COPYRIGHT

Student One: I actually did get caught once at school 'cause I was, like, torrenting, and the whole thing—I don't know if you guys are familiar with torrenting, but you can download it, but you're not supposed to "seed," which means putting it out there so other people can download. Apparently, I've forgot to stop Beyoncé's *I Am...Sasha Fierce*, so I had to sign a letter and send it to the record industry and be like, *I won't do this again.*

Student Two: In my mind, I don't even classify that as criminal, because my dad does it. My parents are performing musicians who've had their stuff out on iTunes and stuff, and iTunes doesn't tell them, so I'm like, *If iTunes doesn't give the artist anything, why would I give iTunes anything?*

Student Three: I don't think I started stealing music until college, and I don't think I'd realized that so many people do it and that it was that easy to do, but one thing that I've noticed is that I only am willing to, I guess, steal certain types of music. I'm a classically trained musician, and I've seen the passion and the effort that it takes to be an artist and to perform, and so for me, stealing their music after the amount of training they've gone through would be very unethical, but if it's Beyoncé or if it's Rihanna or if it's somebody who's not writing their own music, who's stealing everybody else's music in the end and contributing to a gross capitalist system, it's like, *No, you know what? Screw you. I'm gonna take it.* I don't really care as much, quite frankly. It's not "music" music to me.

Student One: **And I think it's interesting what socially decriminalizing something can do. Like what you said—we don't even think of it as a crime. Its actual legality doesn't mean shit.**

LAWYER

MARRIAGE FRAUD; VISA FRAUD; MAKING FALSE STATEMENTS

My prefrontal cortex was not fully developed.

I was young, disenchanted with the college experience and life in general. I wanted to explore.

I took up with a busboy from Syria. Flirtations led to a fling. Pillow talk graduated from sweet nothings to political oppression. He told me about how he and his cousin had fled a flattened town, how their parents feared for their lives.

He told me he was paying a woman a thousand dollars for marrying him so that he could stay in the U.S.

I would marry you for free.

Actually, my cousin needs someone.

The cousin and I got married. I remember the interview well: under oath and not telling the truth. Perjuring myself. To pass the culture test, I tried to recall everything I could from the post-coital conversations with his cousin about the homeland. I guess I was convincing enough.

I didn't think about the legal consequences; I was only thinking about someone who needed help. Just like the church helped with refugees, so I helped.

I began having dreams I was in prison, dreams I would be executed. I didn't tell my parents because I didn't want to worry them.

I went back to school and mostly tried to forget about it. Every now and then I'd receive Valentine's Day cards or love letters from him.

Six years later, I got a divorce document in the mail. There it was: I was divorced.

SEX OFFENSES

People who have been convicted of sex offenses and added to the predatory offender registry are the pariahs of society. Ranging from unimaginable atrocities to ostensibly victimless acts, definitions of criminal sexual misconduct cast an inconceivably wide net. Many youth caught up in the net were first victimized themselves, unfamiliar with appropriate boundaries—some as young as nine reenacting what was first done to them. Others include ten-year-olds who touched each other's bums, juveniles mooning the passing school bus, sexting teens, high school seniors who dated freshmen, college streakers, and people who urinated in a park.

Meanwhile, treatment is alarmingly expensive and the methods are question-able at best. Approximately 800,000 people on sex offender registries stretch state budgets thin, leaving those who would benefit from supervision sharing scant resources with those who don't. People with sex offense convictions or adjudications are often barred from living, working, or being near schools, parks, or other places children may frequent—even when the criminal is a child himself. They are also frequently locked out of college, employment, travel, and innumerable other opportunities life may have to offer. Public registries, social proscription, and the frequently violent response to finding a neighbor on the registry, leave countless people living under bridges, hiding in sugarcane fields, and contemplating whether the daily struggle to survive is worth it.

TEACHER
CRIMINAL SEXUAL CONDUCT

I remember the basement smelled like cat piss and Fritos and that as long as our parents were distracted we could play Tetris until our thumbs were numb and I desperately wanted to rearrange the furniture and photos on the wall so that they would *fit together just so.*

I think our parents were outside. I vaguely recall the soft *thwack* of a croquet game coming from the back yard. No, I can't picture my uncle holding a mallet unless he was tenderizing dinner. My aunt had just left him *again* so he was spending a lot of time with the grill. They must have been getting the burgers ready.

At any rate, there I was with my game set and my cousins and a sudden and irrepressible desire to play doctor. Or rather, patient. I wanted to be poked and prodded and for the love of god these kids were not picking up on my hints. Reluctantly, I showed them what I had seen on TV. They giggled; my impatience swelled. Finally, they tried it on me. I remember wrapping my head in my sister's orange afghan—I wanted to be there and wanted to

be anywhere but there. A wave of laughter—it tickled!—was cut short by a flood of repulsion: what the hell was I doing? I leapt up from the sofa and turned on Mario Kart. What would have happened if my dad—a cop, of course—had come downstairs in that moment? Or worse, my mom?

It's been years since that summer's day. My son turned eleven last month, the same age I was when my cousins and I fashioned a hypodermic needle out of Legos and huddled 'round the sofa.

I'm always terrified of my cousins remembering what happened and calling me out. One's a psychologist now—of course—and likes social media too much to let me relax. Can you imagine? Everyone loves a lascivious teacher pedophile story! I can assure you: I don't sexualize children. I *was* a child. What if my dad had caught us? What if I had been hauled in then? My life would have been over before it began.

COP

CRIMINAL SEXUAL CONDUCT; SALE OF A CONTROLLED SUBSTANCE

Where do I start? You'll have to bear with me, it's a long journey.

I suppose the statutory is as good a place to begin as any. I was 19 and my girlfriend was 15. The age gap was bigger than the magic 24-month difference. She and I had been intimate often. One night, we got busted in the back of my mother's Pontiac Bonneville by law enforcement. But that was back in the day when we said, *Put your clothes back on and go home.* So we did. It's different now.

But before there was sex, there were drugs. By that time, I'd been smoking and selling weed for a few years. Several of us would get together and buy a pound. We'd sell four or five ounces and smoke the rest for free. That went on for years. We got older and got into speed—"white crosses." Same kinda deal. We had enough money—we all worked—we'd go and buy 500 hits, sell two or three hundred, and use the rest to get ourselves high for free.

That went on until I went into the service. Overseas, I roomed with a guy from a very well-connected family from the east coast and he had money to burn. We got into the black market, selling electronics to the local economy for money or trading it for hash. Then we'd sell hash to other sellers, saving enough to get ourselves high for free.

After a while, I was reassigned. I met these local guys one day who told me about a great beach just down the way. The first day I had off, I picked up some local beer, hopped the bus, and hit the beach. The beer was stronger than I had expected and I ended up passing out under the midday sun. Waking up with second-degree burns, I came to the conclusion that maybe drinking was an issue. So I stopped drinking, drugs, everything.

It didn't take me long to realize that I had a lot of money (since I wasn't spending it on booze and weed). You'd think I went straight, right? Nope. I became a loan shark. I'm not good at math (kind of a deficit for a drug dealer) so my rates were simple: 25 percent. I was reasonable. You wanna borrow 20? You pay me back 25.

When I came out of the service, I thought, *I spent the last four years of my life with mental peanuts.* I needed something different, so I went to school.

Shortly after that, I met a woman and started a family.

From there, I decided to follow the family line. My dad is in law enforcement, my brothers are in law enforcement, so now I'm in law enforcement.

It was a natural gravitation to becoming a cop, in spite of spending years living and working on the other side.

I believe we are who we are because of life's experiences. Everyone's got a little story in their history. My experiences give me a unique perspective—professionally and personally—with the people I interact with on a daily basis. Some might call it warped, and sometimes I wonder if it is. But at least it's unique. In this line of work, I think it's an asset.

FORMER MARINE, CORPORATE RECRUITER, FATHER, HUSBAND

I AM MORE THAN MY MUGSHOT

Every choice you make, there are consequences —good and bad. You gotta live with that. And sometimes you don't realize you're making choices until it's too late.

I grew up in a dysfunctional family—which included abuse. At home, away from home: neighbors, alcohol, videotape.

I was a victim until my birthday: then I became a criminal. One moment, one day, one year, one me to the next, it all bled together. I was hurt and I hurt people and I am terribly, terribly sorry.

Someday my son's going to find out, so I work hard every day to make sure that when he sees the whole me, the good outweighs the bad.

If he saw the whole me today, he'd see my record. But he'd also see I'm a Marine and I served our country. He'd see I put myself through college and learned a lot about management and even more about life. He'd see I'm a top-ten recruiter at work, with a corner office. He'd see I love his mom and that I do something every day to make sure she knows. He'd know that I love him more than I thought I could ever love anyone.

And I think he'd be proud.

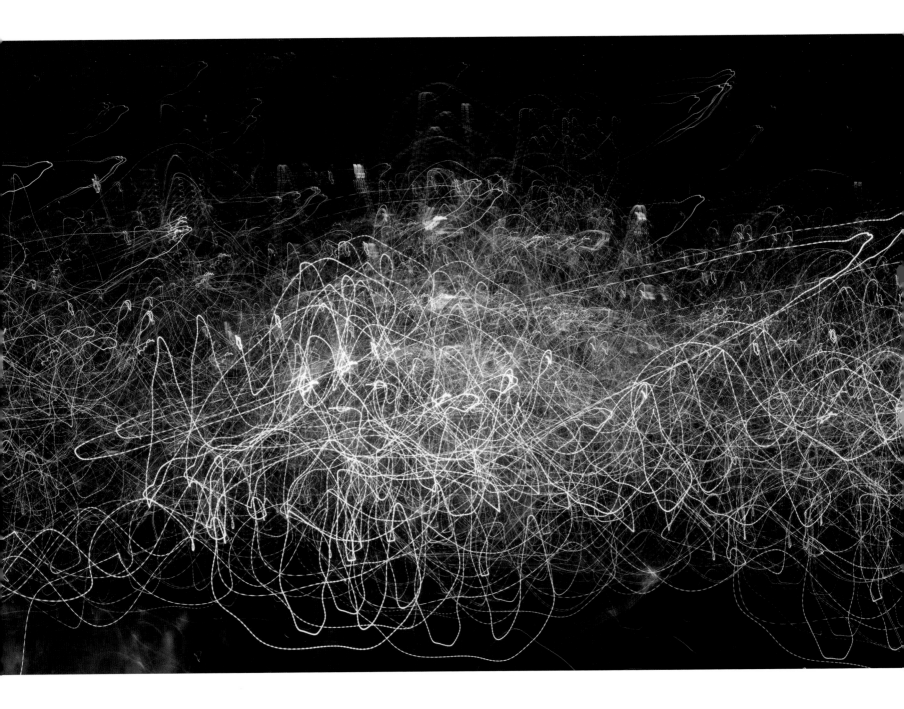

RECENT GRADUATE

PROSTITUTION

This one's still fresh. A while back, I was kind of an escort.

It was in college, and I wanted the money—sometimes for something I needed, one time for a spring break.

But you know there are always those sting operations going on? What if . . . ?

I was a shell of myself: there and not there, me and not me. Yet despite all of the crap I'm dealing with now, I can take solace in the fact

I HAVEN'T HAD THE LUXURY TO FORGET IT— YET. BUT I HOPE TO.

that I'll be able to do what I want to do in life, and that a rough time in college won't ruin all of that.

I haven't had the luxury to forget it—yet. But I hope to.

PARKS EMPLOYEE

INDECENT EXPOSURE; TRESPASSING; POSSESSION OF CONTROLLED SUBSTANCES; MINOR CONSUMPTION

I don't have too many singular, amazing stories. In general, I was an average suburban kid. But that was not inconsistent with breaking the law: **my criminal acts were almost culturally mandated, like rites of passage.**

For example, trespassing was a necessary part of my high school experience. Sneaking into parks after midnight to hook up was the realization of an American trope: you know, going out into the hayfield to mess around. It's this transgression that's sanctioned by our culture. It was relatively innocent—but there are so many ways that, had the circumstances been different, it would have seemed like something so much worse. Of course, there were times when these encounters did involve marijuana or alcohol, so the stakes were a bit higher, although it never really felt that way.

The same can be said for my soft patterns of recreational drug use, although I don't know how valuable it is for you to hear stories of the time I tried cocaine or any other drugs . . .

POLICING
IN AMERICA

Throughout many of the interviews, people recalled being dismissive, openly irritated, and at times even hostile to police when stopped or questioned. These responses might not be commendable, but they're certainly not worth getting killed for. And they weren't: none was arrested, much less tased, choked, or shot.

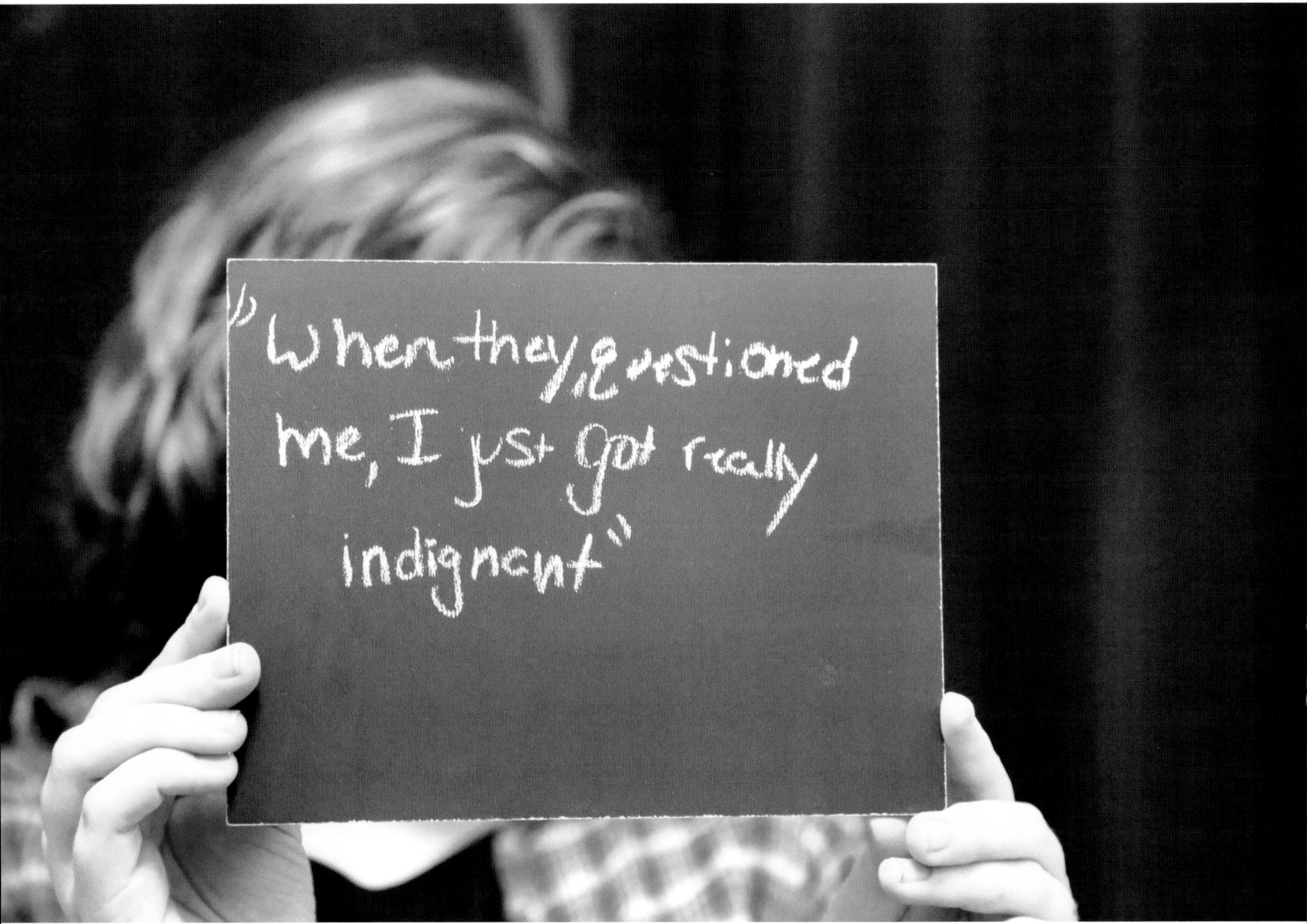
"When they questioned
me, I just got really
indignant"

NOTE:

One all-too-common public reaction to an officer-involved death is to question why the deceased didn't comply. *Why did they talk back? Why didn't they stop? Why did they resist?*

Oscar Grant had been celebrating New Year's Eve with friends when a fight broke out on the train. Several people, including Oscar, were detained and cuffed on the train's platform. Oscar was bound, lying on his stomach when an officer shot him in the back; he died before sunrise. *You shot me*, a witness heard him say. *I got a four-year-old daughter!*

Eric Garner refused to be arrested on the accusation he was selling loose cigarettes. A swarm of officers descended upon him, wrapping their arms around his neck, and forcing his face into the ground. Eric pleaded for breath eleven times. *I can't breathe. I can't breathe. I can't breathe.* He lost consciousness; an hour later, he died.

A 25-year-old Freddie Gray was walking down the street when he briefly locked eyes with patrolling police. He began to run. The police chased him down, searched him, and found a folding knife in his pocket. Video of his arrest shows him limp, screaming in pain. By the time he arrived at the police station, he wasn't breathing. One week later, he died.

Walter Scott was pulled over for a nonfunctioning third brake light. As the officer approached, Walter leapt out of the car and ran behind a building. The officer followed on foot. Moments later five of the officer's eight bullets fired hit Walter in the back. *He took my Taser*, said the cop. A cell phone video shows the officer calmly firing at Walter, fleeing and unarmed. Dashcam video shows that when the officer pulled Walter over, he was listening to Everlast's *What It's Like*, a song about prejudice and empathy: *God forbid you ever had to walk a mile in his shoes / 'Cause then you really might know what it's like to sing the blues.*

Sandra Bland was stopped for failing to signal a lane change. Her subsequent refusal to put out a cigarette in her own car led to the officer aiming his Taser at her and shouting, *I will light you up! Get out! Now!* Three days later, she was found dead in her jail cell.

HIRING MANAGER

TERRORISTIC THREATS; MANUFACTURING OF EXPLOSIVE DEVICES; ASSAULT

My best friend Mike and I wanted to be the next Steven Spielberg. The alley and parking lot across from the town bank made a natural location for the bank robbery scene. Mike's brother had a nylon over his head and an attaché case with fake money sticking out of it; the rest of us were loaded up with masks and fake guns. Mike waved stage directions with his replica .357 BB gun. It never occurred to us that the pedestrians would think it was anything but kids making a film.

Before we knew it, squad cars were coming at us from four different directions. It took about half an hour for the police to stop shouting, put their guns away, and let us up off the pavement. Eventually, they let us go. They even let us finish up.

THIS STORY ISN'T ABOUT BAD THINGS I GOT AWAY WITH; IT'S ABOUT BEING A KID AND THE PRESUMPTION OF INNOCENCE THAT A LOT OF PEOPLE DON'T EVER GET.

This story isn't about bad things I got away with; it's about being a kid and the presumption of innocence that a lot of people don't ever get.

Once there's a record, every youthful misadventure adds further proof that you need more punishment.

IN THE NEWS

Trayvon Martin had Skittles, Jordan Davis, music. Both black teens were gunned down by men who said that they feared for their lives.

It was a wintry Saturday when twelve-year-old Tamir Rice went to a Cleveland city park. On the surveillance video, he looks like countless other young American boys, slightly bored and slightly bemused, playing with a toy gun. He was alone in the park's gazebo when the police car drove over the curb, between the trees and swing set. The squad was still rolling when the officer's bullet ripped through Tamir's torso. He crumpled to the ground. A minute later, Tamir's sister ran towards him; she was tackled, cuffed, and placed in the back seat of the squad. Through the car window, she watched as her baby brother lay dying just a few feet away.

John Crawford III was talking on his cellphone in the pet supply aisle at Walmart when he was killed. Minutes before, he had picked up an unboxed BB gun from a shelf in the sporting goods section; minutes later, he would have joined his girlfriend in picking out the graham crackers, chocolate, and marshmallows for the family cookout. Instead, he was gunned down by police. A fellow customer had called 911, reporting a black man, pointing a gun at people; police opened fire moments after entering the store; the caller later changed his story.

The list of black and brown men and boys gunned down by people within minutes to *seconds* of meeting them, tragically, maddeningly, goes on and on. For many, the presumption of guilt (and danger) is always present: they are seen as always already *criminal*.

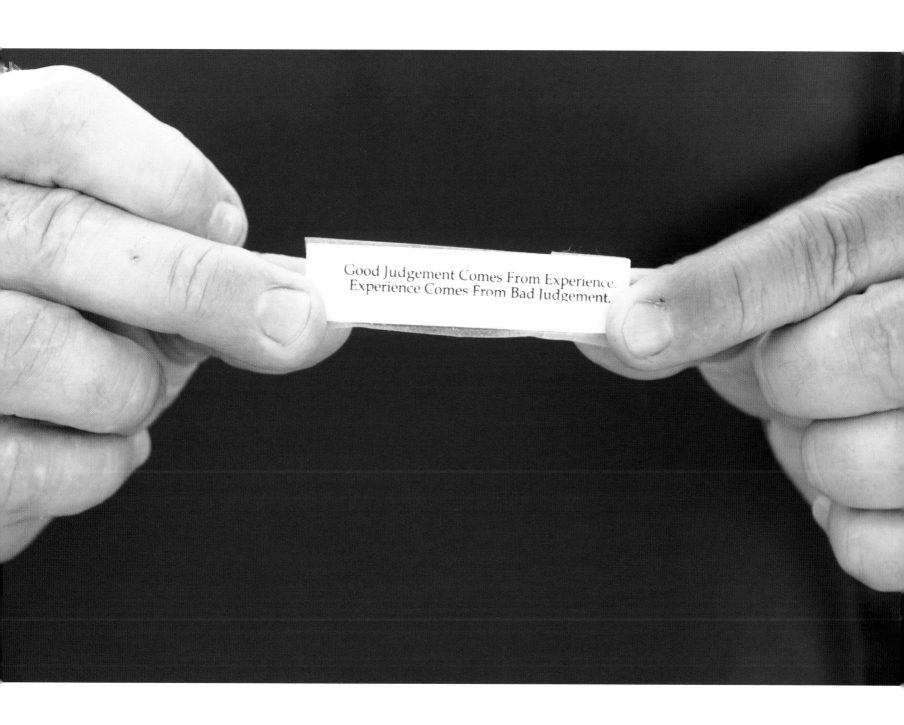

BUSINESS OWNER

TERRORISTIC THREATS; VANDALISM

A lot of it was kid stuff: TP'ing trees, littering front yards with White Castle burger boxes, breaking raw eggs on someone's car. One night we Saran-Wrapped a friend's Toyota with industrial-sized clingy plastic as he watched through the grocery store's sliding glass doors, locked in on the overnight shift and unable to stop us. A cop pulled up mid-way through the job to see what we were doing. *I was young once. Make it quick and get out of here*, he said, driving off. We were white kids in the white part of town, and we were just having fun.

It was in that same white and affluent neighborhood that my friend Nick and I planned another prank: scare a couple of friends while they were hanging out with some girls. We drove over to their house and crept up to the living room window with ski masks pulled down over our faces, realistic-looking water guns in our hands.

We started out stealthily enough, certain they would notice us sneaking up and reward us with shrieks and shouts. But they didn't see us—so we tapped our guns against the windowpane, waved our arms about, and eventually jumped up and down. Despite our efforts, none of them noticed us. Bored, we got back into the car and drove on.

We vaguely registered that there were suddenly a lot of cops around, but didn't think much of it.

A few blocks later we came across a pizza delivery guy. I pulled up next to him as Nick rolled his window down, resting his elbow on the door and raising the gun. We paused for effect and then pulled away.

We continued our disinterested tour for a while, eventually leaving the gated community for The Stretch—a ten-block tract of music venues and boutique shops where everyone went to see and be seen. Three stoplights in, we were pulled over. Apparently while our friends hadn't noticed us, the neighbors had; an APB had gone out an hour earlier for two armed men in ski masks.

My white baby face, letterman's jacket, and compliant response to the police deescalated the situation quickly. At a certain point, I could tell one cop was almost laughing at the comical scene.

Now if we had been two African American teens, we would have been at least booked, probably jailed, and maybe even shot.

Instead, Nick and I got back in the car and drove home.

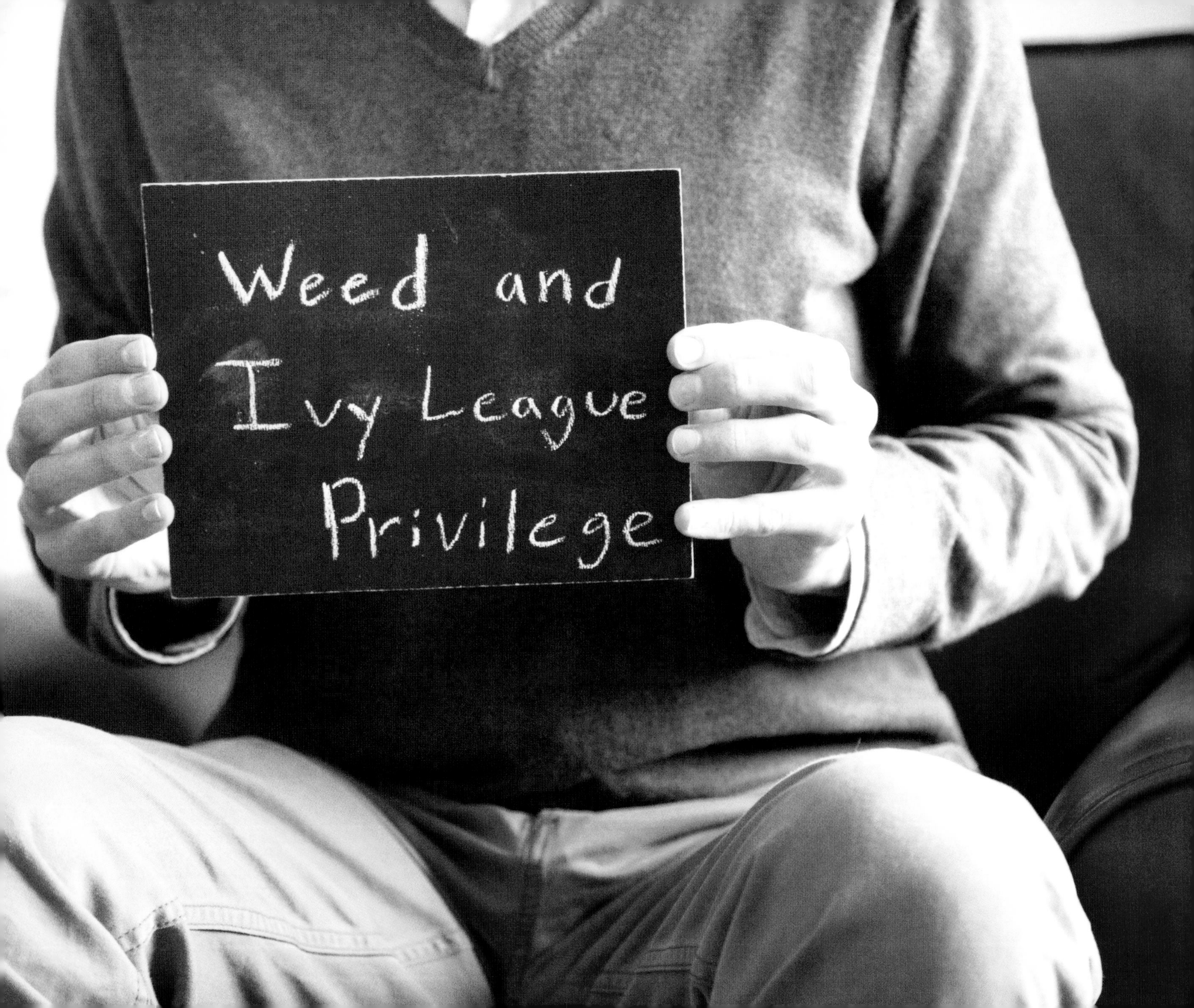
Weed and
Ivy League
Privilege

I used to wear a hoodie and jeans to work.

I work for a caterer on a college campus and would change into my uniform once I got there: black slacks and white button-down shirt. The less you wear it, the longer it lasts, you know?

Anyway, I started getting stopped by campus police on my way in.

Where are you going? What are you up to? What's in the backpack?

Hey, man—I'm just trying to get to work, but they wouldn't listen.

Why don't you step over here? Mind if I look inside your bag?

Yeah, I mind: now I'm late. That would land me another ten minute delay—or worse. I've been cuffed and searched for no reason other than I'm a black man on a very white campus.

I don't wear a hoodie anymore. It doesn't matter if it's 20 degrees outside or 90, I only wear my uniform—that bright-white, ironed shirt vouching for my presence on campus, allowing my existence.

SCHOLAR

POSSESSION OF CONTROLLED SUBSTANCES; PUBLIC INTOXICATION; PUBLIC URINATION; TRESPASSING; DISORDERLY CONDUCT; CRIMINAL INFRINGEMENT OF COPYRIGHT

In retrospect, the same sorts of privileges that shielded me from being caught would have shielded me from being punished.

I grew up in a very affluent town. It was the kind of place where it was easy not to have contact with the police; the few interactions I had were very respectful and innocuous. A tap on the shoulder, a suggestion to go home.

The whole town's economy is based on the university, so there's a disincentive for cops to really act. The school, the students, our parents—it's probably more of a headache to arrest someone than to just let them go.

ENGINEERING STUDENT

FALSE IDENTIFICATION; POSSESSION AND SALE
OF CONTROLLED SUBSTANCES; UNDERAGE CONSUMPTION;
FAILURE TO REPORT INCOME

Start taking notes, because my list is long.

Where I'm from, you can drink alcohol at 18. So when I moved here to go to college, I got a fake ID. I used it for three years—and only stopped using it as often when my 21st birthday got close.

Do I use drugs now? No. I don't think of weed as a drug. And you can't tell me that weed is going to make me stupid: I have a perfect 4.0. My best friend is a med student at one of the nation's top schools—and she smokes all the time.

But back to my list.

I've driven all around the country with weed on me; I've flown with it in my laptop bag. I've consumed mushrooms and sold amphetamine salts to other students on campus. I've worked under the table—and then used the money to party.

I know I've got white privilege. Being white gives me extraordinary power here. *Just be careful*, the cops tell me. *Go home.*

Knowing my privilege is one thing. Now I want to do something about it. I want to help other people. In the position I'm in now—that's something I can do.

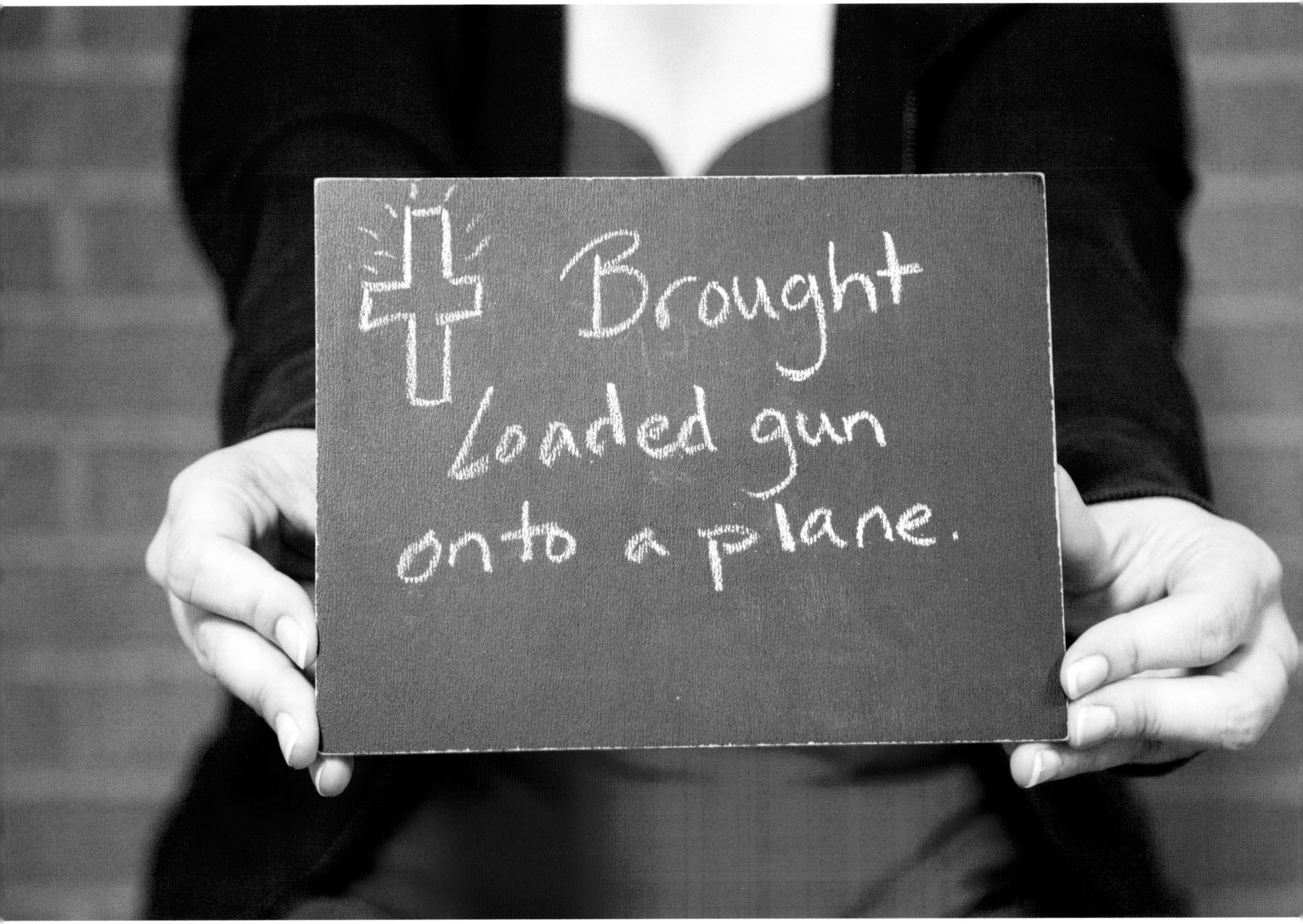
Brought
Loaded gun
onto a plane.

PASTOR

SHOPLIFTING; UNDERAGE CONSUMPTION; RECKLESS DRIVING; POSSESSION OF CONTROLLED SUBSTANCES; CARRYING A WEAPON OR EXPLOSIVE ON AN AIRCRAFT

I have lots of stories—so many aren't even worth telling: shoplifting in high school, underage drinking (like everyone else), driving around with someone in the trunk, and smoking pot (actually, on seminary campus—there's so much drug use on campus). But there's one in particular I wanted to talk about.

I was in school, two hours into the desert, and alone. My husband encouraged me to buy a gun.

I kept the gun in my duffel bag, and the duffel bag in the car. It's also the same duffel bag I'd take on vacation.

I got through airport security with a loaded .365 Magnum Revolver and a six-round speedloader in my carry-on.

On a layover, we left the secure area to see if there were better food options.

Ma'am, is this your bag?

Yep!

We need to talk to you.

Oh, it must be my retainer.

They assumed it was my husband's. Never did they assume ill intent. They were curious about motive, though. Bears? Suicide?

They seized the gun, found a hotel for us, and drove us to it. We were on a flight out of the country the next day.

I was never intimidated or frightened. I was never accused or charged with anything.

I think about it a lot: what could have happened and how incredibly privileged and lucky I am.

I've worked for major corporations, and now I'm a pastor. I doubt I'd be where I am today if I had been seen as anything other than innocent back then.

JOURNALIST

USING ARTIFICIAL LIGHT TO LOCATE ANIMALS; USING MOTOR VEHICLE TO CHASE WILD ANIMAL; HUNTING OUT OF SEASON; REMOVAL AND POSSESSION OF TRAFFIC SIGN; POSSESSION OF CONTROLLED SUBSTANCES

My friend and I got into a lot of mischief the summer between high school and college. I suppose it was sort of a bucket-list before leaving town. One night we shot cats. Well—I didn't shoot the cats, but I did drive, I did roll my window down, and I did shine the spotlight. My friend hit one with a .22. The cat turned out to be an out-of-season fox, which might be worse.

But usually our delinquency was limited to yanking road signs. Not important road signs—just the ones where maybe if you were lost, you would stay that way. County signs, city signs, street signs. At the request of a girl, we decided to steal a neighboring town's street sign. So, late one night, we parked up on this curb in the middle of nowhere and I began unbolting the sign.

I hopped down and flung the bolts in the bushes as the sheriff came racing up, lights off. He wanted to know what we were doing, asked us if we had drugs in the trunk. (We did, but said we didn't. He took our word for it.)

While he was questioning us, he was standing under that road sign. If he had looked up and

THE DOORS WERE ALREADY OPEN AND COPS KNOW BETTER THAN TO SNOOP AROUND IN WHITE PEOPLE'S BUSINESS. YOU DON'T MESS WITH PRIVILEGE. I COULD TELL HE WAS FRUSTRATED, BUT HE LET US GO.

seen the missing bolts, I would have been calling my dad from the county jail. It's crazy—this was the sheriff that I was outsmarting here. (Well, not outsmarting because that sounds cocky. But pretty much *outsmarting*, because I was definitely doing something illegal and he couldn't figure out what it was.)

I told him we were just fixing a light in the trunk. The doors were already open, and cops know better than to snoop around in white people's business. You don't mess with privilege. I could tell he was frustrated, but he let us go.

It's definitely because we were white that he didn't go into further detail.

We drove away scot-free and got stoned again later that night. (Thanks again for not checking the trunk.)

DRAINING AMERICA

Correctional control is expensive in human and financial terms. Each year, the U.S. spends nearly $80 billion locking people up and keeping them under control. Mass incarceration is a financial ecosystem. From wardens who steward public funds and vendors who supply slop to architects of solitary confinement and hardware providers for electronic home monitoring, to beneficiaries of prison labor and the policymakers who ensure the beds are full, entire industries, towns, and careers are built around caging and controlling some of the poorest among us.

Recent budget crises have forced many states to reconsider their incarceration inclination; others turn to private prisons. CoreCivic (formerly Corrections Corporation of America) and The GEO Group, the nation's two largest operators of private prisons, are lining up to feed our carceral addiction, boasting enough beds to cage all of Topeka, Kansas with hundreds to spare. The notion that some can get incredibly rich off the caging of others is reprehensible. With a focus on profit rather than people, perhaps it's no surprise that one such privately operated facility was described by a federal judge as a "cesspool of unconstitutional and inhuman acts and conditions" in which the sum of actions and inactions by the state and private prison company, among others, "paints a picture of such horror as should be unrealized anywhere in the civilized world."

CRIME RATES + REDUCED PUBLIC SAFETY |

Here's some good news: the crime rate today is half what it was at its height 25 years ago. Unfortunately, a common conclusion is that confining people—millions of people—works.

In truth, the relationship between mass imprisonment and crime is far more complex.

For example, in 2015, the Brennan Center for Justice reported that increased incarceration can only account for approximately six percent of property crime reduction in the 1990s and has had little effect on violent crime rates in the previous 24 years. Since 2000, the effect of increasing incarceration on crime reduction "has been essentially zero."

In fact, the reduction may be better explained by a combination of other social factors, such as improvements in the economy, demographic shifts, and changes in policing. States like New York and New Jersey have actually *reduced* their prison populations while experiencing a dropping crime rate.

Meanwhile, Criminologist Todd Clear has found that over-incarceration has actually *increased* crime rates in some areas by eviscerating and destabilizing neighborhoods: "Imprisonment has grown to the point that it now produces the very social problems on which it feeds. It is the perfect storm."

To illustrate how mass incarceration is harmful, Dr. Clear underscores a dominant misperception: criminals "are viewed as people whose net contribution to community life is negative, and so not much will be lost by their being gone."

It's important to remember that people behind bars are fathers and mothers and brothers and mentors and providers, even if they are often also *criminals*.

Removing these individuals from their families and neighborhoods—especially *en masse*—has been devastating.

| PEOPLE HARMED |

Just as the distinction between *clean* and *criminal* falls apart upon closer examination, so often does the dichotomy of *victim* and *offender*. That is, people who have been victimized and people who have committed crimes do not exist in two mutually exclusive categories. Yet our discourse—and our policies—often presuppose they do. As a result, tough-on-crime laws and practices that perpetually punish those with criminal records may be harming people most in need of help.

For example, those most likely to be policed—black and brown and poor individuals, and in particular, impoverished black men and boys—are also the most likely to be victims of violent crime. Additionally, people who are trafficked are often prosecuted for prostitution and additional charges that read like a testament to their pain: drug possession, assault, loitering, trespassing, petty theft, truancy, and possession of a weapon. Victims of domestic violence may be wrongly accused of assault, and young targets of relentless bullying may face significant increases in the likelihood of ending up in prison. Many of those who are incarcerated will become victims of physical, sexual, and mental abuse while they are under the control and supposed care of the state.

After picking up a criminal record, people are frequently locked out of resources, treatment, housing, and broader networks of help because of their criminal pasts. The problem is so prevalent that some states are creating special

expungement orders for individuals whose circumstances indicate a nexus between the criminal offense and their own victimization. Unfortunately, not everyone qualifies, and for those who do, many find the remedy illusory in an age when arrest records seemingly metastasize, becoming available on websites and in newspapers or cached by entrepreneurs.

| DRAINING AMERICA |

Budget reports peg the cost of U.S. incarceration at some $80 billion a year.

But any true tally of the cost of mass criminalization must include the millions of job prospects lost, as people are effectively locked out of the labor force. So, too, should there be a budget line for the immeasurable *dignity* of work, the autonomy, confidence, and stability lost without a steady paycheck; the education, housing, relationships, and general-to-extraordinary life experiences denied to a growing swell of the nation; the endless opportunities precluded to make our workforce and our nation stronger, more diverse, and more dynamic. There should be a column for the broken families ripped apart by incarceration and kept apart by sanctions; another for the lost future income and present security of children whose parents and caregivers suffer under the weight of a criminal record, because this vortex doesn't just swallow individuals—but

families and communities too. Acknowledge the forfeiture of the notion and nation of second chances, and the loss of a true democracy.

There should be an understanding that money spent on incarceration is money that could have gone to other institutions, like education. There should be an acknowledgment that communities currently pay to house, treat, counsel, train, employ, and otherwise transition individuals who are leaving prison or jail, and that more often than not, that burden falls upon poor communities and communities of color.

There should be an attachment to that budget, the photograph of a baby born today, and along with it the projection that he will someday go to prison—a statistic based upon his race, his gender, and his zip code.

For all these collateral costs, our nation is no stronger or safer than when this mass incarceration *experiment* began. This is just the start of the drain mass criminalization has had on America.

| THE WHOLE PICTURE |

Let's return to the graph that opened this book, a tidal wave that shows the U.S. state and federal prison population rate. What doesn't that figure capture?

It doesn't show the population of people in county and parish jails, jails in Indian Country, immigration detention centers, mental health holds, or juvenile detention facilities. It doesn't show the millions of people on probation and parole or the estimated 65 to 100 million people in the U.S. who carry a criminal record, a mark that forever brands them, exiles them, and removes their dignity. That keeps them from volunteering at their child's school, casting a ballot, or being able to get an apartment.

And just as importantly, it doesn't show the nearly three million sons and daughters, countless brothers and sisters, mothers and fathers, spouses and partners, and greater community members of currently incarcerated people, each of whom is impacted by incarceration. It doesn't show the families affected when that person isn't allowed back in. More than *33 million children* have a parent with a criminal record, struggling to find housing, work, and recognized worth.

It doesn't show the devastation or the disparities, it doesn't show the despair.

When the scope of this tragedy is widened to include all of this, you see that the tidal wave is just a drop in the larger ocean of a crisis.

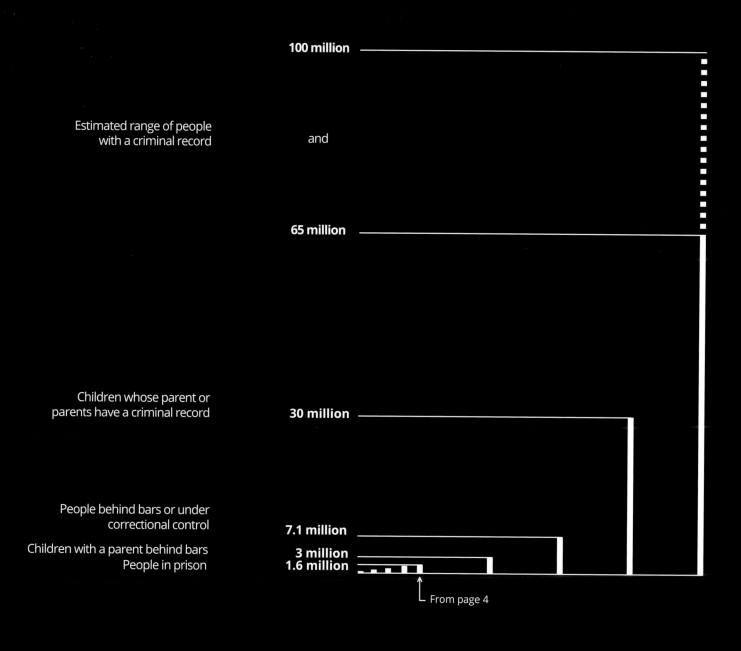

100 million

Estimated range of people with a criminal record and

65 million

Children whose parent or parents have a criminal record

30 million

People behind bars or under correctional control

7.1 million

Children with a parent behind bars
People in prison

3 million
1.6 million

From page 4

RIPPLE EFFECT

More than 2.7 million children in the United States currently have a parent in jail or prison. Most are younger than ten years old. A staggering *one in nine* African American kids has a parent in lock-up. For Hispanic children, it's one in 28 and for white children, it's one in 57.

Across the nation, approximately ten million children have experienced parental incarceration and nearly *half* of America's kids have at least one parent with a criminal record. For millions of parents, criminal records will stymie safe and affordable housing, employment, and countless opportunities to participate in their children's lives—from tucking them in at night to coaching the summer team to joining them at school for lunch. Children meanwhile may undergo the traumas of loss, powerlessness, and instability on top of an increased risk of poverty and the suffocating stigma and shame that comes with having a parent taken away and then not allowed back in.

And while there are millions of children with parents who have been incarcerated, there are millions more whose brothers, sisters, cousins, aunts, uncles, and grandparents have been imprisoned. Each loss can have a profoundly negative effect on child and adult alike—one that reverberates for decades to come.

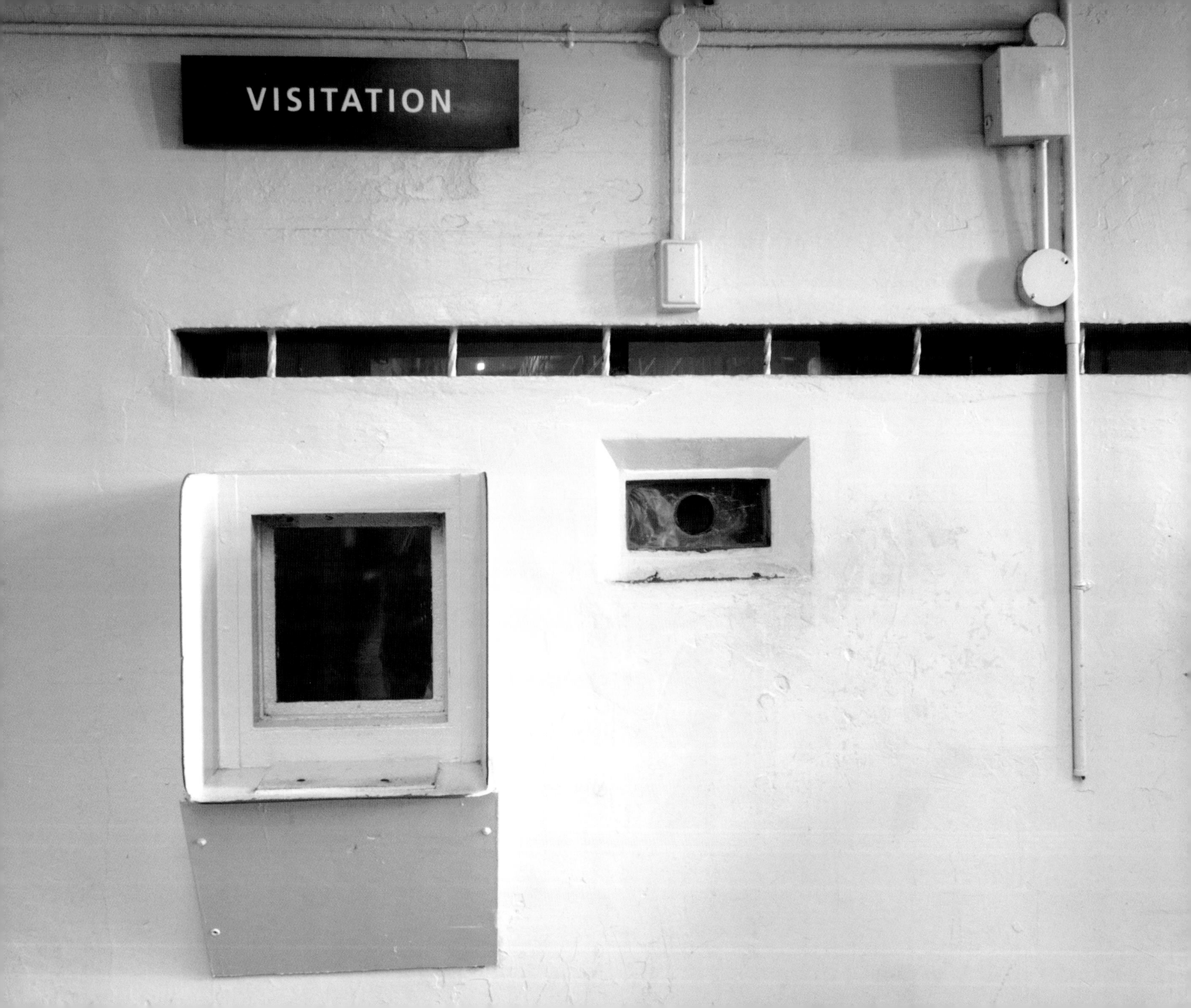
VISITATION

MOM

Once I went in, all communication with my kids was cut off. That hurt
more than anything else. It's been years, and I'm still trying to catch up.

DAUGHTER

Dad and I were wrestling right before he told me.

One minute we were laughing and tumbling the living room. The next, I was stone-still but everything around me was spinning. Lurching. Crumbling.

I just remember thinking it must be so *hard* to go—he must have done something really, really wrong. I didn't realize how easy it was.

I had friends whose parents were divorced, and friends whose parents had died. But no one I knew had a parent in prison. A fog of isolation and shame descended on us.

He's in San Francisco, she'd say—and I know why she did. I don't blame her. The humiliation, the stigma. We weren't allowed to talk about it—but it was all building up inside me and I needed a release valve. I got sick, vomiting my way through fifth grade.

First we visited him in maximum; has your dad ever been stripped searched before he could say hello to you? Minimum was better. Toward the end, we were able to spend the weekend with him in a house on the grounds. It was totally awesome. Dad and I played catch. I got commissary Cherry Coke from the nice guy with long nails and a Jheri curl, and vegetables from the prison gardener—a guy in for mercy killing. We ate SPAM on vinyl placemats, a gift from my grandmother: I ate on Kentucky, my dad, Oregon.

The fog began to lift for me.

It was definitely still a struggle when he got out. The restitution was crushing. My mom lost her job when the papers reported my dad's release; she worked like hell to find another. Dad held multiple jobs at once. But paying fines and fees on top of rent and bills and food—it was a never-ending shitshow. They worked their asses off, they borrowed money, we skimped on everything. But we just couldn't claw our way out.

My whole existence is shaped by it, growing up with that toxic stress. I'm fastidious. I'm very, very driven to have money. Not to be rich, but to be stable. Let's put it this way: if I were a painter or a dancer and I had the opportunity to quit my job and follow my passion—I wouldn't do it. I will never chase a dream.

My friend once told me that I was a dandelion. Some people are orchids, she said. They're fragile. Me? I might get mowed down, but I'm popping right back up. You can't keep me down.

So I suppose I got something out of this. I wish my mom had that. I wish it could have meaning for her in a way that wasn't just pain and shame. She has done amazing things in her life—but it will never be enough. She didn't need this to happen to be a dandelion—she already was one. Now she's a dandelion in a fog.

I wish there were a way to change that.

SON

Saturdays were bacon and eggs and barbecues. Sundays were church after breakfast, fries and fish sticks at noon. Weekends with family were defined by food—even if pops wasn't such a good cook.

Everything was fine until it wasn't. Until the day pops went to work and didn't come back.

I was eight when the breakfasts stopped. Dad went to jail, then prison. Moms would take us kids to visit him on the weekends. In jail, pops was on one side of the scuffed-up plexiglass, and we were on the other. We'd pick up the phone to hear his voice, even though he was just a few feet away. Those were some of the worst times, being so close and so far.

After a while, dad was transferred to prison. In some ways it was easier: we could finally hug him, play chess or checkers, take a picture together. But going through security to see someone you love? No kid wants to go through that. Might as well say I was the one in prison. All of us were.

Seeing pops there for just a few hours hurt so bad I couldn't stop crying. Sometimes the pain would sit in my throat like a rock, sometimes it would fix itself around my heart like a fist, sometimes it would rush through my body, taking me with it, so that I was left hollow and alone.

Still, dad tried. He would use those visits to put some fear into you. The way he talked to you, the way he looked at you. *Going to school? Doing homework?* Even though he was behind bars, he wanted us to do it right.

But I was still struggling. I didn't have friends: I had associates—people I'd see in school and not after. At that point, I was my own best friend.

I was snappin' out—out of frustration, anger, and emptiness. It's all these question marks— *When can I talk to him? When can I see him? When is he coming home?*

I would have given anything for a plate of pops' eggs. I would have eaten breakfast for every meal for ten years if it meant being able to sit across the table from my dad while I ate it.

I'd lash out—we all did. I'd lash out so that someone would be there to comfort me for the next couple of days.

And there were people there. I had an incredible support system: my grandma, my grandfather, uncle, sisters, and brother—even the neighbors were there for us.

Moms was the greatest support of all. I truly believe she's made of steel. She kept us in check, with dinner every night and homework complete. But you can't always talk to your mom about everything, and there was some stuff that was so hard to talk about.

L from Monroe was there too. He used to pick me up and take me to school, come chasing after me if I'd run out, and give me the strength and space to write letters to my dad.

L encouraged me and my brother to focus our energy on sports—basketball, football, biking. He knew we had to keep moving to stay stable.

I'm in my twenties now, and like L, I want to help kids who are going through what I went through—so that they don't have to go through ALL of what I went through.

Dad's home now. I'm a momma's boy, so I'm home too. Saturday mornings, pops and I hang out in the kitchen, where I'm finally able to ask him those questions:

What was it like when you were in prison? Why were you gone so much? What did you do?

The only difference is that now I make the breakfast. (I'm a much better cook.)

DAUGHTER

This is the data I have collected over the last 22 years:

6: The number of years I spent with my father before he was arrested.

3: How many years my Papi spent in jail going from cell to court and back again. My mother and I spent those 3 years traveling in a similar A to B to A pattern: From Detroit to Milan, Michigan to Detroit every Friday, Saturday, and Sunday waiting for his sentencing. Even though I was only 6, then 7, then 8, I can still remember the visiting hours: from 4 until 8; from 8 until 3. We never missed a second.

674: The number of miles between Detroit and the Federal Correctional Institution in Sandstone, Minnesota, where my Papi was sentenced to 15 years. It took my family one year to save enough money to move those 674 miles to be close to him.

Many of these numbers may not mean anything to you, but to me they represent the miles, years and barriers we faced as a family.

949,879: The difference in population from Hinckley, my new home, and Detroit.

According to the 2000 Census, Hinckley's Hispanic population was one percent. My mom, my brother, sister-in-law, cousin, nieces, nephews, and I were that one percent.

44: The number of miles we traveled each weekend to visit my Papi. We would talk about how he was going to stay away from what took him from us and how he would see me graduate high school and go on to college. I used to joke with him a lot and tell him that I wanted to attend an out-of-state school because I thought he called me too much. But he never thought that was funny. I remember him giving me the birds and the bees talk: the only thing he really said was that I shouldn't worry about birds and bees, but think about A's and B's.

I was 13 years old when I started to forget Spanish. My Papi made me read and write to him for 45 minutes every visit until he felt my Spanish was up to par.

2006: The year my Papi came home. I was so happy we were a family again. It didn't hurt that now I could sleep in on the weekend like a normal kid.

My father started looking for work 3 weeks after he was released. He applied to a number of private and public businesses in Minnesota. I remember because I was there: filling out the applications and driving him to drop them off. We never heard from any of them.

It was during this time I started noticing people around town acting differently. They were not as friendly to me as they were before. My friends weren't able to come to my house anymore. Moms and dads who used to cheer me on in track and basketball now seemed reluctant to speak to me.

91: The number of days after my Papi was released before we left Hinckley to search for employment in the Twin Cities.

7: The number of days after the move when my mom was hired at Family Dollar; my Papi was denied. On my mom's first day of work, I decided to skip school and help my dad look for employment. We applied at 10 different locations that day. One of them told my father to call every morning at 7:00 am until he was placed at a site. He was never placed.

30: The number of days it took for the rejection letters to start coming in the mail.

Sixty days later, my Papi and I were still spending countless hours looking for employment. Although this was a frustrating time for us, I had the best laughs with my dad. The car rides are some of my favorite moments. After I would drop him off to drop off the application, he would always emphasize the importance of me going to college because he didn't want to see me struggle like we were now.

90: The number of days after my mom's first day at work, where they both had applied, that she got a 10-cent raise. My Papi was still unemployed. I started to see his frustration as a father and man: he wasn't able to help us with the bills.

91: The number of days after my mom's first day at work that my father decided to go back to his old ways. He knew we could not afford the rent, food, our car, gas and electricity on a single $7.50-an-hour paycheck.

7: The number of months it took before my Papi was charged with intent to sell to an officer.

I felt it was my fault that my dad had resorted back to selling drugs. I thought I really could have helped him find a job. But looking back, all of the odds were against us.

My Papi was acquitted on all charges.

4: Months between my Papi's acquittal and his deportation to Cuba.

3: The number of years I've been in college. My entrance to the University has been my parents' biggest accomplishment. If it wasn't for my Papi pushing me to be everything he couldn't be, I would not be here today.

2,537: The number of miles between where I stand today and where my Papi taxis people from point A to B to A again in a horse-drawn buggy. He earns 10 cents a ride.

MOTHER

You have to learn to forgive yourself.

My son did 15 years of federal time and 10 years of probation—for drugs. I was a single mom, struggling to get by. My son sat in jail waiting for trial, his friends—all white and wealthier—posted bail and got better deals.

You have to get over your guilt.

Have you been to a sentencing before? They don't give the time in years, they give it in months. 180, 220, 300. Try dividing those by 12 when your baby is standing in front of you in an orange jumpsuit with his wrists chained to his ankles and the attorneys are telling you to *shush*. Mathematics is the last thing on your mind.

We spent the next decade and a half going to California, Kentucky, West Virginia, Pennsylvania—anywhere the federal government shipped him. Every scrap of savings, every day of vacation time was spent in the air or on the road, going to lay eyes on my child.

I do prison ministry now, and you know what I tell the guys? *When we, your mothers, were carrying you, when we delivered you, we never thought of our babies as prisoners.*

We have to get over our guilt. That's what I tell the mothers and that's what I remind myself.

MOTHER

Do you have any kids?

It was always the next question.

Yes. A son.

It's true: I have a son. He's my miracle boy, born when the doctors said it wasn't possible.

He's in San Diego.

I'm not proud of lying. But everyone blamed me—my poor parenting must have been the reason my son was incarcerated—so I learned to say what they'd be okay with hearing. I'd already lost one job because of it (*We do, after all, have a reputation to uphold*), and I wasn't going to risk another.

My son was the first person I knew to go to prison. Some people know far more. I know black mothers who visit their sons in prison.

And their nephews, cousins, and brothers. The stories I hear: the *generations* that know this and have felt this.

Visitation is hard on everyone. I've been in the women's bathroom with a dozen mothers cutting the underwires out of their bras—a recent proscription—so that they could see their children. I've witnessed tearful grandmothers turned away after their wedding rings set off security alarms; metal detectors have no sympathy for swollen fingers.

But even still, I have hope. I won't give up. You gotta believe you can change this. Now that I'm retired, I attend community meetings, I call the papers, I storm the warden's office. I do what I can for my son. My only child. My miracle boy.

BROTHER

At ten, I lost my eldest brother to a long prison sentence.

At thirteen, I lost another brother, my best friend, to another long prison sentence.

He got six years. Six years to a 13-year-old kid is forever. Then again, that much time without your brother should feel like forever to anyone.

Attending his last hearing changed my life—but I didn't realize it then.

After my brother was sentenced I gave him a hug, not knowing it'd be the last time in a long time that I would be able to touch him without being searched. As he was led away, I walked over to his attorney. With tears in my eyes, I reached out my hand and said, *Thank you for representing my brother*. The attorney didn't break stride: he gave me a weak handshake—like he didn't even grip my hand or look me in the eyes—and kept moving.

As if this was just another day, and another one biting the dust.

My sadness turned to anger. I realized that to a man like that, my brothers and I were scum that brought nothing of value to the world.

Two days later I was able to visit my brother in prison. In the lobby before we went through security, tears ran uncontrollably down my face. I wasn't crying *per se*—I wasn't even showing any facial expression. I was *staying tough*, but the tears wouldn't stop. Sitting there, I realized I wasn't going to be able to play video games with my brother, go on long drives with him at the wheel, elbow out and hip hop blasting, or just talk—just the two of us, no guards, no guys, no someone-else's-motherbrothergirl trying not to cry next to me in the visitation room. We used to talk about life and about how we had to hustle harder than everyone else just to get by. Those talks are different with an audience. An audience

that doesn't give a shit about you.

Two years later, I was 15 and homeless.

But between that lousy attorney and my brother being locked up, I had never felt more fierce and determined to prove people wrong. It fueled me to graduate high school. Go to college. Go to law school. Show that attorney—and people like him—that I'm not only capable of doing great things despite where we come from, I'm doing them on a much higher level than they could imagine.

I am now the only merger and acquisition attorney of color in the entire metropolitan area, and I am damn good at helping businesses grow.

Here's the thing: I could have done it without the anger. And my brother could have done it, too.

RETHINKING AND REINVESTING

It doesn't have to be like this. In fact, we have seen a massive shift in dialogue, a resounding call to end the era of mass incarceration, mass arrests, and this mass disaster. Politicians from across the spectrum, faith leaders, and business leaders are tuning in, taking note, and saying *enough*. In the nearly 50 years of mass incarceration, there are few clean hands: it took a nation to create this disaster, and it's going to take a nation to end it.

We can learn from other countries. Portugal decriminalized the use of *all* drugs in 2001, and drug use is now considered a public health concern—not a criminal one. Treatment is on the rise, addiction is on the decline, and the number of fatal overdoses has plummeted; at the same time, community relations with police have significantly improved. The unofficial motto of the Norwegian Correctional System is "better out than in," and it permeates every aspect of incarceration: even Halden, Norway's maximum security prison, offers music, sports, and education opportunities. People incarcerated at Halden can spend hours outside each day amid the trees and blueberry forest, disputes are resolved through mediation, and families can visit their loved ones in chalet-style homes, 24 hours at a time.

And we can learn from ourselves. Advocates, activists, agitators, organizations, coalitions, insiders, and outsiders are rising every day to do the innovative, exhausting, and incredibly necessary work to reform the criminal and juvenile justice systems from coast to coast. There's a tectonic shift in progress—and you can help.

You can start at the end. Ban the Box: remove criminal records inquiries from employment, housing, and school applications so that reviewers see an applicant's merits—their skills, commitment, experience, and personality—before being blinded by a criminal history. Support financial incentives for employers who provide second chances. Help create strong, vibrant, and inclusive communities. Reduce the collateral sanctions and consequences that attach to criminal records—including repealing felony disenfranchisement. Expand expungement and pardon legislation to include meaningful remedies to criminal records.

You can start in the middle. Create humane prisons: end solitary confinement; support substantial education and treatment opportunities for people on the inside; ensure that families and friends can stay meaningfully connected. Close private prisons. Eliminate mandatory minimums and other overly punitive sentences.

You can start at the beginning. Eliminate racial profiling; end the "wars" on drugs, mental illness, and homelessness; reroute school-to-prison and cradle-to-prison pipelines to school-to-success and cradle-to-college conduits. Support diversion programs and restorative justice programs and programs that don't depend upon the criminal or juvenile justice system to operate.

Just start. And start *first* by looking in the mirror. Challenge the narrative that has dominated our conversations and concept of criminality: namely, the idea of "clean versus condemned," of "us versus them." Disrupt the notion that people in the criminal and juvenile justice systems are intrinsically different from those who aren't. Understand that some people live without criminal records, but that doesn't mean they don't have criminal histories.

Without a radical reimagining of our criminal and juvenile justice systems spurred by honest considerations of our common criminality, as well as our shared humanity, reform will always fall short.

WHAT'S YOUR STORY?

What do you see when you hear *criminal? Felon? Drug dealer, gang member, thief, assailant, sex offender, bully, fraud, abuser, drunk, vandalizer?* Who do you see? Do you see yourself?

Spend some time thinking about it.

Sit by yourself.

Think of college. High school. Middle school.

Think about a time when you were drunk, or young, or stupid, or rebelling, or exploring, or angry, or in a bad relationship, or hanging out with the wrong crowd. Think of a time when no one was looking, or when they really should have just paid you more, or when it wasn't your idea anyway.

Think of the time no one got hurt, so it should not count.

Or when you gave it back anyway.

Or when they didn't even miss it.

Or when it was just once.

Or when everyone else was doing it.

Or when you felt like you had no choice.

Acknowledge that for every incident you remember, there are many more that you have forgotten.

Contemplate what life would have been like if you were born into a different class or neighborhood or decade. What would life be like if you were a different race? A different gender?

What would life be like if the cop didn't just tell you to *Go home*? Or if an interaction with campus security resulted in jail time and a criminal record, rather than an appointment with admissions? Or how many times the neighbor or the manager didn't even look twice.

Think of how your life would be different had you been caught. Had you been labeled an addict, or an assailant, or a fraud, or a thief.

Count the doors you've walked through unimpeded by your past (school, housing, internships, jobs, licensure, volunteering, travel, voting, just to name a few). What would life be like if you didn't get into school or get that job or those loans or that date? Understand that those doors are closed to millions of people in the United States for engaging in the same or similar behavior to yours.

Think of all of those foreclosed futures, and consider how rich, diverse, dynamic, and equitable our nation could be if we allowed for second chances—and first ones, too.

Be curious. Be vulnerable. Be honest.

So, what's your story?

The endnotes contain additional resources, but here's where you can start.

1. READ, WATCH, LISTEN

read

A Colony in a Nation by Chris Hayes

Are Prisons Obsolete? by Angela Y. Davis

Bastards of the Reagan Era (poetry) by Reginald Dwayne Betts

Between the World and Me by Ta-Nehisi Coates

Burning Down the House: The End of Juvenile Prison by Nell Bernstein

Caught: The Prison State and the Lockdown of American Politics by Marie Gottschalk

Incarceration Nations: A Journey to Justice In Prisons Around the World by Baz Dreisinger

The Innocents by Peter Neufeld and Barry Scheck (Authors), Althea Wasow (Editor), and Taryn Simon (photography)

Just Mercy: A Story of Justice and Redemption by Bryan Stevenson

Juvenile (photographs) by Joseph Rodriguez

Knock Knock: My Dad's Dream for Me (a children's book) by Daniel Beaty

Let's Get Free: A Hip-Hop Theory of Justice by Paul Butler

Locked Down, Locked Out: Why Prison Doesn't Work and How We Can Do Better by Maya Schenwar

Mr. Smith Goes to Prison: What My Year Behind Bars Taught Me About America's Prison Crisis by Jeff Smith

The New Jim Crow: Mass Incarceration in the Age of Colorblindness by Michelle Alexander

On the Run: Fugitive Life in an American City by Alice Goffman

Orange is the New Black: My Year in a Women's Prison by Piper Kerman

The Other Wes Moore: One Name, Two Fates by Wes Moore

Prison Baby: A Memoir by Deborah Jiang-Stein

Prison Writings: My Life is My Sun Dance by Leonard Peltier

Punished: Policing the Lives of Black and Latino Boys by Victor M. Rios

Race to Incarcerate (and a graphic retelling with Sabrina Jones) by Marc Mauer

Understanding Mass Incarceration: A People's Guide to the Key Civil Rights Struggle of Our Time by James Kilgore

Writing My Wrongs: Life, Death, and Redemption in an American Prison by Shaka Senghor

watch

Broken on All Sides: Race, Mass Incarceration and New Visions for Criminal Justice in the U.S. (2012)

Gideon's Army (2013)

The House I Live In (2012)

Mass Drownings (Arthur Longworth CLO Conference 2015)

Pull of Gravity (2013)

The Return (2016)

13th (2016)

A Prosecutor's Vision for a Better Justice System (Adam Foss TED Talk 2016)

Last Week Tonight with John Oliver's videos on prisons, prisoner reentry, mandatory minimums, bail, municipal violations, public defenders, and more

listen

Life of the Law podcast

Michael Santos' Earning Freedom podcast

2. CONNECT TO NETWORKS OF INFORMATION AND CHANGE

All of Us or None
prisonerswithchildren.org

American Civil Liberties Union
aclu.org/issues/mass-incarceration

Bard Prison Initiative
bard.edu/bpi

Brennan Center for Justice
brennancenter.org

BRIDGE and Voices for Racial Justice
voicesforracialjustice.org/our-work/bridge-prison-justice

Center for Community Alternatives
communityalternatives.org

Collateral Consequences
Resource Center
ccresourcecenter.org

Council of State Governments
Justice Center
csgjusticecenter.org/reentry

Defy Ventures
defyventures.org

Drug Policy Alliance
drugpolicy.org

The Education from the Inside
Out Coalition
eiocoalition.org

Equal Justice Initiative
eji.org

Families Against Mandatory Minimums
famm.org

Formerly Incarcerated,
Convicted People & Families Movement
ficpmovement.wordpress.com

The Fortune Society
fortunesociety.org

HIRE Network
hirenetwork.org

Homeboy Industries
homeboyindustries.org

John Jay College of Criminal Justice
Prisoner Reentry Institute
johnjaypri.org

JustLeadershipUSA
justleadershipusa.org

Legal Action Center
lac.org

The Marshall Project
themarshallproject.org

National Employment Law Project
nelp.org

Nation Inside
nationinside.org

Papillon Foundation
papillonfoundation.org

Prison Legal News
prisonlegalnews.org

Prison Policy Initiative
prisonpolicy.org

Safer Foundation
saferfoundation.org

Second Prison Project
secondprison.org

The Sentencing Project
sentencingproject.org

Solitary Watch
solitarywatch.com

Vera Institute of Justice
vera.org

We Are the 1 in 100
iam1in100.tumblr.com

Yes, In My Backyard
yesinmybackyard.org

3. GET CLOSE

Judges often say that people want mercy shown to the defendant they know—their brother, daughter, cousin, neighbor, friend—and vengeance wreaked upon the defendant they don't. Collateral consequences often work the same way: the neighbor who did something stupid, the daughter who was unduly influenced, and the cousin who has been sober for years may be given a second chance and

267

shown mercy through their connections and social safety net. But not everyone has a net. Some people are hanging on by a thread—and a criminal record, along with the anger, fear, and ultimate dehumanization invoked by it—can be the thing that cuts it.

Bryan Stevenson tells us that proximity is key. By being close to those in the criminal justice system, he says, he's learned some basic and humbling truths, including this vital lesson: "Each of us is more than the worst thing we've ever done."

It's time to get proximate. To close the gap. To see that the things that unite us—the hopes and dreams and desires we share as human beings—are far greater than the things that differentiate us.

Hire someone with a criminal record. Rent to someone on probation. Drive families to visit their loved ones in prison. Join study groups in institutions of learning and faith organized by formerly incarcerated people. Follow the lead of the people directly affected by mass incarceration. Stand shoulder-to-shoulder in city hall, your state legislature, and Congress as people with criminal records fight for their right to live full lives.

4. BE AN EMISSARY OF CHANGE

Talk to your family, your colleagues, your classmates, and your friends about privilege, punishment, and disrupting the narrative of what it means to be a "criminal." Talk to your boss and your board about changing policies and practices at work. Call your policymaker about reeling in our criminal code and collateral sanctions, restoring the right to vote, and banning the box. Contact your alma mater about access to education.

Don't stop at raising awareness—be an emissary of changing minds. Don't stop until mass criminalization is a fading image in our nation's rearview mirror.

Finally, invest in change. Support We Are All Criminals and other organizations working to end mass criminalization. We cannot do this work without you.

| THANK YOUS |

I am deeply grateful to so many people for helping make this project, this organization, and now this book a reality.

To the participants: your humor, humility, and honesty are shifting narratives and moving mountains.

To our volunteers, collaborators, and supporters: I am so thankful for your time, talent, and financial support. Special shout-out to the many people who helped turn an unwieldy PowerPoint file and notebooks of scribbles into a book: Emily Christensen, Pramod Subbareddy, Christy Szitta, Richard McElmore II, Barb Nilles, Ingrid Nuttall, Jerome Graham, Nadine Graves, Perry Moriearty, Jennifer Labovitz, Letta Page, Vidya Neni, Dana Leib, Roopal Shah, Kevin Reese, Judge Pamela Alexander, JD Schmid, Lindsay Turner, Jeff Johnson and Andy Weaver, Amrit Dhir, Anna Preus, Ellie O'Neill, Patti and Brian Abrams, Anjali Desai, Scott Beutel, Delaine Snow, John Stuart, Leah Sands, Joel Luedtke, Bernie Luksich, Martha Lee, Mauricio Arango, Myron Orfield, Michelle Phelps, Chris Uggen, Richard Frase, Tholal Ahmed, Joshua Bertsch, Alicia Smith, John Poupart, Dinesh Melwani, Anna Perrotta, Zach Psick, Ebony Ruhland, Josh Esmay, Sarah Davis, Andy Sagvold, Rob Wall, Tom Karls, Morris Sadicario, Bob Johnson, Jason Sole, Jon Vang, Sterling Rozear, Seth Sheffler-Collins, Pat and Marty Baxter, Molly and Ryan Yunkers, Kate Baxter and Dan DeWolf, Tommy Baxter, and Praveen Reddy. Thanks to the Jay & Rose Phillips Foundation and to the Archibald Bush Foundation for supporting this work.

This book is dedicated to the people hurt the most by the irrationality and brutality of our criminal justice system. To my friends, family, colleagues, clients, mentors, and more: your courage, kindness, creativity, brilliance, and tenacity are something to behold.

And to Anthony, thank you for letting me into your world and for changing mine.

CONSIDERATIONS FOR
THE THREE IN FOUR:

What have you had the luxury to forget?

What would life be like had you been caught?

What roles did race and class play in your
ability to get away with it?

CONSIDERATIONS FOR
THE FOUR IN FOUR:

How can you work to close the empathy gap
between the privileged and the punished?

How can you work to end the era of
mass criminalization?

A NOTE ON LANGUAGE:

Ex-con, *felon*, *former felon*, *offender*, *ex-offender*, and *criminal* are stigmatizing terms that define people by a moment in time, by an act or acts, by conduct. Criminals rather than fathers, mothers, brothers, sisters, friends, providers, students, scholars, poets, philosophers, artists, entrepreneurs, leaders, innovators, and more.

As Daryl Atkinson, attorney and inaugural Department of Justice Second Chance Fellow, says: "I'm more than the sum total of my contact with the criminal legal system."

Blair Hickman, "Inmate. Prisoner. Other. Discussed.," The Marshall Project, April 3, 2015, https://www.themarshallproject.org/2015/04/03/inmate-prisoner-other-discussed#.uJziblOCO.

To honor that humanity, I most often use the term *person with a criminal record*. It is far more descriptive than *criminal* (or offender, ex-offender, felon, or former felon), given *criminal* could characterize anybody—not just a person laboring in the shadow of past mistakes and acts.

To describe life with a criminal record, I use the terms *reentry* and *second chances*, but sparingly, as *reentry* suggests the person has left the community due to incarceration (the exception more frequently than the rule) or that the person was previously integrated into the segments of society that he is now seeking to engage.

Second chances imply that a second shot at a full and meaningful life without arbitrary and unjust barriers is all that is required or appropriate, and that everyone started out with a first chance.

Page 5

We haven't always been an incarceration nation: National Research Council, *The Growth of Incarceration in the United States: Exploring Causes and Consequences*, ed. Jeremy Travis et al. (Washington, DC: National Academies Press, 2014), 13.

Decades of bipartisan tough-on-crime: Ibid., 109; U.S. Department of Justice, Bureau of Justice Statistics, *Prisoners in 2014*, by E. Ann Carson, NCJ 248955 (National Criminal Justice Reference Service, 2015), 1, http://www.bjs.gov/content/pub/pdf/p14.pdf; U.S. Department of Justice, Bureau of Justice Statistics, *Correctional Populations in the United States, 2014*, by Danielle Kaeble et al., NCJ 249513 (National Criminal Justice Reference Service, 2015), 5, http://www.bjs.gov/content/pub/pdf/cpus14.pdf.

Black men are more likely to be arrested: *Report of The Sentencing Project to the United Nations Human Rights Committee: Regarding Racial Disparities in the United States Criminal Justice System* (The Sentencing Project, 2013), 1, http://sentencingproject.org/doc/publications/rd_ICCPR%20Race%20and%20Justice%20Shadow%20Report.pdf; The Sentencing Project, *Fact Sheet: Trends in U.S. Corrections* (The Sentencing Project, 2016, updated June 2017), 5–6, http://sentencingproject.org/wp-content/uploads/2015/12/Race-and-Justice-Shadow-Report-ICCPR.pdf; Joshua Aiken, "Era of Mass Expansion: Why State Officials Should Fight Jail Growth," Prison Policy Initiative Press Release, May 31, 2017, https://www.prisonpolicy.org/reports/jailsovertime.html.

Black women and children: Ibid.

One in four people: U.S. Department of Justice, Bureau of Justice Statistics, *Survey of State Criminal History Information Systems, 2012*, by Owen M. Greenspan and Dennis A. DeBacco, NCJ 244563 (National Criminal Justice Reference Service, 2014), 3, https://www.ncjrs.gov/pdffiles1/bjs/grants/244563.pdf; Michelle N. Rodriguez and Maurice Emsellem, *65 Million "Need Not Apply": The Case for Reforming Criminal Background Checks for Employment* (National Employment Law Project, 2011), 3, http://www.nelp.org/content/uploads/2015/03/65_Million_Need_Not_Apply.pdf; "The Importance of Action," The Coalition for Public Safety, accessed July 17, 2017, http://www.coalitionforpublicsafety.org/; "Written Testimony for Amy Solomon, Senior Advisor to the Assistant Attorney General, Office of Justice Programs, U.S. Department of Justice," written testimony presented at the Meeting of EEOC to Examine Arrest and Conviction Records as a Hiring Barrier, Washington DC, July 26, 2011, https://www.eeoc.gov/eeoc/meetings/7-26-11/solomon.cfm.

Page 6

have signaled a much lower tolerance: "Jeff Sessions Orders Tougher Drug Crime Charges," *The Economist*, May 12, 2017, https://www.economist.com/blogs/democracyinamerica/2017/05/drug-war-policies.

Page 17

They say a picture: Delaine Snow, Poems for Parole series, unpublished, 2016.

Page 18

"With a criminal record comes official": Devah Pager, *Marked: Race, Crime, and Finding Work in an Era of Mass Incarceration* (Chicago: University of Chicago Press, 2007), 32–33.

Norman Reimer, Executive Director: *Collateral Damage: America's Failure to Forgive or Forget in the War on Crime* (National Association of Criminal Defense Lawyers, 2014), 9, https://www.nacdl.org/restoration/roadmapreport/.

The National Employment Law Project (NELP) asserts that: Madeline Neighly and Maurice Emsellem, *Wanted: Accurate FBI Background Checks for Employment* (National Employment Law Project, 2013), 10, http://www.nelp.org/content/uploads/2015/02/Report-Wanted-Accurate-FBI-Background-Checks-Employment-1.pdf.

if the record only reports the initial charge: Ibid.

"no single source exists": *The Attorney General's Report on Criminal History Background Checks* (Washington, DC: U.S. Department of Justice, June 2006), quoted in "Amy Solomon," Meeting of EEOC, footnote 10.

Page 19

The American Bar Association (ABA) has begun to compile: National Inventory of the Collateral Consequences of Conviction, niccc.csgjusticecenter.org.

the ABA has identified more than 45,000 sanctions: niccc.csgjusticecenter.org/search (search multiple jurisdictions, no limiting search term).

"Why should someone convicted of possessing drugs": Margaret C. Love, "Managing Collateral Consequences In The Sentencing Process: The Revised Sentencing Articles Of The Model Penal Code," *Wisconsin Law Review* 2015, no. 2 (May 2015): 250.

Because these laws operate largely beyond public view: Jeremy Travis, "Invisible Punishment: An Instrument of Social Exclusion," in *Invisible Punishment: The Collateral Consequences of Mass Imprisonment*, ed. Marc Mauer and Meda Chesney-Lind (New York: New Press, 2002), 15.

Felony disenfranchisement: For more information on disenfranchisement and trends to restore the vote, see "Felony Disenfranchisement," The Sentencing Project, accessed June 28, 2017, http://www.sentencingproject.org/issues/felony-disenfranchisement/.

Maine and Vermont, for instance: Ibid. (click on "Felony Disenfranchisement: A Primer").

while Kentucky, Florida, and Iowa: Ibid.

Page 20

Had the 600,000 Floridians: Christopher Uggen and Jeff Manza, "Democratic Contraction? Political Consequences of Felon Disenfranchisement in the United States," *American Sociological Review* 67, no. 6 (December 2002): 792–93, http://as.nyu.edu/content/dam/nyu-as/faculty/documents/Democratic_Contraction.pdf.

Criminologists have found that people who cast a ballot: Christopher Uggen, Angela Behrens, and Jeff Manza, "Criminal Disenfranchisement," *Annual Review of Law and Social Science* 1 (2005): 311–12, doi: 10.1146/annurev.lawsocsci.1.041604.115840.

A clear path to broader public and political engagement: Kevin Reese (prison organizer), e-mail message to author, June 6, 2016.

"restoration of that right should": Ibid.

"When applied indiscriminately and unnecessarily": Christopher Uggen and Robert Stewart, "Piling On: Collateral Consequences and Community Supervision," *Minnesota Law Review* 99, no. 5 (2015): 1910.

Dr. Travis notes that in this brave new world: Travis, "Invisible Punishment," 19.

In spite of the Department of Housing and Urban Development's repeated calls: U.S. Department of Housing and Urban Development, "Office of General Counsel Guidance on Application of Fair Housing Act Standards to the Use of Criminal Records by Providers of Housing and Real Estate-Related Transactions," April 4, 2016, https://portal.hud.gov/hudportal/documents/huddoc?id=HUD_OGCGuidAppFHAStandCR.pdf; U.S. Department of Housing and Urban Development, Office of Public and Indian Housing, "Guidance for Public Housing Agencies (PHAs) and Owners of Federally-Assisted Housing on Excluding the Use of Arrest Records in Housing Decisions," Notice PIH 2015–19, November 2, 2015, https://portal.hud.gov/hudportal/documents/huddoc?id=PIH2015-19.pdf.

Still, the vast majority of U.S. employers: *Background Checking—The Use of Criminal Background Checks in Hiring Decisions* (Society for Human Resource Management, 2012), PowerPoint report, slide 5, https://www.shrm.org/research/surveyfindings/articles/pages/ criminalbackgroundcheck.aspx.

Page 22

Retired prosecutor Robert M.A. Johnson mused: Robert M.A. Johnson (former Anoka County Attorney), in discussion with the author, 2013.

The Common Application: Juleyka Lantigua-Williams, "'Ban the Box' Goes to College," *The Atlantic*, April 29, 2016, https://www.theatlantic.com/politics/archive/2016/04/ban-the-box-comes-to-campus/480195/ (quoting the Common Application).

no empirical evidence showing students with criminal records: Marsha Weissman et al., *The Use of Criminal History Records in College Admissions Reconsidered* (Center for Community Alternatives, 2010), 3, http://www.communityalternatives.org/pdf/Reconsidered-criminal-hist-recs-in-college-admissions.pdf.

while there is evidence that education: Alan Rosenthal et al., *Boxed Out: Criminal History Screening and College Application Attrition* (Center for Community Alternatives, 2015), 45, http://communityalternatives.org/pdf/publications/ BoxedOut_FullReport.pdf.

"All it takes is one procrastinating person": Participant, in discussion with the author, 2015.

Page 23

"[d]espite the lack of official conviction record": Pager, *Marked*, 95.

"Today it is perfectly legal to discriminate": Michelle Alexander, *The New Jim Crow*, rev. ed. (New York: New Press, 2011), 2.

"We have not ended racial caste": Ibid.

Page 27

a 68-year-old man was fired: Ed Payne, "A 'nickel-and-dime' crime almost 50 years ago gets 68-year-old employee fired," CNN, August 30, 2012, http://www.cnn.com/2012/08/30/us/iowa-fired-for-a-dime/index.html.

Page 51

"America's public enemy": President Richard Nixon, "Remarks About an Intensified Program for Drug Abuse Prevention and Control.," speech, White House Briefing Room, June 17, 1971, transcript, The American Presidency Project, University of California, Santa Barbara, http://www.presidency.ucsb.edu/ws/?pid=3047.

Page 52

In The New Jim Crow, *a searing indictment:* Alexander, *New Jim Crow,* chapter 1.

Brown v. Board of Education: 347 U.S. 483 (1954).

"Any candid observer of American racial history": Alexander, *New Jim Crow,* 21.

"We knew we couldn't make it illegal": Dan Baum, "Legalize It All: How to Win the War on Drugs," *Harper's Magazine,* April 2016, http://harpers.org/archive/2016/04/legalize-it-all/.

Even when President Ronald Reagan ran: Alexander, *New Jim Crow,* 49.

"In the era of colorblindness": Ibid., 2.

Page 67

"[N]o one has ever lost an election": Jeff Smith, *Mr. Smith Goes to Prison: What My Year Behind Bars Taught Me About America's Prison Crisis* (New York: St. Martin's Press, 2015), 115.

Page 68

"People who commit crimes should be caught": William Clinton, "Remarks on Signing the Violent Crime Control and Law Enforcement Act of 1994," September 13, 1994, in *Public Papers of the Presidents of the United States: William J. Clinton, 1994, Book II-August 1 to December 31, 1994* (Washington, DC: Government Printing Office, 1995), 1540–41.

"the crest of a national tide": "An Invitation," *Justice in Focus: Crime Bill @20* (Vera Institute of Justice, 2014), https://www.vera.org/justice-in-focus-crime-bill-20.

"We basically took a shotgun": Andrew Cohen, "Bill Clinton and Mass Incarceration," Brennan Center for Justice, October 14, 2014, https://www.brennancenter.org/analysis/Bill-Clinton-Mass-Incarceration.

state legislatures pump out more and more laws: See, e.g., Paul H. Robinson and Michael T. Cahill, "The Accelerating Degradation of American Criminal Codes," *Hastings Law Journal* 56, no. 4 (March 2005): 634 (referring to legislatures as "offense factories"); State v. M.D.T., 831 N.W.2d 276, 301 n.14 (Minn. 2013) (Anderson, J., dissenting) (Minnesota Supreme Court Justice Paul Anderson decried his state's ever-expanding criminal code, noting that since 1965, Minnesota had added more than 200 pages—often with multiple statutes per page—to a single criminal code chapter); Jarrett Skorup, "How to Deal With Michigan's Vast Criminal Code," *Michigan Capitol Confidential,* February 12, 2015, http:// www.michigancapitolconfidential.com/20989 (Michigan created approximately 270 offenses in just six years); Jeff Welty, "Overcriminalization in North Carolina," *North Carolina Law Review* 92, no. 6 (2014): 1942 (North Carolina enacted 101 new felonies and 105 new misdemeanors in six years).

the more than 4,000 federal offenses: John S. Baker, "Measuring the Explosive Growth of Federal Crime Legislation," *Engage* 5, no. 2 (October 2004): 23.

"if one only has a hammer": Marc A. Levin, "At the State Level, So-Called Crimes Are Here, There, Everywhere," *Criminal Justice* 28, no. 1 (Spring 2013): 1, https://www.americanbar.org/content/dam/aba/publications/criminal_justice_magazine/sp13_state_level.authcheckdam.pdf.

Page 69

courts' calendars are jammed: Robert C. Boruchowitz, Malia N. Brink, and Maureen Dimino, *Minor Crimes, Massive Waste: The Terrible Toll of America's Broken Misdemeanor Courts* (National Association of Criminal Defense Lawyers, 2009), 7, https://www.nacdl.org/WorkArea/linkit.aspx?LinkIdentifier=id&ItemID=20808.

For immigrants, a misdemeanor conviction: Jenny Roberts, "Why Misdemeanors Matter: Defining Effective Advocacy in the Lower Criminal Courts," *UC Davis Law Review* 45, no. 2 (December 2011): 298.

"may lose or be unable to get public housing": Ibid., 288–89; see also Jenny Roberts, "Crashing the Misdemeanor System," *Washington and Lee Law Review* 70, no. 2 (2013): 1089–1131.

Despite being staffed with adept and dedicated attorneys: Geoff Burkhart, "Public Defense: The New York Story," *Criminal Justice* 30, no. 3 (Fall 2015): 23, https://www.americanbar.org/content/dam/aba/administrative/legal_aid_indigent_defendants/ls_sclaid_def_nystory.authcheckdam.pdf.

In the world of misdemeanor McJustice: Alisa Smith and Sean Maddan, *Three-Minute Justice: Haste and Waste in Florida's Misdemeanor Courts* (National Association of Criminal Defense Lawyers, 2011), 9, https://www.nacdl.org/reports/threeminutejustice/.

Misdemeanor or felony, perhaps it's no surprise: U.S. Department of Justice, Bureau of Justice Assistance, *Plea and Charge Bargaining,* by Lindsey Devers (Bureau of Justice Assistance, 2011), 3, https://www.bja.gov/Publications/PleaBargainingResearchSummary.pdf (90 to 95% of cases); Erica Goode, "Stronger Hand for Judges in the 'Bazaar' of Plea Deals," *New York Times*, March 22, 2012, http://www.nytimes.com/2012/03/23/us/stronger-hand-for-judges-after-rulings-on-plea-deals.html?_r=1 (97% of federal cases and 94% of state cases).

Page 90

Nationwide, law enforcement made: U.S. Department of Justice, Federal Bureau of Investigation, *Crime in the United States, 2014*, Uniform Crime Reports online, Fall 2014, Table 29, https://ucr.fbi.gov/crime-in-the-u.s/2014/crime-in-the-u.s.-2014/tables/table-29.

In 2016, one in five incarcerated people: Peter Wagner and Bernadette Rabuy, *Mass Incarceration: The Whole Pie 2017* (Prison Policy Initiative, 2017), second slide group, first graphic, accessed July 6, 2017, https://www.prisonpolicy.org/reports/pie2017.html.

According to the American Civil Liberties Union (ACLU): *Marijuana Arrests by the Numbers* (American Civil Liberties Union), slideshow, slide 1, accessed July 17, 2017, https://www.aclu.org/gallery/marijuana-arrests-numbers.

that year, cops made a pot arrest every 37 seconds: American Civil Liberties Union, *The War on Marijuana in Black and White: Billions of Dollars Wasted on Racially Biased Arrests* (American Civil Liberties Union, 2013), 4, https://www.aclu.org/files/assets/aclu-thewaronmarijuana-rel2.pdf.

Between 1980 and 2015, there were six times as many arrests: Wagner and Rabuy, *The Whole Pie*, second slide group, third graphic.

While neither use nor dependency: Redonna K. Chandler, Bennett W. Fletcher, and Nora D. Volkow, "Treating Drug Abuse and Addiction in the Criminal Justice System: Improving Public Health and Safety," *Journal of the American Medical Association* 301, no. 2 (2009): 183, doi:10.1001/jama.2008.976.

individuals serving time for a property or person crime: U.S. Department of Justice, Bureau of Justice Statistics, *Drug Use and Dependence, State and Federal Prisoners, 2004*, by Christopher J. Mumola and Jennifer C. Karberg, NCJ 213530 (National Criminal Justice Reference Service, 2006), 5–7, http://www.bjs.gov/content/pub/pdf/dudsfp04.pdf.

the high cost of illegal drugs: Paul Butler, *Let's Get Free: A Hip-Hop Theory of Justice* (New York: New Press, 2010), 52.

After all, most people who consume drugs: Carl Hart, *High Price: A Neuroscientist's Journey of Self-Discovery That Challenges Everything You Know About Drugs and Society* (New York: HarperCollins, 2013), 306.

Meaningful employment is one of the most attractive: Carl Hart, "Let's Quit Abusing Drug Users," filmed September 2014, TEDMED video, posted September 2014, http://www.tedmed.com/speakers/show?id=308946.

The human cost of the misguided: Hart, *High Price*, 306.

Black and white people use and sell drugs: Alexander, *New Jim Crow*, 99.

on average, a black person is 3.73 times: ACLU, *The War on Marijuana*, 4.

Those disparities continue through criminal charging: Gwen Rubinstein and Debbie Mukamal, "Welfare and Housing: Denial of Benefits to Drug Offenders," in *Invisible Punishment*, 40.

the majority of illegal drug users and dealers are white: Alexander, *New Jim Crow*, 98.

"The day that we bring the troops": Butler, *Let's Get Free*, 55.

Some states are moving toward decriminalizing: ACLU, *The War on Marijuana*, 113.

many more jurisdictions—including the federal government—are not: Jon Gettman, *Racial Disparities in Marijuana Arrests in Virginia (2003–2013)* (Drug Policy Alliance, 2015), 2, https://www.drugpolicy.org/sites/default/files/Racial_Disparities_in_Marijuana_Arrests_in_Virginia_2003-2013.pdf (stating that, for example, while marijuana arrests were down 6.5 percent nationwide between 2003 and 2014, possession arrests in Virginia skyrocketed by an alarming 76 percent. During that same time period, arrests of black people for pot possession increased by more than 100 percent, and accounted for nearly half of the state's possession arrests. Virginia's general population was 20 percent black during this time period.).

the new U.S. Attorney General, Jeff Sessions: "Jeff Sessions Orders," *The Economist*.

At least three former presidents seem to be proof: Olivia B. Waxman, "Bill Clinton Said He 'Didn't Inhale' 25 Years Ago—But the History of U.S. Presidents and Drugs is Much Older," *Time*, March 29, 2017, http://time.com/4711887/bill-clinton-didnt-inhale-marijuana-anniversary/.

Page 111

This is particularly true for transgender women of color: *Unjust: How the Broken Criminal Justice System Fails Transgender People* (Center for American Progress and Movement Advancement Project, 2016), 3, http://www.lgbtmap.org/file/lgbt-criminal-justice-trans.pdf.

the American criminal justice system not only fails: Ibid.

Page 123

Our nation's recent response to a rise: Ekow Yankah, "There Was No Wave of Compassion When Addicts Were Hooked on Crack," *PBS NewsHour* video, aired March 29, 2016, and transcript, http:// www.pbs.org/newshour/bb/there-was-no-wave-of-compassion-when-addicts-were-hooked-on-crack/.

"Back then, when addiction was a black problem": Ibid.

"Suddenly, crime is understood as a sign": Ibid.

Page 142

the lifetime likelihood of imprisonment for white men: The Sentencing Project, *Fact Sheet: Trends in U.S. Corrections*, 5.

women's imprisonment rate increased: The Sentencing Project, *Fact Sheet: Incarcerated Women and Girls* (The Sentencing Project, 2012, updated November 2015), 1, http://www.sentencingproject.org/doc/ publications/cc_Incarcerated_Women_ Factsheet_Sep24sp.pdf.

According to The Sentencing Project, the racial disparities: The Sentencing Project, *Fact Sheet: Trends*, 5.

One out of three women incarcerated in Montana: Montana Department of Corrections 2015 Biennial Report (Montana Department of Corrections, 2015), G-5, https://cor.mt.gov/Portals/104/Resources/Reports/2015BiennialReport.pdf.

two-thirds of people in jail report: Alexander, *New Jim Crow*, 155.

The significant and enduring economic repercussions: The Pew Charitable Trusts, *Collateral Costs: Incarceration's Effect on Economic Mobility* (Washington, DC: Pew Charitable Trusts, 2010), 18, http://www.pewtrusts.org/~/media/legacy/uploadedfiles/pcs_assets/2010/collateralcosts1pdf.

"[w]e may try to comfort ourselves": Marc Mauer, *Race to Incarcerate*, rev. ed. (New York: New Press, 2006), 215.

The U.S. is the world's warden: Michelle Y. H. Lee, "Does the United States really have 5 percent of the world's population and one quarter of the world's prisoners?" *The Washington Post* online, April 30, 2015, https://www.washingtonpost.com/news/fact-checker/wp/2015/04/30/does-the-united-states-really-have-five-percent-of-worlds-population-and-one-quarter-of-the-worlds-prisoners/.

mass incarceration is relatively new: The Sentencing Project, *Fact Sheet: Trends*, 1, figure 1.

In 2014, that number was more than 1.5 million: Carson, *Prisoners in 2014*, 1.

With an additional 731,000 in jail: Ram Subramanian et al., *Incarceration's Front Door: The Misuse of Jails in America* (New York: Vera Institute of Justice, 2015), 4, https://www.vera.org/publications/incarcerations-front-door-the-misuse-of-jails-in-america.

The federal prison population swelled: Nathan James, *The Federal Prison Population Buildup: Options for Congress*, CRS R42937 (Washington, DC: Congressional Research Service, 2016), 1, http://www.fas.org/sgp/crs/misc/R42937.pdf.

During a 21-year stretch: Keely Herring, "Was a Prison Built Every 10 Days to House a Fast-Growing Population of Non-Violent Inmates," *PolitiFact*, July 31, 2015, http://www.politifact.com/truth-o-meter/statements/2015/jul/31/cory-booker/was-prison-built-every-10-days-house-fast-growing-/.

Page 144

California's penchant for incarceration: Brown v. Plata, 563 U.S. 493, 539–41 (2011).

noting that people in prison: Ibid., 510.

"Prisoners are crammed into spaces": Ibid., 502.

prior to the early 1990s, people behind bars: Joshua Page, "Eliminating the Enemy: The Import of Denying Prisoners Access to Higher Education in Clinton's America," *Punishment and Society* 6, no. 4 (October 2004): 357–58, doi:10.1177/1462474504046118.

Congress passed legislation denying: Ibid., 357–59.

Even today, some states are disbanding: Marie Gottschalk, *Caught: The Prison State and the Lockdown*

of American Politics (Princeton: Princeton University Press, 2015), 82.

Sociologist Joshua Page studied the public discourse: Page, "Eliminating the Enemy," 360.

A Prison Policy Initiative report finds that: Wagner and Rabuy, *The Whole Pie*, text and note 2.

the Vera Institute of Justice notes: Subramanian et al., *Incarceration's Front Door*, 5.

"Just a few days in jail": Ibid.

As Vichal Kumar with the Neighborhood Defender Service of Harlem: Vichal Kumar, e-mail message to author, May 2, 2016.

add 41,000 more people locked up on immigration holds: Wagner and Rabuy, *The Whole Pie*, first slide group, first graphic.

Page 145

Each has been called our nation's largest mental health institution: Michael Arceneaux, "Why Are The Three Largest Mental Health Care Providers Jails?," NewsOne Original, accessed July 17, 2017, http://newsone.com/2744141/prisons-mental-health-providers/; Renee Montagne, "Inside The Nation's Largest Mental Institution," National Public Radio online, August 13, 2008, http://www.npr.org/templates/story/ story.php?storyId=93581736; Matt Ford, "America's Largest Mental Hospital is a Jail," *The Atlantic*, June 8, 2015, http://www. theatlantic.com/politics/archive/2015/06/americas-largest-mental-hospital-is-a-jail/395012/.

In the 1970s, a social movement: Montagne, "Inside The Nation's Largest."

two million people with mental health concerns: "Jailing People with Mental Illness," National Alliance on Mental Illness, accessed July 3, 2017, https://www.nami.org/Learn-More/Public-Policy/Jailing-People-with-Mental-Illness; Leah G. Pope et al., *First-Episode Incarceration: Creating a Recovery-Informed Framework for Integrated Mental Health and Criminal Justice Responses* (New York: Vera Institute of Justice, 2016), 4, https://www.vera.org/publications/first-episode-incarceration-creating-a-recovery-informed-framework-for-integrated-mental-health-and-criminal-justice-responses.

nearly three-fourths of women and more than one-half of men: U.S. Department of Justice, Bureau of Justice Statistics, *Mental Health Problems of Prison and Jail Inmates*, by Doris J. James and Lauren E. Glaze, NCJ 213600 (National Criminal Justice Reference Service, 2006), 1, http://www.bjs.gov/content/pub/pdf/mhppji.pdf.

Jails and prisons are now de facto health care providers: National Research Council, *Growth of Incarceration*, 213.

Violent and inhumane conditions: Jamie Fellner, *Callous and Cruel: Use of Force Against Inmates with Mental Disabilities in US Jails and Prisons* (Human Rights Watch, 2015), para., 2, https://www.hrw.org/report/2015/05/12/callous-and-cruel-use-force-against-inmates-mental-disabilities-us-jails-and.

people with mental illnesses tend to be held longer: "The Problem," The Stepping Up Initiative, accessed June 19, 2017, https://stepuptogether.org/the-problem.

seventy percent of those with a serious mental illness: National Research Council, *Growth of Incarceration*, 207.

Take, for instance, one gentleman who: Participant, in discussion with the author, 2015.

a quarter of the 498 people shot and killed: "Fatal Force," *The Washington Post* online, accessed July 5, 2017, https://www.washingtonpost.com/graphics/national/police-shootings-2017/.

Surveys suggest that police may perceive: Amy C. Watson and Anjali J. Fulambarker, "The Crisis Intervention Team Model of Police Response to Mental Health Crises: A Primer for Mental Health Practitioners," *Best Practices in Mental Health* 8, no. 2 (December 2012), "Author manuscript," available in PubMed Central on December 1, 2013, 71, http://www.ncbi.nlm.nih.gov/pmc/articles/PMC3769782/.

some jurisdictions are investing in efforts: "What is CIT?" National Alliance on Mental Illness, accessed July 17, 2017, https://www.nami.org/Law-Enforcement-and-Mental-Health/What-Is-CIT.aspx.

"tragedy of national proportions": "Stop Criminalizing Mental Illness," National Alliance on Mental Illness, accessed July 3, 2017, https://www.nami.org/Press-Media/Press-Releases/2000/Stop-Criminalizing-Mental-Illness#sthash.6o1DDmWK.dpuf (statement by NAMI Executive Director Laurie Flynn to the U.S. House of Representatives Judiciary Subcommittee on Crime, September 21, 2000).

"It is a trend": Ibid.

Page 147

At any given time, thousands of incarcerated women: Stephanie Fritz and Kevin Whiteacre, "Prison Nurseries: Experiences of Incarcerated Women During Pregnancy," *Journal of Offender Rehabilitation* 55, no. 1 (2016): 2, doi :10.1080/10509674.2015.1107001.

Most of these newborns are taken: Ibid.

People serve more and more time: *Old Behind Bars: The Aging Prison Population in the United States*, (Human Rights Watch, 2012), 24, https://www.hrw.org/sites/default/files/reports/usprisons0112webwcover_0_0.pdf.

Criminologists, meanwhile, will point you to the "age-crime" curve: Sarah Shannon and Sarah Lageson, "Discovering Desistance," *The Society Pages*, March 22, 2013, https://thesocietypages.org/specials/discovering-desistance/; Fergus McNeill et al., *How and Why People Stop Offending: Discovering Desistance* (Institute for Research and Innovation in Social Services, 2012), 3, http://www.iriss.org.uk/resources/how-and-why-people-stop-offending-discovering-desistance.

in 2010 there were 26,200 people: *Old Behind Bars*, 18.

Experts project that by 2030: American Civil Liberties Union, *At America's Expense: The Mass Incarceration of the Elderly* (American Civil Liberties Union, 2012), 5, https://www.aclu.org/files/assets/elderlyprisonreport_20120613_1.pdf.

There are nearly 160,000 lifers: The Sentencing Project, *Life Goes On: The Historic Rise in Life Sentences in America* (The Sentencing Project, 2012), 1, http://sentencingproject.org/doc/publications/inc_Life%20Goes%20On%202013.pdf.

This population has more than quadrupled: Ibid.

right now in the U.S., there are at least 41,000 people: Elizabeth Gudrais, "The Prison Problem," *Harvard Magazine*, March–April 2013, 41, http://harvardmag.com/pdf/2013/03-pdfs/0313-HarvardMag.pdf.

Elderly men and women unable to climb: Sari Horwitz, "The Painful Price of Aging in Prison," *The Washington Post* online, May 2, 2015, http://www.washingtonpost.com/sf/national/2015/05/02/the-painful-price-of-aging-in-prison/.

"Our federal prisons are starting to resemble nursing homes": Ibid.

Page 148

"Living on probation is like living in a netherworld": Jason Sole (author and activist), in discussion with the author, 2016.

Recently, the U.S. prison population began to show: Michelle S. Phelps, "The Paradox of Probation: Community Supervision in the Age of Mass Incarceration," *Law & Policy* 35, no. 1–2 (January–April 2013): 51–52, doi:10.1111/ lapo.12002.

Sociologist Michelle Phelps notes the decarceration is spurred: Ibid., 52.

the United States' probation rate is more than five times: Mariel Alper, Alessandro Corda, and Kevin Reitz, *American Exceptionalism in Probation Supervision* (Robina Institute of Criminal Law & Criminal Justice, 2016), http://robinainstitute.umn.edu/publications/data-brief-american-exceptionalism-probation-supervision.

it's no longer just a matter of mass incarceration: Phelps, "The Paradox," 53.

Generally, people "on paper" must submit to a search: See Fiona Doherty, "Obey All Laws and Be Good: Probation and the Meaning of Recidivism," *Georgetown Law Journal* 104, no. 2 (2016): 317–22, for examples.

The result is "an almost farcical level": Ibid., 294.

"probationers must be good people": Ibid., 295.

Given that eight or nine out of ten probationers: Alicia Bannon, Mitali Nagrecha, and Rebekah Diller, *Criminal Justice Debt: A Barrier to Reentry* (Brennan Center for Justice, 2010), 4, http://www.brennancenter.org/sites/default/files/legacy/Fees%20and%20Fines%20FINAL.pdf.

others, homeless and jobless, are instructed by probation officers: State v. Brown, No. 62–CR–11–1058, 2016 WL 1290973, at *1 (Minn. Ct. App. April 4, 2016) (unpublished). See also U.S. Food and Drug Administration, Center for Biologics Evaluation and Research, "Deferral of Current and Recent Inmates of Correctional Institutions as Donors" recommendation letter, from Director of CBER to All Registered Blood Establishments, June 8, 1995, accessed July 5, 2017, https://www. fda.gov/downloads/biologicsbloodvaccines/guidancecomplianceregulatoryinformation/otherrecommendationsformanufacturers/memorandumtobloodestablishments/ucm062637.pdf. (recommending deferring donors who have spent more than 72 consecutive hours in lock-up in the past 12 months. Author's note: Because spending a long weekend in jail is anything but a rarity for probationers, many are disqualified from even this.)

Page 151

One-third of all U.S. young adults have been arrested: Robert Brame et al., "Demographic Patterns of Cumulative Arrest Prevalence by Ages 18 and 23," *Crime & Delinquency* 60, no. 3 (2014): 471–472, doi: 10.1177/0011128713514801.

Page 152

Kids are arrested, detained, adjudicated, and expelled: See, e.g., Nicole Flatow, "Report: Mississippi Children Handcuffed in School for Not Wearing a Belt," *ThinkProgress*, January 18, 2013, http://thinkprogress.org/justice/2013/01/18/1466001/report-mississippi-children-handcuffed-in-school- for-not-wearing-a-belt/ (throwing peanuts; not wearing belt); Christopher Ingraham, "Virginia School Suspends an 11-year-old for One Year Over a Leaf That Wasn't Marijuana," *Wonkblog* (blog), *The Washington Post* online, March 16, 2015, https://www.washingtonpost.com/news/wonk/wp/2015/03/16/virginia-school-suspends-an-11-year-old-for-one- year-over-a-leaf-that-wasnt-marijuana/ (an 11-year-old was suspended for a year and charged with marijuana possession after bringing not-marijuana to school. A single leaf that tested negative for pot three times nevertheless fell under the state's zero-tolerance policies on "imitation drugs." The child, once in the gifted-and-talented program, now has panic attacks and fears his dreams of college are foreclosed).

While white youth are more likely: Motoko Rich, "Analysis Finds Higher Expulsion Rates for Black Students," *New York Times*, August 24, 2015, http://www.nytimes.com/2015/08/25/us/higher-expulsion-rates-for-black-students-are-found.html.

In total, black and Native American students: U.S. Department of Education, Office for Civil Rights, *Civil Rights Data Collection Data Snapshot: School Discipline* (Office for Civil Rights, 2014), 1, http://ocrdata.ed.gov/Downloads/CRDC-School-Discipline-Snapshot.pdf.

black girls are suspended at greater rates: Kimberlé W. Crenshaw, Priscilla Ocen, and Jyoti Nanda, *Black Girls Matter: Pushed Out, Overpoliced and Underprotected* (African American Policy Forum and Center for Intersectionality and Social Policy Studies, 2015), 16–17, http://static1.squarespace.com/static/53f20d90e4b0b80451158d8c/t/54d2d37ce4b024b41443b0ba/1423102844010/BlackGirlsMatter_Report.pdf. (Author's note: *Black Girls Matter* lists examples of incidents that read like surreal fiction: a 12-year-old girl facing expulsion and criminal charges after writing *hi* on a locker room wall; another 12-year-old threatened with expulsion unless she changed the look of her natural hair; a 16-year-old arrested for dropping a piece of cake on the cafeteria floor; a six-year-old arrested for throwing a tantrum.)

Following expulsion, youth are more likely: Rich, "Analysis Finds Higher Expulsion."

It's no small number of kids: U.S. Department of Justice, Office of Juvenile Justice and Delinquency Prevention, *Juvenile Court Statistics 2013*, by Sarah Hockenberry and Charles Puzzanchera (National Center for Juvenile Justice and Office of Juvenile Justice and Delinquency Prevention, 2015), 6, http://www.ojjdp.gov/ojstatbb/njcda/pdf/jcs2013.pdf; "OJJDP Statistical Briefing Book," Office of Juvenile Justice and Delinquency Prevention website, August 05, 2013, https:// www.ojjdp.gov/ojstatbb/structure_process/qa04102.asp?qaDate=2012.

Not all of these kids end up in custody: *The Comeback States: Reducing Youth Incarceration in the United States* (National Juvenile Justice Network and Texas Public Policy Foundation, 2013), 21–22, http://www.njjn.org/uploads/digital-library/Comeback-States-Report_Final.pdf.

there are tens of thousands in adult prisons and jails: Wagner and Rabuy, *The Whole Pie*, third slide group, first graphic.

African American, Latino, and Native American youth: The Annie E. Casey Foundation, *Juvenile Detention Alternatives Initiative Progress Report 2014* (Baltimore: Annie E. Casey Foundation, 2014), 5, http://www.aecf.org/m/resourcedoc/aecf-2014JDAIProgressReport-2014.pdf.

Page 153

Detention can have profound and deleterious effects: Jennifer Gonnerman, "Before the Law," *The New Yorker*, October 6, 2014, http://www.newyorker.com/magazine/2014/10/06/ before-the-law.

Take Kalief Browder, a 16-year-old: Ibid.; "'Time: The Kalief Browder Story' Depicts Issues With Solitary Confinement," *All Things Considered*, Michel Martin interview with Jenner Furst, March 4, 2017, http://www.npr.org/2017/03/04/518527689/time-the-kalief-browder-story-depicts-issues-with-solitary-confinement.

Soon after his release, Kalief took his own life: Ibid.

Among the 34,000 in juvenile detention: Wagner and Rabuy, *The Whole Pie*, third slide group, first graphic.

"At the same time the 'super-predator' war amplified": Perry L. Moriearty and William Carson, "Cognitive Warfare and Young Black Males in America," *Journal of Gender, Race and Justice* 15, no. 2 (2012): 283–84.

At-risk vs. at-promise: "At Promise Youth," UCSB Sustainability, accessed June 29, 2017, http://www.sustainability.ucsb.edu/at-promise-youth/.

Our children vs. their children: Barry C. Feld, *Bad Kids: Race and the Transformation of the Juvenile Court* (New York: Oxford University Press, 1999), 7.

Missing, as former President Obama said, the margin of error: Michael Calderone, "Vice Went To Prison With Obama. Now It's Going Deep Into Inmate Issues.," *Huffington Post*, September 22, 2015, http://www.huffingtonpost.com/entry/vice-obama-prison-documentary-hbo_us_55fd7c1ee4b00310edf74566.

Consider the kids kept in solitary confinement: Gonnerman, "Before the Law."

Consider the thousands of individuals sentenced to die: Josh Rovner, *Juvenile Life Without Parole: An Overview* (The Sentencing Project, 2017), 1, http://www.sentencingproject.org/publications/juvenile-life-without-parole/.

"I suspect that all the crimes committed": Karl Menninger, *The Crime of Punishment* (Bloomington: AuthorHouse, 2007), xv.

Page 156

Kids as young as ten: "OJJDP Statistical Briefing Book."

Yet we've learned a lot about brain development: "Juvenile Justice & the Adolescent Brain," Massachusetts General Hospital Center for Law, Brain & Behavior, accessed July 17, 2017, http://clbb.mgh.harvard.edu/juvenilejustice/.

Page 163

"In the era of mass incarceration, labeling": Victor M. Rios, *Punished: Policing the Lives of Black and Latino Boys* (New York: New York University Press, 2011), 45.

Page 167

Criminologists point to employment, marriage, education: John H. Laub and Robert J. Sampson, "Understanding Desistance From Crime," *Crime and Justice* 28 (2001): 1–69, https://dash.harvard.edu/bitstream/handle/1/3226958/sampson_understandingdesistance.pdf?sequence=4; Page, "Eliminating the Enemy," 367–68.

"it implies valuing people for who they are": Fergus McNeill et al., *How and Why*, 4 (emphasis removed).

Page 176

A teenager in Florida was expelled: Tim Elfrink, "Florida School Responds to Criticism for Expelling Student Over Science Project: 'There Are Consequences to Actions,'" *Miami New Times*, May 1, 2013, http://www.miaminewtimes.com/news/florida-school-responds-to-criticism-for-expelling-student-over-science-project-there-are-consequences-to-actions-6556028.

Kids should learn: Ibid.

Page 193

"many males—especially black males—are navigating": "Study: Half of Black Males, 40 Percent of White Males Arrested by Age 23," University at Albany news release, on the University at Albany website, accessed July 3, 2017, http://www.albany.edu/news/45558.php (quoting study author Robert Brame).

"Fully 80 to 90 percent of American teenagers": Nell Bernstein, *Burning Down the House: The End of Juvenile Prison* (New York: New Press, 2014), 8.

For kids who get a pass: Ibid.

Page 210

Ranging from unimaginable atrocities: Sarah Stillman, "The List," *The New Yorker*, March 14, 2016, http://www.newyorker.com/magazine/2016/03/14/when-kids-are-accused-of-sex-crimes.

Approximately 800,000 people on sex offender registries: "Number of Registrants Reported by State/Territory," Parents for Megan's Law and The Crime Victims Center, accessed July 17, 2017, https://www.parentsformeganslaw.org/public/meganReportCard.html.

Public registries, social proscription: Stillman, "The List."

Page 225

Oscar Grant had been celebrating: Dalia Hashad, "Another Year, Another Unarmed Black Man Killed by Police," Amnesty International, January 7, 2009, http://blog.amnestyusa.org/us/another-year-another-unarmed-black-man-killed-by-police/.

Eric Garner refused to be arrested: Al Baker, J. David Goodman and Benjamin Mueller, "Beyond the Chokehold: The Path to Eric Garner's Death," *New York Times*, June 13, 2015, https://www.nytimes.com/2015/06/14/nyregion/eric-garner-police-chokehold-staten-island.html.

A 25-year-old Freddie Gray: Sheryl Gay Stolberg and Ron Nixon, "Freddie Gray in Baltimore: Another City, Another Death in the Public Eye," *New York Times*, April 21, 2015, https://www.nytimes.com/2015/04/22/us/another-mans-death-another-round-of-questions-for-the-police-in-baltimore.html; "Freddie Gray Case Ends With No Convictions of Any Police Officers," *New York Times*, July 27, 2016, https://www.nytimes.com/interactive/2015/04/30/us/what-happened-freddie-gray-arrested-by-baltimore-police-department-map-timeline.html.

Walter Scott was pulled over: Krishnadev Calamur, "S.C. Dashcam Video: A Broken Tail Light, A Routine Traffic Stop, A Fleeing Man," National Public Radio, April 9, 2015, http://www.npr.org/sections/thetwo-way/2015/04/09/398615265/s-c-dash-cam-video-a-broken-tail-light-a-routine-traffic-stop-a-fleeing-man; Michael S. Schmidt and Matt Apuzzo, "South Carolina Officer Is Charged With Murder of Walter Scott," *New York Times*, April 7, 2015, https://www.

nytimes.com/2015/04/08/us/south-carolina-officer-is-charged-with-murder-in-black-mans-death.html.

Sandra Bland was stopped: Abby Ohlheiser and Abby Phillip, "'I Will Light You Up!': Texas Officer Threatened Sandra Bland with Taser During Traffic Stop," *Washington Post*, July 22, 2015, https://www.washingtonpost.com/news/morning-mix/wp/2015/07/21/much-too-early-to-call-jail-cell-hanging-death-of-sandra-bland-suicide-da-says/?utm_term=.7cac5c23d3c5 (including dashcam video).

Page 226

Trayvon Martin had Skittles: Adam Weinstein et al., "The Trayvon Martin Killing, Explained," *Mother Jones*, March 18, 2012, http://www.motherjones.com/politics/2012/03/what-happened-trayvon-martin-explained/.

Jordan Davis, music: Kristal Brent Zook, "The Lessons of Jordan Davis's Murder, Revisited," *The Nation*, November 23, 2015, https://www.thenation.com/article/the-lessons-of-jordan-daviss-murder-revisited/.

It was a wintry Saturday when twelve-year-old Tamir Rice: Shaila Dewan and Richard A. Oppel Jr., "In Tamir Rice Case, Many Errors by Cleveland Police, Then a Fatal One," *New York Times*, January 22, 2015, https://www.nytimes.com/2015/01/23/us/in-tamir-rice-shooting-in-cleveland-many-errors-by-police-then-a-fatal-one.html; Elliot McLaughlin, "Tamir Rice's teen sister 'tackled,' handcuffed after his shooting, mom says," *CNN*, December 9, 2014, http://www.cnn.com/2014/12/08/us/cleveland-tamir-rice-mother/index.html.

John Crawford III was talking: Elahe Izadl, "Ohio Wal-Mart Surveillance Video Shows Police Shooting and Killing John Crawford III," *Washington Post*, September 25, 2014, https://www.washingtonpost.com/news/post-nation/wp/2014/09/25/ohio-wal-mart-surveillance-video-shows-police-shooting-and-

killing-john-crawford-iii/?utm_term=.89b1e4ae2ff2; Jon Swaine, "Video Shows John Crawford's Girlfriend Aggressively Questioned After Ohio Police Shot Him Dead in Walmart," *The Guardian*, December 14, 2014, https://www.theguardian.com/us-news/2014/dec/14/john-crawford-girlfriend-questioned-walmart-police-shot-dead; Jon Swaine, "Doubts Cast on Witness's Account of Black Man Killed By Police in Walmart," *The Guardian*, September 7, 2014, https://www.theguardian.com/world/2014/sep/07/ohio-black-man-killed-by-police-walmart-doubts-cast-witnesss-account.

Page 239

Each year, the U.S. spends nearly $80 billion: Melissa S. Kearney et al., *Ten Economic Facts about Crime and Incarceration in the United States* (The Hamilton Project, 2014), 13, https://www.brookings.edu/wp-content/uploads/2016/06/v8_THP_10CrimeFacts.pdf.

Page 240

CoreCivic (formerly Corrections Corporation of America) and The GEO Group: Jeff Sommer, "Trump's Win Gives Stocks in Private Prison Companies a Reprieve," *New York Times*, December 3, 2016, https://www.nytimes.com/2016/12/03/your-money/trumps-win-gives-stocks-in-private-prison-companies-a-reprieve.html; see http://www.cca.com/who-we-are (more than 80,000 beds); https://www.geogroup.com/locations (approximately 100,000 beds).

"cesspool of unconstitutional and inhuman acts": Order Approving Settlement at 5, DePriest v. Epps, No. 3:10-cv-00663-CWR-FKB (S.D. Miss. Mar. 26, 2012), Docket Entry/ECF No. 75, available at http://www.aclu.org/files/assets/order.pdf.

the crime rate today is half: Matthew Friedman, Ames C. Grawert, and James Cullen, *Crime Trends: 1990–2016* (Brennan Center for Justice, 2017), 1, https://www.brennancenter.org/sites/default/files/publications/Crime%20Trends%201990-2016.pdf.

in 2015, the Brennan Center for Justice: Dr. Oliver Roeder, Lauren-Brooke Eisen, and Julia Bowling, *What Caused the Crime Decline?* (Brennan Center for Justice, 2015), 15, https://www.brennancenter.org/sites/default/files/analysis/What_Caused_The_Crime_Decline.pdf.

Since 2000, the effect of increasing: Ibid.

the reduction may be better explained: Ibid., 8–15.

States like New York and New Jersey: Ibid., 4.

"Imprisonment has grown to the point": Todd R. Clear, *Imprisoning Communities: How Mass Incarceration Makes Disadvantaged Neighborhoods Worse* (New York: Oxford University Press, 2009), 3.

"are viewed as people whose net contribution": Todd R. Clear, "The Problem with 'Addition by Subtraction': The Prison-Crime Relationship in Low-Income Communities," in *Invisible Punishment*, 181.

As a result, tough-on-crime laws: Janet L. Lauritsen, Robert J. Sampson, and John H. Laub, "The Link Between Offending and Victimization Among Adolescents," *Criminology* 29, no. 2 (May 1991): 267, doi: 10.1111/j.1745-9125.1991.tb01067.x.

those most likely to be policed: Susan Herman, "Seeking Parallel Justice: A New Agenda for the Victims Movement," speech, National Press Club Luncheon, December 15, 2000, transcript, The National Center for Victims of Crime, accessed July 3, 2017, https://victimsofcrime.org/media/newsroom/ speeches-and-testimony/parallel-justice.

Victims of domestic violence may be wrongly accused: Jeffrey P. Greipp, Toolsi Gowin Meisner and Douglas J. Miles, *Intimate Partner Violence Victims Charged With Crimes: Justice and Accountability for Victims of Battering Who Use Violence Against Their Batterers* (Aequitas, 2010), 17–18, http://www.aequitasresource.org/Intimate_Partner_Violence.pdf.

young targets of relentless bullying: "Being Bullied Throughout Childhood and Teens May Lead to More Arrests, Convictions, Prison Time," American Psychological Association press release, August 1, 2013, on the American Psychological Association website, http://www.apa.org/news/press/releases/2013/08/ being-bullied.aspx.

some states are creating special expungement orders: E.g., Minn. Stat. § 609A.03 subd. 6a (2016).

Page 242

Budget reports peg the cost: Kearney et al., *Economic Facts*, 13.

or the estimated 65 to 100 million people: Rebecca Vallis et al., "Removing Barriers to Opportunity for Parents With Criminal Records and Their Children," Center for American Progress, December 10, 2015, https://www.americanprogress.org/issues/poverty/reports/2015/12/10/126902/removing-barriers-to-opportunity-for-parents-with-criminal-records-and-their-children/; Rodriguez and Emsellem, *65 Million*, 3.

doesn't show the nearly three million: The Pew Charitable Trusts, *Collateral Costs*, 18.

More than 33 million children: Lottie Joiner, "How Families Pay the Never-Ending Price of a Criminal Record," *The Atlantic*, December 15, 2015, https://www.theatlantic.com/politics/archive/2015/12/how-families-pay-the-never-ending-price-of-a-criminal-record/433641/.

Page 245

More than 2.7 million children: The Pew Charitable Trusts, *Collateral Costs*, 18.

Most are younger than ten: The Annie E. Casey Foundation, *A Shared Sentence* (Baltimore: Annie E. Casey Foundation, 2016), 2, http://www.aecf.org/m/resourcedoc/aecf-asharedsentence-2016.pdf.

A staggering one in nine: The Pew Charitable Trusts, *Collateral Costs*, 4.

Nearly half of America's kids have: Vallis et al., "Removing Barriers."

Page 262

Portugal decriminalized the use: *Drug Decriminalization in Portugal: A Health-Centered Approach* (Drug Policy Alliance, 2015), https://www.drugpolicy.org/sites/ default/files/DPA_Fact_Sheet_Portugal_Decriminalization_Feb2015.pdf.

Treatment is on the rise: Ibid.

The unofficial motto of the Norwegian Correctional System: Jessica Benko, "The Radical Humaneness of Norway's Halden Prison," *The New York Times Magazine*, March 26, 2015, https://www.nytimes.com/2015/03/29/magazine/the-radical-humaneness-of-norways-halden-prison.html?_r=1#.

Ban the Box: Michelle N. Rodriguez and Beth Avery, *Ban the Box: U.S. Cities, Counties, and States Adopt Fair Hiring Policies* (National Employment Law Project, 2017), http://www.nelp.org/publication/ban-the-box-fair-chance-hiring-state-and-local-guide/.

Page 268

"Each of us is more than": Bryan Stevenson, *Just Mercy: A Story of Justice and Redemption* (New York: Spiegel & Grau, 2015), 17–18 (emphasis removed).